HISPANIC TELE-VISIONS IN THE UNITED STATES

Eleven Essays on Television, Discourse, and Cultural Identity

Critical Bodies
Joseph J. Pilotta, *series editor*

HISPANIC TELE-VISIONS IN THE UNITED STATES

Eleven Essays on Television, Discourse, and Cultural Identity

Elizabeth M. Lozano
Loyola University Chicago

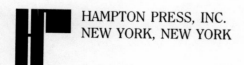

HAMPTON PRESS, INC.
NEW YORK, NEW YORK

Printed in the United States of America

Library of Congress Cataloging-in-Publication Data

Lozano, Elizabeth M.
    Hispanic tele-visions in the United States : eleven essays on television, discourse, and cultural identity / Elizabeth M Lozano, Loyola University, Chicago.
        pages cm — (Critical bodies)
    Includes bibliographical references and indexes.
    ISBN 978-1-61289-128-6 (hardbound) — ISBN 978-1-61289-129-3 (paperbound)
    1. Hispanic Americans on television.   2. Ethnic television broadcasting—United States.   3. Ethnicity on television.   4. Hispanic American television viewers. I. Title.
    PN1992.8.H54L69 2013
    791.45'652968073—dc23   2013023523

Hampton Press, Inc.
307 Seventh Ave.
New York, NY 10001

Contents

II
THE EXPLORATORY TOOLS
Textual Analysis

III
READING THE ARCHIVE
Hispanic Tele-Visions

List of Figures

Acknowledgments

Writing this book has required a constant questioning of my own discursive procedures and a risky venturing in an unknown territory. It also has been exhilarating, as I moved through it in the company of Kevin Williams, who brought to this beloved task the richest insights and observations.

Neither this book nor the years of academic work that preceded it could have been accomplished without the presence of Algis Mickunas as professor, mentor, and friend. To him, to a teaching that never ceases to create, to a life that brings inspiration to those who long for the impossible, I dedicate this work. Finally, I wish to thank my sister Ana Maria, a true soul mate as lovely as she is brilliant; my mother Diana, who taught me the art of looking inward; and Hernán, the first human to suggest I may have a thing for words.

Preface

This book is a moment in an ongoing intellectual journey that started two decades ago, in Colombia, when I turned my attention to television and its semiotic structures. In those days, I participated in a Pan-Latin American study of *telenovelas*, conducted by Cultural Studies scholar Jesus Martín-Barbero, which studied Colombian, Brazilian, Mexican, and Venezuelan "melodramatic serials." When I came to the United States in 1987, I did not have to look too far from the living room to determine my thesis research focus. In fact, I think I had little choice. I needed to continue what I had started in Colombia—a most unexpected intellectual journey that was providing me with most unexpected intellectual rewards (and pains). The comparative textual analysis (i.e., Latin American/Anglo American melodramatic serials) that I did at the time has proven fundamental to almost everything I have done afterward, even when it does not relate specifically to melodrama or television.

"Hispanic television" appeared clearly framed as the phenomenon—or the cultural site—whose presence I needed to interrogate. This was a cultural industry whose products were alien to me in their very outspoken efforts to call me up, by my name. Here is a television system created for U.S. Hispanics; the visiting South American, the national Spanish American, the expatriated Central American, the colonized Puerto Rican, the reborn Cuban, the annexed Mexican. This TV system speaks "our" language, tells "our" jokes, celebrates "our" talent, and broadcasts "our" news. A TV system, that is, whose existence depends on the existence of "us," and that, therefore, posits interesting, existential, metaphysical, and political questions—Who are we? What do we look like? What do we want? What belongs to us?—and offers some categorical answers to those questions. We know that we are because television is speaking to "us" right now and because we are . . . on TV (and radio and magazines). Hispanic television and other Spanish-speaking media outlets intend to give us a recognizable face, that of José and María Pérez, Hispanic, USA. In the process of "mirroring" us, Hispanic television shapes, defines, and builds that face.

The discourses that traverse Hispanic television—and the conditions of their possibility—carry implications that go well beyond the issue of the production and consumption of television. Television can be seen and studied as cultural "evidence" of nationalistic discourses, hegemonic narratives, mythical explanations, and collective assertions of imagined and imaginary communities. Hispanic television, therefore, can be studied as archival and forensic evidence of the discursive regimes and social practices in which national, regional, racial, ethnic, and gender categories are constituted and legitimized.

The chapters in this book intend to explore these issues and see Hispanic television as a *revelatory node* whose many threads lead us to unravel a multiplicity of interconnected cultural issues. Some of the key questions that I will address include: What does Spanish-language television "televise"? How does it frame "reality"? What social reality does it legitimize? How does it relate to the "reality" of English-speaking television? How does this television speak about, and to, its audiences? How can semiotics and poststructural theory be used to design a methodology that could analyze television not as a collection of texts but as a site of textual production?

The Book's Plan

The Context

Taking to heart the idea of exploration as a spatial, temporal, and symbolic pursuit, I start the book by defining the context and cultural field in which Hispanic television takes place. I discuss a number of theoretical and cultural issues that both contextualize and provide depth to the cultural field in which Hispanic television emerges. Among these are the (a) constitution of the "Hispanic" and the "Latino" as social categories, (b) rhetorical construction of the "American" as a social and a political category, (c) narratives that articulate nation and origin in Latin America and in the United States, (d) nature of Hispanic television as culture industry and televisual apparatus, and (e) discourses that unfold in Hispanic television's programming.

The Textual Space

The book situates "Hispanic television" in relation to the mainstream television of the United States, and in relation to "American television," the television consumed and produced in the Americas.[1] Thus, its territory of exploration could be called "American Tele-Visions" or the U.S.-based, broadcast bilingual vision of *America*.

Speaking of television as a *territory* of exploration proposes a paradoxical category or a twisted analogy, at the same time that it suggests the ways in which traditional categories of analysis become problematized by new social practices. Ideas of space, place, and time; of reality and representation; of identity, nationality, and origin; and of border, boundary, and difference are being transformed and redefined by new diasporas and diasporic journeys; by new ways of city dwelling and political expression, new forms of cultural allegiance, and new logics of representation.

Television is a *place* of postindustrial dwelling[2] and an audiovisual setting that engages and transforms lived and practiced space, providing text and discourse with material density, with the weight and texture of that which is experienced. Television is an active producer (and reproducer) of nationalistic aspirations and a contested arena for the representation, documentation, and legitimization of social identities. To study television is to study a privileged "documenting" device; a site in which "social reality" is *envisioned*, presented, articulated, segmented, tamed, and polished. Such documenting labor might appear particularly apparent in U.S. Hispanic television, as it is actively engaged in the act of "creating" the *Hispanic/Latino*, the audience it is designed to address. In the act of addressing it, an ethnicity, a community, and a subculture are legitimated—and proven empirical, concrete, and material.

Analyzing a Televisual Textuality: Data, Scene, and Sites

Univision is the most watched Spanish broadcast network in the U.S. With "52 million viewers and counting," says Guthrie with charming hyperbole, the network is becoming "the brand most recognized and trusted by Latinos— second only to the Church" (2012). Telemundo is Univision's most important competition, with a coverage of 94% of Hispanic households, and a distribution arm that syndicates its Spanish programming to more than 100 countries in over 35 languages (Corporate Information, 2013).

Whereas Univision has very strong production ties to Mexico's powerful network Televisa, Telemundo has production studios in Miami and Colombia and ties to Televisa's rival TV Azteca. Both networks trace their beginnings to a single channel created in the mid-50s. In the case of Univision, it was a San Antonio, Texas, channel owned by Mexican media entrepreneurs. For Telemundo, it was a channel in San Juan, Puerto Rico, owned by Angel Ramos, a local media industrialist.

The late 1980s were very significant for both networks. In 1987, the single Puerto Rican station Telemundo Canal 2 was sold to U.S. investors and the Telemundo network was created. Similarly, Univision changed name, ownership and status in 1987. Until 1987 Univision was known as SIN, the Spanish International Network, an enterprise owned by Televisa. After a decade of lawsuits and a final FCC order to change its foreign-controlled ownership, 10 SIN stations were sold to Hallmark Cards and First Capital Corporation and became the Univision network (Rubin, 1986). In 1992 Hallmark sold Univision to a group led by a Hollywood producer, Jerrold Perenchio, Univisa's owner Emilio Azcarraga, and Gustavo and Ricardo Cisneros from the Venezuelan network Venevision (Murray, 1994). Currently, Univision is owned by Broadcasting Media Partners (BMP), a U.S. investor group, whereas Telemundo is owned by NBCUniversal (History, 2013; Telemundo corporate, 2013; The Univision Story, 2013).

The televisual analysis that follows is based on the programming of Telemundo and Univision ranging from 1988 to 2011, and it focuses particularly on Univision's Canal 44 in Miami and Canal 66 in Chicago. Within the range of the overall programming, or what I will call *televisual textuality*, I dwell more particularly on "limit programming." That is, not only that which is "typical" or average programming, but that which *marks* the different boundaries and limits of the legitimate and acceptable within the televisual flow. I refer to *telenovelas*, the Latin American TV genre *par excellence*; news shows that anchor the "real"; the talk and variety shows imported from the U.S. mainstream to speak to a "Hispanic" audience; and the advertising aimed at creating, shaping, and educating a market. These are all fundamental components of this Hispanic television "textuality," which constitutes historical, cultural, and popular "archives." The *textual* analysis is complemented by *contextual* information provided by the Hispanic press, magazines, newspapers, TV supplements, popular journals, and Internet sites; and the *intertextuality* provided by Hispanic narratives, in poetry, literature, film, and music.

A "Third Text"?

Based on the textual and discursive analysis of Univision and Telemundo, I highlight some of Hispanic television's emergent discourses and ponder their relationship to Latin American and U.S. mainstream dominant discourses. Studying television as an archive and using the concepts of *mestizaje*, hybridization, and syncretism, I suggest that Hispanic television can be seen as an emergent "third text," neither Latin American nor Anglo American, but both, less and more. A new culture, a new language, a new nationalism, and a whole array of new contradictions are announced and manifested in Spanish-language television; simultaneously legitimized and limited by the market, but superseding and overflowing it in unexpected ways.

Notes

1. Taking it literally, American television is television produced, broadcast, and consumed in the Americas.

2. In *An ontology of everyday distraction*, Morse (1990) refers to the "intuition" expressed "from time to time in critical literature—that television is similar or related to other, particular forms of transportation and exchange in everyday life" (p. 193). Morse compares television to the freeway and the mall, as places for distracted attention, for staying-in-transit, for dwelling-in-movement.

I

EXPLORING THE TERRITORY

The Rhetorical Power of Naming

1

Of U.S. Television and Américan Invention

Weaving A Hispanic Textuality

I have chosen to call the object of study of this book "Hispanic" television instead of "Latino" or "Spanish-language" television. The decision has important implications. I am using *Hispanic* as an adjective that denotes language (and connotes culture), but not as a noun that indicates ethnic membership. In the

Figure 1.1. Selena Vive! ([Photo by Business Wire] Getty Images Publicity/Getty Images.) February 4, 2005. During a press conference, Univision announces a 10th anniversary tribute concert to honor the Tejano music superstar Selena. Pictured: Mexican-American actor Edward James Olmos, who portrayed Selena's father in the film *Selena*.

same way that there is a *Hispanic literature*, written in Spanish and originating in any of 20 countries, there is, one can argue, *Hispanic* television. Such television may originate in Spain, South, Central, or North America, include any combination of those regions, and constitute national or transnational systems that have the Spanish language as a commonality.

In this case, the label "Hispanic television" is not intended to carry with it a *presupposed* cultural identity or "ethnic" features (e.g., we know what "Hispanic" means in U.S. official circles, therefore we should know what "Hispanic television" is all about). Instead, I would like to "let" the Spanish-speaking television system of the United States state what it stands for, and what social and cultural features it would claim as its own. I intend to "read" (visually, aurally, linguistically, and textually) the self-referential statements of U.S. networks Univision and Telemundo, deconstruct their narratives, and reconstruct their discourses.

If in the Latin American context the label *Hispanic* or *Hispano* does not and could not denote "ethnic" membership, in the United States, the term has been used to denote an ethnicity since the 1970s. This adds another semantic dimension to the label *Hispanic television*, for in the U.S. context, speaking Spanish (or having ancestors who did) is a marker of ethnic affiliation and becomes, therefore, a cultural and social profile. This profile includes characteristics such as *familismo, personalismo*, and fatalism (Fullerton & Kendrick, 2000); *machismo*, Catholicism, and traditional medicine practices; low education attainment and high birth rates; limited access to health insurance (*Hispanics in the U.S.*, 2009); and lower mortality rates than those of other U.S. residents (Lara, Gamboa, Kahramanian, Morales, & Hayes Bautista, 2005).[1] On many occasions, the public usage of "Latino" and "Hispanic" becomes indistinguishable in their *denotative* meaning, but the labels maintain divergent political and cultural *connotations*. That which Lara et al. (2005) call "Latino" is precisely what Dr. Elena Rios, president of the National Hispanic Medical Association, calls "Hispanic."

Latino (or Latino/a; Latina/o) is a term often favored by cultural studies and scholars in the humanities, as well as cultural workers and activists. The label carries a more "progressive," indigenous connotation and emphasizes geopolitical origin—Latin America—instead of singling out language as the privilege marker of cultural identity ("Hispanic" includes Spain and excludes Brazil, a rather surprising move for many of those included and excluded). In contrast, Hispanic is the term preferred by social scientists because, according to Fullerton and Kendrick (2000), "it is neither offensive nor politically linked" (p. 131). This explanation would surely surprise the many for whom "Hispanic" is indeed an offensive ("I am not from Spain") and politically charged ("made up by the U.S. census") term.

The discursive collapsing of the distinct labels *Hispanic* and *Latino* into a single signified denotation may explain why it comes as a surprise to many in my Chicago milieu that Brazil is part of Latin America. If a Hispanic is a Latino and a Latino originates in Latin America, then it would follow that all Latin Americans are Hispanic, and thus speak Spanish. Brazil is therefore extraordinarily excluded from the map, as are Amerindian peoples who speak Nahuatl, Guaraní, Quechua, or Mayan as their mother tongue.

Latina is indeed how I have always described myself, as a Colombian citizen and as an alien residing in the United States; a short form for the label *Latin American*, which encompasses the peoples from Brazil and Argentina to Mexico and Cuba. The label I used to describe myself in Colombia, however, has little resemblance to the *Latina* of the United States because its context, history, and politics differ. In 2000, the U.S. census seemed to solve the tension between the labels by using *Hispanic* and *Latino* as interchangeable terms. It also included only two ethnicities, Hispanic/Latino or Non-Hispanic/Latino, thus defining all other groups as races. A Hispanic/Latino, therefore, may be White, Black, Asian, Native American, Pacific Islander, or Other. To say that there are more Latinos than Blacks in the United States is, therefore, a logical impossibility because one is an ethnicity, the other is a race, and Latinos can be Black. The classification seems to suggest that Latinos are the only group that cannot be identified by physical features, while all "races" can. The conceptualization of race and ethnicity is murky at best, and the census appears to acknowledge this, with consequences remarkably poetic.

In fact, based on the 2000 census, one can conclude that the Hispanic/Latino person is not: (a) a person of "color" (92.5% of Latinos self-identify as White), (b) someone who speaks Spanish (she may know only English or speak Portuguese, French, Aymará, or other Amerindian languages), (c) a Latin American (he may come from Spain), or (d) an immigrant (Latinos may be Native American, Puerto Rican, or seventh-generation Mexicans from any of the annexed states such as Arizona, California, Colorado, New Mexico, and Texas). It is no less than remarkable that an ethnicity could be "identified" with boundaries as porous as this, and that it indeed "works" well enough to create a consumer market, a political constituency, and a mass-mediated imagined community.

The U.S. Hispanic/Latino Ethnicity

Even though it has been ignored by official history, the Hispanic contribution to the formation of the United States constitutes an underground force which has constantly reemerged in the history of this country through multiple cultural expressions. . . . The unknown details of this history have been emerging as the population grows and hundreds of thousand of immigrants keep arriving. (Quinientos años de herencia hispana, 1992, p. 7, my translation)[2]

The United States is the third largest Spanish-speaking country in the world (after Mexico and Colombia), and the "Hispanic/Latino" has become its largest "ethnic minority" in the new millennium. In 1990, there were 22,354,059 persons of Hispanic origin living in the United States (Quinientos años de herencia hispana, 1992). In 2000, that population had reached more than 35 million, and it was approximately 15% of the U.S. population by 2010. It is expected that there will be almost 60 million Hispanics in 2020 (U.S. Census Bureau, 2007).

The above information has an air of self-evidence. However, it rests on the assumption that the "Hispanic" and the "Latino" are nonproblematic categories. However, the "Hispanic" as an ethnicity was born in the 1970s by an explicit, official decision from the U.S. government and the Census Bureau. The Hispanic was declared in existence (i.e., discovered and invented) by an official act of naming—an act not unlike that by virtue of which "America" came to exist; a New World for, and by, the Old World. Proposing an ironic reading, we could say about "Hispanics" what Marcel Duchamp said about art and Baudrillard said about reality. Hispanic is what we choose to call "Hispanic." There is no Hispanic outside the text, so to speak. No empirical reality corresponds to the label—but its imaginary and symbolic power is undeniable (see Žižek, 1991/2008). The Hispanic then and the Hispanic/Latino now is as real as its popular representations, its icons, its mythology, and its mass-mediated narratives. The Hispanic does not precede its inscription in the cultural text—it is constituted in the act of inscription, in the act of public naming. Thus, to study what has been publicly labeled Hispanic does not imply as much to observe an "empirical" reality out there, but to grasp the logics of a rhetorical field. A field, that is, in which regional, national, and local differences and identities are constituted, inscribed, and legitimated.

To say that the Hispanic is not an empirical reality does not mean that it is less real than other ethnicities—or races. Aren't all nationalisms fundamentally grounded on the performative act of naming? Are there objective, neutral, and context-free ways of marking the borders between ethnicities or races? Is Tiger Woods Asian, Black, or White? Does Barack Obama belong to the "Pacific Islander" race because he was born in Hawaii? Do actors Anthony Quinn and Alexis Bledel, writers Junot Díaz and Isabel Allende, activist Cesar Chavez and politician Bill Richardson share the same ethnicity? (Yes, they do. They are all Latinos.) Is Shakira *still* Colombian?

The Hispanic/Latino label reveals, in a particularly strong manner, the discursive apparatus required for the maintenance, legitimation, and proper identification of ethnicities and nationalities.

Hispanic Topographies

The "Hispanic" and the "Latino" are umbrella terms under which arguably different groups are identified as one ethnicity. This situation has provoked ardent discussions and debates throughout the decades, as some critique either the label's homogenizing or imperialistic undertones or defend its unifying and empowering implications (see Bean & Tienda, 1987; Civica Americana, 2008; Gimenez, 1989; Mohr, 1990; Nicolini, 1986; Rojas, 2004; Rosales, 1990). Because of its history in the United States, the *Hispanic* label connotes conservative leanings and acculturation, whereas *Latino* has often suggested progressive politics and cultural resistance. However, in principle, either label could be liberating or reactionary, empowering or oppressive. A Paraguayan is not a Brazilian is not a Mexican is not a Chicano. A Colombian may be quick to point out that the Colombian Coast is not the Colombian Andes, and that we (Colombians) are a plurality of regions barely contained within one state. Overwhelmed by the homogenizing and reductive power of the national label, a Mexican Zapoteca Amerindian from Oaxaca could argue similarly. Oaxaca is quite different from Juarez and both from Mexico City. However, we could be just as quick to point out that "we" do have things in common and that those commonalities override countries and unify the region under a sort of Latin American complicity.

The *Hispanic* label has been for decades the preferred choice of demographers, social scientists, advertisers, and the press. It is the choice of *Broadcasting and Cable*, and of *Advertising Age*, which over the decades has given us increasingly large supplements on "marketing to Hispanics," the fastest growing market in the United States ("Hispanic Broadcasting & Cable," 1995; "Hispanic Fact Pack," 2007; "The Hispanic Market," 1988; "Marketing to Hispanics," 1987, 1994). It was also the choice of Univision and Telemundo, as they positioned themselves within the U.S. market, because Spanish is the core characteristic of their networks, and from speech an ethnic demographic is derived.

The "Hispanic" that emerges from advertising has some central characteristics that we could come to recite with closed eyes: Catholicism, machismo and *familismo*, multigenerational households, and very strong familial ties. We could also spice up the demographics with a few other elements. Salsa, siesta, fiesta, taco, sombrero, bandido, J. Lo, ranchera, and Selena come to mind. These ingredients are as present in the Pepsi Hispanic commercials and Univision's advertising as they are in the Hollywood greaser movies, the *New York Times*, and the *Wall Street Journal*.[3]

Thus, we are informed that "Hispanic media see siesta ending" (Fisher, 1994a), and that there are "myths and realities" in the Hispanic market, which the Strategy Research Corporation will spell out for us ("Marketing to Hispanics," 1994). That might explain why "Buy me Arepa and Buena Noche" (1993) is a way of naming the market because we learn, informed by Hispanic Market Connections, that "Hispanics tend to preserve their cultural values, traditions and identities" (an advertisement in "Marketing to Hispanics," 1994, p. S7). Those values appear summarized in the need to put more "salsa" in your advertising[4] and could explain why you should use *GSRK Advertising* to reach Hispanics:

> What can two men raised on rice and beans and groomed at Procter and Gamble and Doyle Dane Bernbach bring to your hispanic marketing effort?
>
> *Highly creative advertising that works. . . .*
>
> Both men are fluent in Spanish and live their Hispanic traditions and customs everyday. ("Marketing to Hispanics," 1987, p. S12)

Despite its problems, the *Hispanic* seems to be the preferred label in social scientist circles, even by researchers who argue that it does not "exist" as an ethnicity. The efficiency of the term seems to come from the fact that it describes simultaneously a difference and a common ground between Anglo Americans and Latin Americans. The Spanish language is an "obvious" difference between the Anglo and the Latin American and can represent or stand for other differences as well.[5] However, that language is spoken, lived, and performed in a U.S. context. Thus, the "U.S. experience" becomes the common ground between the Anglo American and the U.S. Hispanic, and the social difference between the Latin American and the Hispanic. The "Latin American ancestry," in contrast, stands as a central marker of cultural difference between the Hispanic and the Anglo. The Hispanic is, therefore, an "in-between" category whose constitution demands the co-presence of the Latin American and the Anglo American, while requiring a distance from both (see Chapters 2 and 3). As such, the term makes important discursive and rhetorical sense. It manages to highlight, quite clearly, a zone of conflict and tension. "Hispanic" is a linguistic borderland, a historical meeting ground, a cultural cross-pollination, and a social, ongoing *mestizaje*. The Hispanic is as "Anglo" as it is Latin American. This proposition takes us into a new realm of political, semiotic, and experiential difficulty (to which I return in later chapters).

As with the case of the terms *homosexual* and *gay*, choosing "Hispanic" over "Latino" tends to suggest detachment, even objectivity, but just as much a lack of sympathy or empathy. As in the case of *gay*, the Latino label was fought for from within, and thus it suggests sympathy and political correctness. However, these differences do not always work in this way. At an academic forum in which I participated a few years ago, a well-respected professor of Spanish, herself Anglo-American, argued that these terms did not differ in meaning. To her, they were fully interchangeable. This argument would make sense because the labels *Hispanic* and *Latino* do not demand of her any action or interrogate her identity, as she is a member of the U.S. mainstream. The forum's audience members, self-identified Chicanos, Puerto Ricans, Dominicans, Guatemalans, and Mexican Americans, vehemently begged to differ. Many of them spoke no Spanish, and thus being identified by that language made no sense. Others had never traveled south of the border, had no immediate family outside the United States, and saw little meaning in being called Latinos. Others preferred to call themselves Chicanos or Puerto Ricans. Yet others wished to be seen as Americans, no hyphens added.

South, North, Both, and Neither

> In contrast with Blacks, a minority racially defined, Hispanics are distinguished from other groups by their coming from Spanish-speaking countries where the black, white and Indian races have been mixing in different proportions for five centuries. Thus, as a minority Hispanics are defined by their cultural heritage and tradition, their language, and, consequently, by their values. The above is perfectly normal for that is what we have in common. But, how about our differences? (Quinientos años de herencia hispana, p. 25, my translation)

The 2000 U.S. Census Bureau describes the Hispanic/Latino as "a person of Cuban, Mexican, Puerto Rican, South or Central American, or other Spanish culture or origin regardless of race" (Griego & Cassidy, 2001, p. 2). This includes the population of Mexican origin (66.9% of Hispanics), whose settlements in the United States could be traced back at least two centuries; Puerto Ricans (8.6% of the Hispanic population), whose land was designated U.S. territory in 1898 and a semiautonomous commonwealth in 1952; Cubans (3.7% of the Hispanic population), who arrived in large numbers in the 1960s and 1980s; and Central and South Americans, who arrived especially during the 1980s and comprise 14.3% of the Hispanic population (Quinientos años de herencia hispana, 1992; Ramirez & de la Cruz, 2002). Finally, there are the ones classified as "others" (6.5% of the Hispanic population), who see themselves as belonging to more than one of these regions or to another "Spanish culture," such as Spain.

The social and historical differences among U.S. Mexicans, Cubans, and Puerto Ricans are worth considering. Mexican Americans or *Chicanos* (preference for one or another term is also a political statement) understand themselves less as immigrants than as colonized North American peoples. Historically, the entry of Mexican Americans into the United States came about through "conquest and subordination" (Bean & Tienda, 1987):

> Unlike other immigrant groups who voluntarily migrated to the United States and whose sense of peoplehood and ethnicity was shaped by the immigration process. . . . Mexicans residing in U.S. territory at [the time of Guadalupe Hidalgo treaty] had neither cause nor power to challenge the new Anglo rulers. Not only did a rapid and clear break with the parent country occur, together with ensuing socioeconomic and cultural subjugation, but the land itself that the indigenous population considered its own was often lost. (pp. 17–18)[6]

Puerto Ricans, in turn, have an ambiguous relationship with the "mainland," as they see themselves treated as second-class citizens, people who belong but are not included, aliens in a land that is nominally their own. As the Puerto Rican poet and playwright Tato Laviera (1985) observes:

> AmeRican, yes, for now, for i love this, my second
> land, and i dream to take the accent from
> the altercation, and be proud to call
> myself american, in the U.S. sense of the
> word, AmeRican, America! (p. 95)

Puerto Ricans, say Bean and Tienda (1987), have with the United States "common citizenship, common defense, common currency, and a common loyalty to the value of democracy" (p. 23). However, as an "unincorporated territory" of the United States, the island residents may not vote in U.S. presidential elections, are not represented in the U.S. Senate, and have a non-voting Resident Commission in the House of Representatives (Bea, 2005).

The experience of Cubans deeply differs from that of Puerto Ricans and Mexicans. In marked contrast to the reception and perception of Mexicans and Puerto Ricans, "the arrival of the Cubans involved the United States in the largest refugee aid operation in its history to that point" (Bean & Tienda, 1987, p. 29). They are exiles, the ones who fled from dictatorship to the freedom of democracy; the ones who embody the American dream of opportunity, success, and freedom. In contrast with the Puerto Rican experience, Cubans can speak of a U.S. government that gave them help in starting businesses, trained their children in the new language, and allowed them to convert Miami, in three decades, into a Cuban enclave economy. In fact, according to the U.S. Census Bureau, more than half of all Cubans in the United States live in Miami County (Hispanic Heritage Month, 2007). This situation partially explains the high level of Cuban political power in Florida in particular, and in the United States in general, for this high concentration facilitates action and cohesiveness. It should be pointed out, however, that to speak of a "Cuban," "Puerto Rican," or "Mexican" experience in the United States is not necessarily less problematic than to speak of a "Hispanic" experience. Much more (and less) than nationality comes into play in the constitution of common experience.

Besides the aforementioned nationalities, the U.S. Census mentions two other "groups" of Hispanic/Latinos: the Central and South Americans and "others." The main immigration flows from Central and South America have been those of Nicaraguans, Salvadorans, and Dominicans, as well as Argentineans, Brazilians, Ecuadorians, Peruvians, and Colombians. In their case, nationality has been substituted by "region" as the descriptor of origin and immigrant identity. Interestingly, the "Central-South American" category, which was used in the 1970 U.S. Census, had to be dropped as an ethnic descriptor, for many thought that it referred to the south or center of the United States (Bean & Tienda, 1987; Gibson & Jung, 2005). Thus, Texans, Californians, Arizonans, and, sometimes, Midwesterners classified themselves as "Hispanics," assuming that the coordinates of the continent were actually references to their country's geography.[7] The U.S. de facto appropriation of the continental name "America" has more than an anecdotal value in the symbolic economy of the cultures of this continent. It carries a power of mythical proportions and very material implications (I return to this issue in Chapter 3).

Hispanic Television

The Hispanic/Latino "question" has become increasingly notorious in U.S. public discourses—in political debates, in pop sociology and psychology, in front-line news, in popular iconographies, and in advertising. In 1994, the World Cup soccer tournament, held for the first time in the United States, placed Univision and other Hispanic media outlets at the U.S. mainstream center. For the first time, the Hispanic TV networks were held as the prime experts by other U.S. networks for a U.S. event of national and international appeal. Univision and Telemundo had the veteran expertise, the trademark "goooool" cries, and the skill to transform, through narration, an otherwise alien game into a highly charged drama full of passion and suspense. In the summer of 1995, another "crossover" took place. The Tejana singer Selena accomplished a posthumous jump into mainstream stardom.[8] To its editors' surprise, the April 17, 1995, issue of *People* magazine featuring Selena on the cover sold out. *People* followed with a commemorative photographic issue of her life, "Selena 1971–1995: Her Life in Pictures," only the third time the magazine had done so in its history. *People en español* was launched shortly after (Mitchel, 1995). Fittingly, Univision sponsored an "all star" concert in her memory ten years later (see Figure 1.1.)

In that same August, the mayor of Chicago announced a rather compelling statistic. The heat wave that had killed almost 600 Chicagoans that summer affected the Hispanic population the least. *Familismo* was the argued reason: close-knit families, protection of the elderly, and continuous communication among family members. In 2007, Univision "made history" when the finale of the telenovela *La fea mas bella* reached higher ratings than any of the shows for that day on the English-speaking networks ABC, CBS, NBC, FOX, and CW (Dempsey & Schneider, 2007). *La fea* was the Mexican version of *Ugly Betty*, which is in turn the Anglo American version of *Betty La Fea*, a Colombian telenovela whose plot has met with record ratings in two languages and three countries.

In 2007, for the first time Univision aired a U.S. presidential political debate in Spanish (Montanaro, 2007). Having all political candidates participate in a Spanish forum in which they are the ones in need of a translator reaffirmed not only the strategic importance of the Hispanic/Latino voter, but also the political power of Spanish and the place of Univision as a national media powerhouse. In this and other cases, Hispanic television becomes the legitimate mass-mediated ambassador of an "ethnic" constituency.

These very different situations and events are revealing of the status of the "Hispanic/Latino" in national iconographies. They suggest the multiple forms of Hispanic presence in national consciousness and its process of legitimation within official discourses.

Interestingly enough, advertising and marketing publications have been particularly outspoken pioneers in officially announcing—and legitimating—the actual existence of the Hispanic/Latino, a fact made irrevocably "real" by their "newly discovered" purchasing capability. If you can buy, you undoubtedly exist; you have passed a strict test of objective existence in the marketplace. Thus, regardless of political, social, or cultural tensions and ambiguities, once the Hispanic/Latino becomes a "market," its presence is not only worth noticing, but also wooing and respecting as a new market force—a new potential consumer group. Thus, the Hispanic consumer—and, by extension, the places and spaces of its "dwelling"—is dealt with as "a best-kept secret" and "a new frontier." A new colonizing expedition has been under way, its front lines officially reported by marketing and advertising publications.

This new frontier in U.S. marketing has been steadily announced for more than 30 years. As a 1988 headline for *Television/Radio Age* put it, "Advertisers are learning to speak Hispanic—the hard way." The new market requires a new language, a new casting, and a few, rather specific, hot ingredients, such as hot salsa, hot music, and hot bodies. An advertisement for the March

1988 premier issue of *Hispanic Media and Markets* reminds us that, most importantly:

HISPANIC IS HOT!

A hot market that's exploding.
Exploding with over $134 billion of buying power.
Reaching this market has been difficult—until now. . . .
("Marketing to Hispanics," 1987)

Once your existence has been proven in the marketplace, you are worth being studied, culture and all, so that we can figure out your ways, your taste, your style, your (consuming) rituals, your fears, and your accents. In the process of studying the new market, the new ethnic group is constructed—in the very process of depicting, addressing, labeling, and classifying. Spanish-language media advertise themselves by proclaiming to know Hispanic/Latinos better than others, and social scientists often restate what advertisers have been stating explicitly and implicitly all along. In fact, social-scientist research on Hispanics often seems to paraphrase or work under the same basic principles that advertising geared toward Hispanics does (Lozano, 2008). Thus, the Hispanic "profile" is as reiterated in demographic journals as it is in *Advertising Age* or AT&T commercials.

What Is There to Be Studied About Hispanic Television?

The fields of marketing and advertising were prompt to acknowledge the presence of the Hispanic media and their consumers (Dávila, 2001). Social scientists followed through with analyses of that media from the perspective of social behavior and media effects (see e.g., Aguirre & Bustamante, 1993; Allen & Clarke, 1980; Blosser, 1983, 1986, 1988; Eastman & Liss, 1980; Faber, O'Guinn, & Meyer, 1986; Goldsen & Bibliowicz, 1976; Sobel, 1990). Quantitative, content analyses of Hispanic television have also been conducted occasionally on aspects ranging from the portrayal of men and women in commercials (Fullerton & Kendrick, 2000), to the representation of gender and class (Glascock & Ruggiero, 2004) or social groups in primetime television (Mastro & Ortiz, 2008), to the analysis of election-related news coverage (Hale, Olsen, & Fowler, 2009).

When studied, Hispanic television has been mostly a concern of sociologists, psychologists, and economists, who see in this "ethnic media" an anomaly, a political menace, a vehicle of enculturation, a barrier/aid to education, or an instance of capitalistic exploitation/democratic progress. Early communication studies treated "the Hispanic/Latino" as they treated other "minorities" (including children)—as the "exceptional" group that might be, in consequence, exceptionally affected by the media. Because all are exceptional and "marginal,"

Latinos, African Americans, and Asian Americans find themselves sharing the same charts, the same research questions, and the same sociological assumptions. Under their identity as minorities, these groups are homogenized into a measurable difference. Typical questions to be posited while dealing with the television viewing of Hispanics include, for example:

1. Does television fulfill the informative needs of the community, and thus, is the community "satisfied" with the contents of television?

2. How can television be used for educative purposes, as well as for the purposes of enculturation and mainstreaming?

3. Does "ethnic" television represent the community "better" than mainstream television and media?

4. How can the community be targeted more efficiently in mainstream or ethnic television for the sake of selling, educating, or informing?

5. How can the excessive watching of television be controlled, especially the "wrong kind" of television (e.g., daytime talk shows and *telenovelas*)?

6. Which Hispanics watch which programs, for what reasons, and how does their viewing compare with the habits, schedules, and demographics of the "mainstream" audience and other "minorities" (e.g., African Americans)?

7. What is the influence of television on the minority's self-esteem, identity, and adaptation to the larger society?

Traditional mass communication and social science studies grounded on a neopositivist paradigm have approached television as a presence that is necessary to register but not to interrogate, for what is important are the effects television causes (i.e., its social role), not the cultural dynamics that it expresses, reveals, creates, or legitimizes. Thus, it is understood that the "mystery" of television resides in that people actually watch it (and thus one wants to know what happens as a consequence), not in that "watching TV" is seen as a mystery, as an external influence over an otherwise (so it seems) well-defined reality. Within this context, television is an invisible *agent* (i.e., one cannot study it; instead, one studies what it does, what it affects, and what it influences). The invisible thing cannot be directly studied; it has no place, it occupies no space, it has no time. One can only address the invisible by indirection, through its effects—its traces on the sand, its weight on the ground, and its impact on the environment.

The fields of marketing and advertising conducted the first studies of the Latino media market (Dávila, 2001), and social science studies followed with attempts to measure and evaluate the media's impact on communities. In contrast, critical and cultural studies have been particularly slow in addressing such media, from the perspectives of consumption, production, or textual analysis. Critical and cultural studies have greatly contributed to the study of Latino cultural and aesthetic manifestations, and, in particular, to Chicano and Chicana studies. Important contributions have been made to the study of Chicano and Chicana history, geography, art, oral storytelling, literature, and film (e.g., Calderón & Saldívar, 1991; Durán & Bernard, 1982; Fabre, 1988; Fregoso & Chabrám, 1990; Moraga, 1986; Rosales, 1990). However, critical studies of Hispanic television and other Spanish-speaking media have been rare. Some of the most noteworthy contributions include Dávila (2001), Levine (2001), Rodriguez (1999a, 1999b), and Rojas (2004).

Darlene Dávila's (2001) *Latinos INC: The Marketing and Making of a People* is an ethnographic and historical account of marketing to Latinos in the United States and the practices of the Latin American "corporate intellectuals" in charge of such processes. América Rodriguez (1999a, 1999b) focuses on a "cultural and economic" analysis of Latino news. Rodriguez discusses the construction of a Latino identity in the United States in relation to language, race, and class as used in Spanish-language journalism. The formation of a Latino identity is also a theme of central importance to the present study and to Elana Levine's (2001) critical study of Telemundo's programming. Levine sees in Telemundo's programming evidence of the construction of a "syncretic" Latino identity (vs. a more unstable "hybrid" identity). Finally, Rojas (2004) uses Bourdieu's theory of practice and a combination of textual and ethnographic methodologies to study Latinas' practices of television consumption. She specifically studies Latinas' negotiation and evaluation of talk shows on Univision and Telemundo.

The aforementioned studies, each one of which breaks ground in its own right, show us the richness of the field of investigation and help us see as well how much remains unexplored and unknown. I do hope that my own research contributes a textual and poststructural approach to the study of Hispanic television that may complement emergent ethnographic and critical approaches to the study of Spanish-language media, and that it proves provocative or suggestive enough for others to further the inquiry.

Aside from the tremendous excitement, freedom, and nervousness that come with exploring unknown territory, one may also experience a sense of puzzlement that Spanish-language television has been so slow to attract critical attention. Although there is, no doubt, a plethora of interrelated reasons for its relative invisibility, one may suggest that the subject of study is a veritable academic "no man's land." That is, a site paradoxically too mundane and too foreign to attract analysis; a dumping ground of Anglo advertising and Latin American clichés, which neither the United States nor the Latin American mainstream would call its own. Hispanic television is too similar to U.S. mainstream television to warrant distinct analysis, but too distant from it to be manageable unless one herself is bilingual, holds some membership in its ethnic consumer niche, and has the appropriate scholarly credentials.

Those who might be more interested in studying Hispanic television (e.g., Latin American and Latino Studies scholars) have as their priority the investigation of forms of cultural expression, such as music, theater, film, and poetry, which could be more readily seen as "Latino creations." Univision, recently bought by a Californian millionaire with strong ties to Israel and Telemundo, owned by NBC, are clearly not independent Latino creations. Whereas the latter can be claimed to be authentic (as in the case of street theater), enlightened (as in the case of literature and poetry), or "vernacular" (as in the case of *corridos* or oral storytelling), the former, television, is neither vernacular nor authentic or enlightened. It is an industrial production, and, as such, it does not stand out because of its originality or existential merits. It does not speak with the angst, rebelliousness, ingenuity, or originality of the community.

Whereas it is clearly significant to study the work of writers, poets, and painters, it might appear quite pointless or even redundant to write critical essays on television shows that by definition are nonoriginal, mass-produced objects for the consumption of mass audiences (or "ethnic" audiences, in this case). What could possibly be said about Hispanic television that is not self-evident? Why spend any time on the critical analysis of television when so many aspects of cultural and social life are demanding our attention? As a consequence, hardly any attention has been paid to the textual analysis of Hispanic television, its discursive regularities and narrative themes.

The invisibility of Hispanic television is the invisibility of those exceptions that can be found in any preestablished universe or system of reference and that can be dispensed with by seeing them as "nonsignificant" or aberrant. This is, quite literally, "border" television: It does not fit well under our preestablished notion of U.S. American television or Latin American television. Hispanic television is Anglo television broadcast in a dialect; blatant mainstream commercialism without the mainstream; culture industry without best-seller hype or block-buster notoriety; neither national nor international but both; local and regional, pan-American and U.S. region-specific. Hispanic television is regular enough not to be noticed and aberrant enough not to be counted. Hispanic television is not only marginal, it is also particularly banal or "crappy," in the words of Laura Martínez, a blogger for *Advertising Age*:

> We [Latinos] now have more of nothing to watch. Or rather, there are now more Spanish-language [TV] "choices" serving me—and my people—with

the same crap we are used to: dating contests, gossip and paparazzi shows, court fights, reality TV, wrestling and, of course, lots and lots of T&A. In a nutshell: the exact same things I grew up watching on Mexican TV, now expanded and proudly Made in the USA. (Martinez, 2007)

Given the aforementioned, one can see a final objection to studying Hispanic television. What is Hispanic about Spanish-speaking television? Isn't "Hispanic television" an a priori category, a label with no more substance than its rhetorical effort to identify itself with a "community" and sell in its name? If this is the case, Hispanic television is not invisible; it just does not *exist*. After all, how is Hispanic television different from "Latin American television" or "Anglo American network television translated into Spanish?" As I proceed with this investigation, I would like to keep open the possibility that "Hispanic television" might be no less or more than a Spanish translation of the English networks or a U.S.-based Latin American system. These possibilities are important and relevant in their own right. Whether Hispanic television turns out to be one or the other, both or more, its broadcast presence is already offering a position, a reading, a vision, and an embodiment of "American television."

Notes

1. In their review of the literature on Latino health, Lara et al. (2005) argue that the more acculturated a Latino becomes, the higher his or her degree of health care but worse his or her health behavior. For example, highly acculturated Latinos have a higher degree of substance abuse and a poorer diet than less acculturated Latinos.

2. A pesar de haber sido ignorada por la historia oficial, la contribución hispana a la formación de Estados Unidos forma una corriente subterránea que ha resurgido constantemente en la historia del país a través de múltiples expresiones culturales. . . . Los detalles desconocidos de esta historia han ido aflorando a medida que la población crece y cientos de miles de inmigrantes siguen llegando.

3. For a brilliant analysis of Latino images in U.S. cinema, see Charles Ramirez Berg (2002).

4. "Need some salsa in your advertising?," a Del Valle, Macedo, and Associates advertisement, *Advertising Age* (in "Marketing to Hispanics," 1987).

5. This, of course, depends on which perspective we take. From the U.S. American perspective, Spanish is the difference between Anglo and Latin Americans. From the Latin American perspective, *English* is the difference. Thus, if we were to apply the same classificatory logic of the Hispanic label, we could imagine an ethnicity constituted by the "Mexican peoples of U.S. descent." If such a Mexican ethnicity were identified by English, its language of origin, this group would be called "Anglo." Once identified as "Anglo," this Mexican ethnic minority would automatically share "ethnicity" with all peoples whose origin can be traced to any of the English-speaking countries of

the world, from India to Australia. What seems implausible (or plainly hilarious) in the case of this imaginary ethnicity becomes naturalized in the case of the *Hispanic*.

6. In 1848, the United States annexed what at the time was about one-third of the Mexican territory. Although the Guadalupe-Hidalgo treaty guaranteed that Mexican properties would be respected, many Mexican ranches and properties were expropriated by the Anglo colonizers, and Mexicans found themselves in an alien territory, governed by another language and another law (Quinientos años de herencia hispana, 1992).

7. The Hispanic/Latino category is officially broken down into the subcategories Mexican, Puerto Rican, Cuban, South and Central Americans, and "others." We could propose a similar breakdown for the *Anglo*, the imaginary Mexican "ethnicity" I suggested earlier. We would say that the *Anglo*, although characterized by a common language and heritage, is very *diverse* in its composition. We would point out that the Anglo ethnicity is actually constituted by these subcategories: (a) Californians, (b) New Yorkers, (c) Midwesterners, (d) British, (e) Others. This categorization is as logically implausible as it is rhetorically sound. The subcategories break any principle of noncontradiction, parallelism, symmetry, or consistency. However, these are the principles on which "scientific" data on the empirically verifiable "ethnic" group are collected, classified, and evaluated. Clearly, a distinct map of the country, the continent, or the world is drawn in the ways human groups are divided, categorized, distinguished, or melted down.

8. On a special report on the "booming" Hispanic market, Channel 66 News (Noticias 66, Univisión-Chicago) mentioned this rather accidental manner in which *People* magazine discovered the "power" of the yet-to-be-conquered Hispanic market. It is getting harder to miss the importance of the Hispanic market, concluded the report.

2

A View from Latin America

Markers of Difference and Identity

In the previous chapter, I discussed the official invention of a Hispanic/Latino ethnicity in the United States—its symbolic power, its empirical inexistence, and its almost poetic ideological paradoxes. One could imply from this "invention" that the U.S. Latino is indeed a lie or a fabrication, whereas other U.S. ethnicities or American nationalities such as Colombian or Mexican may be more empirically real. However, an ethnicity or a nationality are never empirically given, objective realities, but collectively sanctioned identities based on intersubjective experience, social practices, and legitimating discourses. These identities are phenomenological, semantic, and semiotic in nature, and they engage simultaneously individual experience, group sense-making, and collective power dynamics. The issue at stake, therefore, is less whether an ethnicity such as the "Latino" really "exists" and more how it has been made "real" and in whose name.

Let me speak to you first as a Mexican and then as a Latin American, said Carlos Fuentes in his famed address to the 1983 Harvard Commencement (1988, p. 199). His address both praised the United States for its cultural, scientific, and political contributions to the world and critiqued its interventionist policies in Latin America. Fuentes called on the United States to treat Latin American countries as friends and neighbors instead of satellites (the Soviet Union loomed large at the time). He spoke just as strongly on behalf of Mexico as he did on behalf of Nicaragua, El Salvador, and other countries in Central and South America. For Fuentes, as for many other Latin American writers, artists, and theoreticians, "Latin America" is both a geopolitical region defined by its colonial and neocolonial relations to Europe and the United States and an overarching culture constantly created and re-created in the complicity of a common history and the tension of a great polyphonic diversity.

As a Mexican, Fuentes spoke of the history and culture of a specific nation-state. As a Latin American, he spoke of a shared background, a crisscrossing of stories and histories, and a symbolic territory whose limits are as empirically imprecise as its experience is compelling. He may be hard pressed to identify what it exactly means to speak like a Latin American. And yet, he *speaks as* a Latin American, and he does so without much hesitation, for Latin America is a common symbolic referent and experiential background for most of those who live south of the U.S. border and a few of those to the east (Cuba, Dominican Republic, Puerto Rico).

I find myself speaking in these pages as a Latin American first and as a Colombian second. Although I am not certain of the *substance* of a Latin American speech, I know its *practice* is a fundamental part of my lived cultural awareness. I find this continental cultural identity no less perplexing or compelling than my nationality, for identifying oneself as a Colombian requires as much a leap of imagination as seeing oneself as a Latin American. A Latin American (or a Colombian) cultural identity is not defined by essential attributes (e.g., that which we positively are), but by markers of difference (e.g., that which we are not; that which constitutes "us" in relation to others in a field of differences).

I cannot speak of Latin America but as a Colombian. This is my nationality, the country I know best, and the region from which "Latin America" as a cultural field unfolds for me. Conversely, I make sense of Colombia within a larger Latin American field, so that both co-constitute one another. These identities are not independent nor are they interchangeable. They are overlapping cultural dimensions that unite "us" in our distinctive traits, divide us in our similarities, and construct, through identity and difference, a common background of cultural awareness.

Under closer inspection, that clearly defined geopolitical unit, Colombia, reveals itself to be heterogeneous to the point that some scholars argue for the need to speak of "Las Colombias," in plural, to acknowledge its regional, ethnic, racial, economic, and cultural diversity. As in the case of Latin America, when I speak of Colombia, I invoke a general cultural field, neither directly experienced nor fictional, but collectively imagined. In my case, Colombia unfolds as a generality from my lived experience in Bogotá and Cali, two large cities that cannot claim to "represent" Colombia, and from my position as an urban, middle-class female intellectual. These markers of identity greatly influence my experience and understanding. I have little to no experiential knowledge of the Colombian Pacific and Atlantic coasts; of its southern jungles and vast eastern plains; of its fishing towns, banana plantations, emerald mines, and coastal carnivals. Were I an Afro-Colombian peasant residing in the war-torn Urabá region of the northwest, my lived experience of Colombia would be dramatically different. I would find Bogotá as culturally remote as Miami and as physically unreachable as Panama City.[1] I would find "Colombia" to be as fictitious and intriguing as the evening melodramas; not an "imagined community" in the celebrated words of Anderson, but an *imaginary community* or a slightly odd fabrication in somebody else's imagination.

Difference in Identity

"Just tell them who we are and that we are not all alike," said an interviewee to Shorris (1992) when he was preparing his book, *The Latinos: A Biography of the People* (p. XV). Two things are striking in this request. First, the interviewee expresses a desire to let the U.S. non-Latino mainstream (i.e., "them") know that Latinos encompass different cultures and peoples. A Cuban is not a Mexican is not a Puerto Rican is not a Chilean. Second, the interviewee does not hesitate to say "us" in her request. We are not the same, but it is among "us" that we differ, in the same way that siblings are not identical or that the panels in a well-sewn quilt remain distinct. The emphasis here is less on the fact that "we are not the same" than on the failure of *them* to appreciate the nuances of a family or the richness of a quilt.

Acquiring or being given an identity is simultaneously being positioned in a field of differences and resisting a homology as either Other or the Same. Being called Hispanic (or Latino or Colombian) situates us within an ethnosociological map that designates demographics, origins, and history; and that defines, in social practice, our bodies, faces, and habits.

Identity in Difference

The Colombian writer Gabriel García Márquez has stated on numerous occasions that he is more a *costeño* than a Colombian. He is a "native of the Coast," and as such he might have more in common with other Caribbean peoples, whether Colombian, Venezuelan, or Cuban, than with the inland people from the cold Andean mountains of Colombia.

García Márquez's statement is revelatory at least in two ways. First, it uncovers the cultural alliances that break the smooth surface of unified nation-states. Second, it highlights an in-between region that cuts across political borders as the space in which cultural identity emerges. This space articulates cultural identity as an *integration in difference*, an acknowledgment of differences that supersede them.

This relationship between identity and difference is fundamental to understand the ways in which Latin American political borders are simultaneously boundaries and bridges, as they *highlight* the commonalities of those who do not share the same nationality, and the differences among those who do.

García Márquez has recounted both in his novels and interviews his first impressions of Bogotá as an alien city. The Colombian capital he recalls in the 1950s was a cold, somber, and foggy city of tight morality, obsessive religiosity, and extreme decorum. A place, said García Márquez, where men always dressed in gray and women only ventured outside their houses to attend funerals. The Colombian capital contrasted sharply with his native Aracataca on the Colombian Atlantic coast and the Caribbean towns after which his mythical Macondo was modeled. In the coastal town, heat covered everything with a veil of unreality, rain had more constancy than the law, sorcerers protected reason from rational superstition, and the smell of human passion was as penetrating as that of ripe fruits.[2] In a vivid manner, García Márquez is describing the profound distance between two places fully alien to one another yet forced into "oneness" by the accidental arrangement of political borders.

One could say, as Fuentes (1988) put it, that Latin American societies "are marked by cultural continuity and political discontinuity" (p. 205). The differences between *costa* and *cordillera* are not, in fact, only a matter of topography but also of collective memory. At the time of the European invasion of the 15th century, one's location on the high Andes or the lowlands, the eastern plains, or the western mountains would have strongly correlated with different indigenous cultures and linguistic families, such as the *Chibcha*, the *Quimbaya*, and the *Tayrona* in what would become Colombia. After the invasion, those regions generated their own specific forms of social hierarchy and cultural myth, as well as styles of human exploitation and production, whether of sugar, gold, bananas, cocoa, or tobacco. This long, "topographic" memory has a historical and social depth that is not defined by, or circumscribed to, nations or states. It cuts across national boundaries and proposes a map of Latin America whose borders differ fundamentally from those officially sanctioned.

Music is an eloquent expression of these continental interconnections. *Tangos* and *milongas*, born in the slums and brothels of Buenos Aires and Montevideo at the turn of the 20th century, are as important to Buenos Aires as they are to Medellín, Colombia. The place where famous tango singer Carlos Gardel died in 1935, Medellín rivals few places in terms of its traditional affection for tangos and of its public display of tango as a city's musical icon.

Contemporary *salsa* was born in the New York mixing of Afro-Caribbean and African American rhythms (from *son* and *mambo*, Rhythm and Blues, and jazz). It is as much Cuban and Puerto Rican as it is *Nuyorican*; a U.S. meeting ground of the African diaspora, in English and in Spanish. However, a non-coastal Colombian city, closer to the Pacific than to the Atlantic, proudly calls itself "the capital of salsa." In Cali, Colombia, salsa is in the fabric of everyday life; listened to in buses and restaurants, danced to most weekdays, celebrated in an annual festival, and recently despised by a new generation for whom other musical diasporas have arrived: *Hispanic Hip-Hop*, *Rock en Español*, and Dominican *Raeggetón*.

Similarly, the Amerindian music of Bolivia, Peru, and Paraguay was adopted by Chilean, Guatemalan, and Nicaraguan folk singers and transformed by the Cuban New Song movement (*Nueva Trova Cubana*). In turn, Cuban *danzón* was adopted as its own by Mexico in the 1920s; Mexican *rancheras* are a necessity in Colombian celebrations, and Colombian *cumbias* are best-sellers in Ecuador. While Brazilian Caetano Veloso interprets Mexican and Venezuelan traditional music, the music from the Venezuela plains (*música llanera*) popularized by Simón Diaz is reinterpreted as salsa, jazz, or folk by Argentine, Cuban, Puerto Rican, and Panamenian musicians.

These are musical expressions of a Latin American cultural territory whose map is not based on political divisions, but on designs of collective memory and popular cross-pollination.[3] In that map, the South-Pacific city Cali is closer to Cuba than the Caribbean Cartagena, the northern Medellín neighbors the southern Buenos Aires, and the Cuban Silvio Rodriguez plays the Andean rhythms that the slain Chilean singer songwriter Victor Jara used to sing about Cuba. Such interconnections allow one to speak of "Latin America" in spite of the clear differences among the countries of the region. This vital map suggests the figure of a cultural tapestry whose texture can only be seen or sensed in the crisscrossing of its multiple threads. Not one aspect or thread suffices to account for the quilt's texture.

Cultural Boundaries, Tapestries, and Quilts

A culture can be compared to a tapestry in which threads can be followed in many directions, from their points of convergence to their lines of divergence; from their dispersed networks to their dense knots. Depending on what threads are followed, diverse patterns become apparent. Although we can have a distinct sense of the tapestry as a whole, its knots and patterns are shapes without precise boundaries. As in the case of the tapestry, a culture's contour is *nowhere* in particular, for it is the very crisscrossing of the woven net (Lozano & Mickunas, 1992).

The contact with an alien cultural field renders one's own visible and reveals as conventional that which we might have assumed as natural. Walking for the first time on a surface to which our feet are not accustomed, exploring a city whose conventions are unfamiliar, or speaking a foreign language bring to the fore the nuances of our own vocabulary, posture, and habit. To recognize a discourse as foreign is to grant the familiar a finite contour. The experience of the alien and the proper (and of the alien *in* the proper) allows us to see as well how differing discourses overlap and intersect, being already transformed and opened by our presence. No awareness of "culture" could be possible without the presence of the foreign. Thus, cultural boundaries are actively and constantly traced, defined, and transformed; as the alien becomes familiar, the external is embodied, and the foreign is translated. The "essence" of a culture is not different from its field of action, and its identity, always motivated and porous, extends as far as its surface goes. We recognize "our culture" (whatever this happens to be) in the face of that which is unexpected, meaningless, or abnormal; in that which might turn out to be normal for others.

It is possible to speak of a Western culture while simultaneously acknowledging, for example, the presence of the French and German traditions. The latter do not deny or contradict the former, for France and Germany share commonalities as Western nations and differences as cultural traditions. Similarly, it is possible to speak of a Latin American culture without denying the strong presence of the Mexican, the Brazilian, or the Cuban nationalities. A Latin American culture is coextensive with and inseparable from the differing nations and regions that we claim constitute Latin America and from the symbolic values we have collectively assigned to it. Accordingly, the limits and boundaries of what we can call a Latin American culture are given by a multiplicity of political, historical, linguistic, and narrative criteria, which may vary over time and place. For example, is English-speaking, Central American Belize a part of Latin America? Is Puerto Rico simultaneously a U.S. territory and a Latin American island? Under which conditions does French Guiana or English-speaking Guyana count as Latin American?

A Latin American "culture" disappears in the face of the distinctiveness of its inclusions (e.g., the Argentine or Mexican nationalisms) and the arbitrariness of its exclusions (why do we include the Dominican Republic but seldom Haiti?). But Latin America emerges as a cultural formation in the face of its distinctiveness from Western Europe or Southeast Asia.

Because a culture is traced in that which "marks it" as other, that which emerges as Latin American would differ depending on whether I am contrasting its different regions, understanding it within the designs of Western Modernity, or comparing it with the Indian, Arabic, or Japanese cultures.

A Latin American culture appears when the given background is global and the reference is another "externality," such as Europe or the United States. The cultures of Latin America, in contrast, appear when the given background is regional (i.e., Latin America itself) and the references are "internal" or local. I recognize the Colombian in the face of the Peruvian, but I lose it in the presence of *la Zona Cafetera*, *el Magdalena medio*, or *la Costa Atlantica*, all very distinct Colombian regions. Once I take a unitary whole as a given, its heterogeneous nature comes to the fore; once I take heterogeneous pieces as the given, their commonality comes to the fore. A quilt is an alliance of distinct pieces. We can see the quilt and its singular pieces, and we can see one through the other.

As with the quilt, we can simultaneously recognize Latin America—or Colombia—and miss it if we are expecting it to be a homogenous territory. This does not imply the inadequacy of the categories "Latin American," "Colombian," or "European," but their intentional and ideological nature (i.e., they are always articulated in a field of action and discourse). Only if these are seen as positive and closed objects of investigation, which therefore adhere to a binary logic of "either/or," do they become inadequate categories, as their intentionality is overlooked. What we call a culture is less a mapped geography than a lived territory of uneven plateaus, depressions, and mounds that are disclosed in our wandering and transformed by it.

A culture presupposes a sense of lived complicity that can be traced in discourse and practice. However, the awareness of such complicity only comes to the fore in the presence of the *other*, the different, the outsider. This awareness can only emerge—as a matter of knowledge—when it is brought to the fore by the presence of something that forces the comparison and the recognition of the proper or the normalized.

The Latin American and the Anglo American

Say what you must about the Spanish colonial era; there was this extraordinary catholic achievement: races were mixed, first in rape, then in conversion and marriage, now in memory. Today 90 percent of Mexico is mestizo. By contrast, consider Puritan America: The Indian and the pilgrim drew apart and have regarded each other with suspicion over centuries. It was in Puritan America that "diversity" became a national virtue, and miscegenation became a sin and a crime. Paradoxically, I remain truest to Mexico, least the American, when I accept the inevitability of assimilation in my life. I am most Mexican when I refuse to use the past as a shield against my new American influence. (Rodríguez, 1989, p. 10)

Latin America can be considered simultaneously postindustrial and nonmodern, capitalistic and feudal, Western-rationalist, and magic-realist. Its mestizo Catholicism is a magic practice that pervades social life beyond the religious realm; its democracies could not be understood without aristocracy; its capitalistic practices embrace neoliberalism and exercise paternalism and *clientelismo*.[4] Not unlike Protestantism in the United States, Latin American Catholicism becomes an ethics of daily life, a fundamental way of living, coping with, and understanding the environment.[5]

Concepts and practices central to Protestant ethics—or to the project of Western modernity with which it is intertwined—such as the autonomy of the individual, the body as private property, or the Law as the ultimate social mediator are absent from, or questioned by, the very logic of daily life in most Latin American settings (Lozano, 1994). Social life is governed instead by (Catholic) rules of loyalty, friendship, dignity, solidarity, and generosity (Kuznesof, 1989). Jorge Luis Borges captured this difference between civil society and community when he described the Argentinean. "Unlike North Americans and almost all Europeans," said Borges (1952/1981a), "the Argentinean does not identify himself with the state."

> The Argentinean is an individual, not a citizen. Aphorisms like Hegel's—The State is the reality of the moral idea—seem like a vicious joke. Films made in Hollywood repeatedly portray as admirable the man [. . .] who tries to make friends with a criminal so he can turn him over to the police later; the Argentine, for whom friendship is a passion and the police a mafia, feels that this "hero" is an incomprehensible cad. (Borges, 1952/1981a, pp. 167–168)

In the same manner that State, Law, and Property do not have in Latin America the status they carry in Western Europe or the United States, "reality" is a field that unfolds with a higher degree of ambiguity and porosity than a "modern" consciousness might willingly accept. In this respect, the Latin American field of experience carries with it a peculiar postmodern logic, which does not come "after," but precedes and co-constitutes the modern. Dichotomies such as fact/fiction, poetry/history, and description/evaluation do not carry oppositional but overlapping valences. Such a situation can be well grasped in García Márquez's *magic-realism,* which the author would say is not fantastic storytelling but faithful chronicle of a complex reality. What is more "absurd," one may ask: That the virginal Remedios the Beauty "ascended to heaven in body and soul" or that a nocturnal train carried the corpses of "more than three thousand people, workers, women, and children" to be discarded "into the sea like rejected bananas"? (García Márquez, 1970, pp. 256, 309, 312).[6] Both accounts can be understood as real-magic. The former is the magic of the mestizo sagas, in which religion is endowed with Spaniard mysticism and Indian-African shamanism. The latter is the magic of "Mr. Brown" and "Mr. Herbert," the U.S. businessmen who organized the exploitation of bananas in *One Hundred Years of Solitude*'s Macondo. The magic of the *gringos* is the *technology* that endowed them with:

> Means that had been reserved for Divine Providence in former times . . . to change the pattern of the rains, accelerate the cycle of harvests, and

move the river from where it had always been and put it with its white
stones and icy currents on the other side of the town. (García Márquez,
1970, p. 233)

The technological magic (or Habermas' "instrumental reason") endows
the "magician" with the ability to control, suppress, or deactivate those
things that stop him from performing his alchemy. As opposed to the magic
of technology, which grants the subject control and power over the world,
the magic of Macondo is the magic of the world over which humans have
little or no power.

In this experience of reality, the rational cannot be without the magical,
the analytical without the fantastic. Routine is reinvented every morning,
chance is the only predictable event of daily action. Instead of being structured linearly or progressively, as a sequence of past, present, and future,
social time is a field that extends in multiple directions, neither of which
is future, neither of which is "just" past. Paraphrasing Borges, Alazraki
(1988) has written that "things are their dusty future." Time is a consuming
fire and a sweeping river, but "I am the fire . . . I am the river" (Alazraki,
1988, p. 48). Because our very substance is time, it cannot be measured in
homogenous particles or standard sequences. Time is the time that I am,
the populous time of action, pleasure, devotion, struggle, or labor. To plan
the future is, therefore, an ineffective alchemy, an act of rhetoric, and an
inept attempt to control the voluptuous. One deals with the uncertain as the
only thing one can rationally expect, for the texture of the world is ahuman
(Lozano & Mickunas, 1992).

From a "magic-realist" standpoint, the Anglo-American is a magic world
in which the superstition of linear time actually works as a power over reality.
As a Colombian entering the United States for the first time 20 years ago,
I found surprising the predictability of U.S. daily life, which frees one from
continuously deciphering an unpredictable daily life. Well-established routines,
standard procedures, and ritualized mechanisms convert the cultural *polysemic
signs* into *monosemic signals*. As with any effective magic, the technologically
constituted world restricts multilayered actions to the enactment of precise
performances that produce specific results. In *One Hundred Years of Solitude*,
Mr. Brown knows where the river should be to produce better and improved
bananas. He therefore moves the river.

The *bricolageous* daily life of Colombia emphasizes the resourceful response
to the surprising event, an ongoing "original" response to an unpredictable
context, and ever-emerging situations.[7] Interpretations of action are multiple
and indefinite, and every activity is performed as a variation. Within this
context, the U.S. Magic land is pleasant and soothing; a relief. Technological

magic provides for security, order, and predictability, and it encourages trust in a system that appears to go on, regardless of human inclination, distaste, or passion. However, it also regulates polysemy, establishes manuals for daily action, and restricts expressivity to functional ends.

To the multivalent reality and the voluptuous time, the high modern U.S. society offers a quantifiable reality, segmented and compartmentalized, and a homogenous time that is alien to intensities, elongations, or mutations. Time is consistent, directional, and scarce. It is always running ahead, breathless and merciless, requiring everyone to engage in a race for which there is no end but only interruption. The present is but a moment toward the future, an ephemeral instant in the achievement of the reality "ahead." Thus, to the Borgesian view that "we are all that we will be, all that we have been," the Modern time proposes the "that's just history" view of Bush's unavoidable directionality.

These exclusionary forms of time encounter and juxtapose one another in the cultural experience of the Hispanics, the Latino-Americanos. The tensions between these cultural understandings of time and action are expressed by Latina writer María Lugones (1990) when she writes,

Siempre hay tiempo para los amigos.

> I see you next Tuesday
> at 5:15.

Vente y tomamos un café y charlamos
mientras plancho la ropa.

> I'll call you Monday
> evening to let you know for sure
> that I am coming.

Ay, mujer, te ves triste,
te sientes bien?
Me duele mucho la cabeza y
estoy un poco sola y cansada.
Dura la vida, no?

> Hi, how are you? Fine, and you?
> Fine, thank you.

(pp. 53–54)[8]

The Myth of Origin

Harvey (1991) has noted the ambivalence that Peruvian Andean communities experience between the Spanish heritage and their indigenous Inca identity. The Peruvian Andean community is aware of two pasts:

> One associated with the Quechua language combines a positive evaluation of their powerful autochthonous ancestors with a negative view of the Spanish invaders. The other, associated with the Spanish, presents the Spanish-speaking state as a positive, civilizing force acting on the ignorant backwardness of the superstitious indigenous people. (Harvey, 1991, p. 6)

This sense of ambivalence is a characteristic structure of the Latin American, mestizo mythical consciousness. Regardless of their skin color or ethnic background, in discourse, most Latin Americans take symbolic side with the conquered, the Indian. Whereas the U.S. mainstream narrative of national origin recalls that "we came here and settled down," the Latin American story remembers "when they came and invaded us." The Spaniard and Portuguese conquistador is an outsider, an invader, and a rapist, but "we" speak his language, worship his god, and value his "civilized" heritage. Latin Americans embrace our colonized mother but do not take "seriously" her gods, her language, or her "old-fashioned," uncivilized customs. Her myths, rituals, and knowledge are *nostalgically* remembered but hardly ever practiced.

The mythical origin of U.S. Americans is located in the "Continent," the outside-U.S. world; their future is in the frontier. In contrast, both the origin and the future of Latin Americans (which are the same) are located in the American land. "We," Latin Americans, were born out of the rape and invasion of "our" land. "We," Anglo Americans, were born out of self-determination, endurance, heroism, and conquest of wild and inhospitable lands. The mythical father of an Anglo American is the frontiersman, the cowboy who wins against all odds, fights the Indians, saves the girl, and rides toward the sunset, the last frontier. The mythical father of a Latin American came for the gold, presented us with God and King, and left.

The polar complementarity of the Anglo and the Latin American myths of origin allows these two cultural formations to position each other as current expressions of the myth. Latin Americans "fit" in the U.S. image of frontier conquering. Anglo Americans "fit" in the Latin American description of conquerors. If the mythical father of a Latin American is a Spaniard soldier who came to steal gold, the United States is his brother, the Uncle, the modern-day postcolonizer. The United States is a constant cultural and political invader, a presence that permeates Latin American media, art, technology, and politics.

Although envied, admired, and emulated for its technological prowess and efficiency, it is despised for its superficiality, hypocrisy, and greed. The Latin American who comes to the United States is entering the land of the frontiersman, and thus repeating the journey of the colonized and the colonizer. She is both, in a tension hardly ever resolved. The Latin American must embrace the pragmatic style of the once despised invader and share with him the logic of action, individuality, and pragmatism. However, such a pragmatic embrace does not nullify the discursive *mythos*. The Latino/Latina immigrant speaks publicly in Anglo American codes, but speaks domestically with Latin American complicities.

A culture is not given by abstracted identities but constituted as a conventional (not arbitrary) and lived space *created* in discursive, political, and dialogic action. Therefore, in becoming a part of the United States, one rearranges narratives, styles, and expectations. As Penelope's cloth, a culture is continuously woven and continuously reconstituted. There is no positive edge, no clear marker to the beginning or end of the weaving. To enter the new cultural space of the United States is to learn anew one's own culture and transform both cultures from within (Lozano, 1994).

> I was a boy. Short. Fat. I kept to myself. Coveted. I did not go to the junior prom. I was dark and thought myself ugly in a world that rewarded blondness. . . . Many years afterward I became a writer because I hungered for communal assurance. Applause. The good review. It was your understanding that I desired. . . . So I wrote of my Mexican house, but in the words of the city. I end up here. I end up speaking your language, not the language of my childhood. You—strangers—hold my polished secrets in your silent stare. (Rodríguez, 1989, p. 13)

Notes

1. Traveling from the Urabá region to Bogotá could take two or three days by land. In contrast, no roads connect Panama and Colombia. Even if Urabá is close to Panama, the only way to reach Panama City would be to take a plane from a major city such as Medellin. This proposition is unlikely for a poor peasant.

2. I am paraphrasing passages from García Márquez's (1970) *One Hundred Years of Solitude*.

3. This cross-pollination can be seen in *melodrama* as a narrative and an expressive style. Melodrama is expressed in music and oral storytelling (such as in tangos, vallenatos, and narco-corridos), in mass-mediated narratives such as *telenovelas*, and in the political rhetoric of *populismo*. It is, according to Martín-Barbero (1989), one of the forces that integrate Latin America from "below." That is, it is a way in which

traditions, cultural legacies, and social needs are expressed, transformed, and repossessed by common people. It is a form of *mestizaje*, the European-African-Indian mix of Latin America, in which conflicting languages and practices find a common ground of expression.

4. *Clientelismo* is an informal political system in which political favors are exchanged for votes. The politician sees his or her constituents as "clients" and relates to them accordingly.

5. Catholicism is the predominant religion in most Latin American countries. However, the presence of Protestantism is growing, particularly in Brazil, Chile, Guatemala, and Puerto Rico.

6. The infamous "Masacre de las Bananeras" to which this episode in *One Hundred Years of Solitude* refers occurred in the plantations of Balboa, Colombia, in 1928. Peasant workers were demanding better working conditions from their employee, the United Fruit Company. They gathered in a public plaza to protest and were besieged and killed by the Colombian army. A 1991 Colombian/British documentary, *Mi Macondo/My Macondo*, sets up to trace the accuracy of García Marquez's account and engages in a search of "Macondo" (Weldon, 1991), the mythical town in which the book's narrative takes place. Macondo, said García Márquez, is a state of mind. We Colombians are constantly creating Macondo—and re-creating the Massacre of the Bananeras in every act of State violence.

7. I find the concept of "bricolage" as used by Lévi-Strauss (1968) and others quite appropriate to describe the cultural dynamics of daily life in Colombia. Bricolage is "making do" with whatever is available—creating tools from odd materials, improvising detours or stories as they are needed, and responding tactically to the always surprising environment.

8. The italicized verses say, roughly translated: There is always time for your friends/Come by and we get a coffee and talk while I iron the clothes/ Ay, woman, you look sad, are you O.K.? I have a headache and I am a little lonely and tired. Life is hard, isn't it?

3

From the United States to America and Back

The Power of Rhetorical Naming

In the Cheech Marin film *Born in East L.A.*, Rudy, a U.S. born, L.A. resident mistakenly deported to Mexico, is trying to earn some money to come back to the United States (Marin, 1987). Paid to attract people to a night club, he stands in front of the place, trying to convince passers-by to come in. A couple approaches, and Rudy touches the man's shoulder. The man pulls his body away and responds angrily, "Don't touch me! I'm an American citizen." This is a poignant, funny, and revelatory scene, particularly for the viewer who has experienced being positioned simultaneously in and out of "America," as a Latin American, a Mexican American, an Asian American, and so on. Our laughter (or anger) at this scene may be deeper if we can recognize the two contrasting codes of public comportment being enacted. One is Anglo American and demands not to be touched; the other, Latin American, demands interpellation. Rudy, a Mexican American, is the meeting place of these codes: an embodied borderline.

Rudy does not speak Spanish "too well," he had reminded his mother a few days earlier, when she asked him to pick up his cousin Javier who is visiting the United States for the first time. A raid by "la migra" at the toy factory where he is picking up Javier gets Rudy and dozen others deported. Rudy was born in L.A., where he works as a mechanic and lives with his Mexican mother. He is shocked by his detention and has a hard time remembering who the president of the United States is.

Immigration officer (IO): Where were you born?

Rudy: What?

IO: Read my lips, El Paco. Where were you born?

Figure 3.1. Rudy (Cheech Marin) instructing OTMs in *Born in East L.A.* (1987).

Rudy: I was born in East L.A., man.

IO: Sure, sure. If you were born in East L.A., then who's the president of the United States?

Rudy: I-I don't know, that guy, that guy who was on T.V., the guy in the cowboy hat . . . he used to be on "Death Valley Days" . . . uh, John Wayne!

IO: Get him out of here.

Rudy insists that he is an American citizen ("Where did you learn to speak English so well?" asks one official). But his failure to remember the president's name, which in any other situation might have been the expression of a misinformed citizen, corroborates in this case the suspicion that Rudy is an illegal Mexican worker. "Get your hands off me! I am an American citizen!" Rudy has yelled at the U.S. officers taking him away. Later, in Mexico, he becomes the object of such a request.

The fact that the "American citizen" who Rudy has touched is an African American only emphasizes the ironic nature of the situation.[1] The "American citizen" cannot recognize in Rudy the citizenship that they both share. Rudy's face and body announce South of Rio Grande, non-American, Mexican. Rudy might be an L.A. native and a citizen of the United States, but the signs that are inscribed in flesh, the semiotics of the body, always overflow and contradict the abstractions of Law and State. The African American "defends himself" against Rudy in Mexico the same way Rudy did in L.A. against the immigration police. Both try to appeal to their privileged legal status as U.S. citizens, and both find this privilege denied by their skin. Since this Black man is (despite "appearances") an American citizen, Rudy does not have over him the same cultural "rights" he would have over Mexicans. Paradoxically, it is outside of the United States that this African American can claim the "American" right not to be touched. While in Mexico he is an American citizen, whereas in "America" he is a citizen only ambiguously, and he, most definitely, may be touched. The non-White descendant of African slaves is never entirely free from designating the puritanical outside, standing at the border, and marking the margin. The African American and the Chicano reveal the embodied codes of "Americanhood," and by so doing expose the semiotics inscribed in flesh and the "superfluidity" of the body. Gloria Anzaldúa (1987) expresses this embodied "borderline" with singular force:

> 1,950 mile-long open wound
> > dividing a *pueblo*, a culture,
> > running down the length of my body,
> > > staking fence rods in my flesh,
> > > splits me   splits me
> > > me raja   me raja
>
> > This is my home
> > this thin edge of
> > barbwire
>
> (pp. 2–3)

"Don't touch me, I'm an American citizen." Being an American citizen, I have a body that stands as a private property, a law that has wrapped up my body with a "no trespassing" cautionary sign, and a State that behaves as my body guard—particularly if I am outside U.S. boundaries. My (American) citizenship protects me wherever I go, and, as a nomadic institution, it allows me to reconstitute around myself the civic and political space with which I am familiar. As a transnational national, the American can travel most of the globe as a nomad, moving from space to space without ever changing place, rearranging landmarks to fit his or her known territory. It is possible to travel the world without leaving *America*. There is always the Hilton and McDonald's to keep oneself attuned to home. There is always, in short or large supply, American Express, Madonna, blue jeans, Superman,

CNN, *Time*, Bush, Clinton, or Obama news, Stephen King's latest best seller, and Spielberg at the multiplex.

Sometimes it is hard to tell the "world" and "America" apart. Sometimes the world becomes a metonymy of "America," which in turn becomes a metonymy for the United States, which in turn may stand for New York, L.A., or Atlanta.

Heterogeneous Logics

Rudy is an outsider and an insider, whether in Tijuana or California. He is not fully an American, not quite a Latin American, not "one of us" either side of the border, but an embodied site of tension between the two. One deals with this tension every day, in the Tex-Mex music, in the Hispanic markets, in the voting districts, in the bilingual neighborhoods, in the transformation of barefoot Colombian rocker Shakira into blonde Miami pop singer Shakira, and on television commercials abundant on siesta, fiesta, and salsa.

Rudy is also a new integration; a son of East L.A., a place where to be considered a rightful native one must "be brown" or act brown (Marin, 1987). It is limiting to call Rudy a Hispanic or circumscribe his experience to that of Mexican Americans. It is just as rhetorically charged to call him Latino. His cultural experience emerges as a result of an ambivalent pull and push among several forms of ethnic or national identity: Mexican, Mexican American, Latin American, Latino, Chicano, American, and *vato* from L.A.[2] As is the case with the "United States" and "America," the "Latino" and the "Hispanic" categories increasingly constitute two planes of signification that are "consistent" and sedimented enough to signify in their own terms as two different semantic fields (I discuss the concepts of semiotic planes and semantic fields in Chapter 5).[3]

This semantic and semiotic tension makes apparent the discursive slippages that occur while trying to define semantic fields whose rhetorical force supersedes any "rational" taxonomy of exclusions and inclusions. To become aware of these slippages, it is important to make explicit the distinction between *America* the continent and "America" the U.S. mythical identity—that which Baudrillard (1988) has called the "Astral America" of Hollywood imagination.

America, the Discourse

In the United States and increasingly in Europe and Latin America, *The United States* and *America* are used synonymously. However, the (symbolic) boundaries of America do not correspond to the (geopolitical) boundaries of the United States. These terms, in fact, open two different semantic fields; they invite us into two different discursive nets. While it is common and comfortable to refer to the *American* dream, the *American* lifestyle, or the *American* culture, it seems quite awkward to refer to the U.S. dream or the U.S. culture. In contrast with "America," the United States begs for pluralization—in the name of its diversity of cultures, dreams, lifestyles, and states.

Indeed, one may ask, what is the culture, the style, or the memory that unites the states of the union, and their relentless population of visitors, natives, settlers, and nomads? Could one claim that there is a tradition that is representative of the United States? Is it the West African, the West European, the British, or the Native American? In fact, if there is a culture in the United States, such culture is the *American*. It is neither one of these traditions, nor a particular memory, but another logic of cohesion, a *discourse* that is both a "master practice" and a mythical narrative.[4] Because "Americanhood" is a matter of social and discursive practice, it is quite possible to be fully an American and not a native of the United States—conversely, one may be a U.S. native and barely an American. As a performative condition, "Americanhood" requires actors and stages more than natives or citizens. In order for "America" to work, the would-be American must accomplish a "rite of passage" and be "melted" into the melting pot. Through this melting, the multiplicity of the United States is turned into the unity of America, a "representation."

One could say that "Americanhood" is an especially democratic affiliation, for in principle, it would be open to anyone who has the skills necessary to play and perform (as opposed to being open only to those with the "natural" right of birth or settlement). But, as in the case of a performance or a play, there are actors better suited for the role and actors who barely meet the casting needs. In the United States, some can play "American" better than others. The Whiteness of Europe is a plus, as is a certain body shape and style (tall is favored over short, big over frail) and the ability to speak "American" fluently. The WASP continues to be an ideal casting for "the American."

The United States, in contrast, is constituted by a multiplicity of cultural backgrounds and traditions that inflect one another and articulate the culture from within, not as exceptions to the rule, but as the conditions for the existence of the rule. While "America" renounces difference (i.e., all differences are understood as components of the *Same*), the United States is a union of things dissimilar, diverse, nonequivalent, and unfinished (under the Same, things arise in their diversity and nonequality). Puerto Rico, Hawaii, Alaska, Appalachia, the Southwest, and the Deep South are all regions of a Union-State that otherwise claims for itself a homogenous symbolic landscape.[5]

Both Rudy and the African-American couple are U.S. citizens. But they fail to meet the expectations of the homogenized "American citizen" representation. Between "America" and the "United States," and in their contrast, one can hint at the presence of two discourses: an affirmative discourse and its negative, the same and its contradiction. According to the former, there is an "American culture" in which everybody's cultural background "melts" into a mainstream that erases differences and makes us all equal. "America," the mythical land, is a nation built with the hard work of (freedom-loving) immigrants who left behind their "old countries" and built from scratch an alliance, a common ethics, and a common pragmatic language. But the fine surface of this discourse is continuously irrupted by "others": groups, ethnicities, and cultural traditions such as the Indian, the Kenyan, the Mexican, and the Vietnamese, which are neither dissolved within a "mainstream" nor relegated to the status of a curiosity (Lozano, 1994).

The mythical land appears always more clear from the distance, when seen through the melting pot, and in the implosion of signification that Mickey Mouse, Star Wars, the Forefathers, and Madonna imply. It becomes diluted, in contrast, on the streets, in the experience of walking Chinatown in San Francisco, La Pequeña Habana in Miami, the hills of Appalachia, the Indian and Pakistani neighborhoods of Chicago, the Native American reservations, and the multilingual New York. On the streets, neat oppositions disperse and explode in shapes that are not yet categorical instances of identity and difference. At this level, the limits of the American culture are the limits of the mass-mediated global village. Indeed, often the latter melts into the former to the point that the "American" might be recognized in its global accent and the global might be recognized speaking American. This "utopic" identity attracts and repulses because it constitutes, to paraphrase Ricoeur (1992), differences as *indifference*.

CNN's *World Report* is an interesting exemplar of this process. A four-hour, weekend program initiated in 1987, *World Report* "provides TV viewers around the world with the unique opportunity to see other countries as they see themselves." The official CNN website adds that this program "has brought together thousands of journalists from over 350 broadcasters in more than 150 countries and territories, giving them a global forum to report the news as they see it, to the rest of the world" (CNN website, 2009). The "rest of the world" is either assumed to speak English or to be marginal to its own news reports and to the "world" itself.

The global forum is made up of broadcasters brought together to show their countries as they "see themselves," in the *lingua franca* of CNN, to an audience to which the world reports. "World report" is indeed a magnificent forum and a fascinating source of information about the ways televisual semiotic codes are developed, standardized, and legitimized. The program can be argued to restate the United States to the status of an unprivileged country among many. However, in "World Report," the "world" reports to the United States in English and in an effort to reach U.S. audiences. Thus, one would have to conclude that either (a) the United States is "outside" of the world, (b) the United States is the only one that is truly in the world (and is receiving reports from those outside), or (c) "America" constitutes the standard against which one measures "reality," and particularly the reality of other countries.

Categorical Sedimentations

The United States of America *is* a nation-state under a common government and *are* a coalition of states under a common name. As such, it has some interesting parallels with other unions of states, empires such as the Roman, the Soviet, the Spanish, and the British. Under the Soviet Union, the Russians were the part that stood for the whole, the particular universal. Thus, one could assume that Soviets spoke Russian and that Russia extended through Lithuania, Czechoslovakia, and Afghanistan. Under the equation of state and language and under the sameness of nation, a difference is instituted as identity and center, while other differences become regional, marginal, or alien. Thus, to describe a Catalan person as a Spaniard who speaks a language other than Spanish requires (a) defining the Catalan language as a regionalism, and (b) imposing a region, the province of Castilla, as the norm, from which Castillian (as Spanish) emerges. Spain collapsed its cultural and linguistic differences into the universality of "Spanish," which in turn became the language of most countries in America and the Caribbean, which prompted, in turn, the usage of the label "Hispanic" to define all those U.S. residents who originate from Latin America.

After a century and a half of formal separation and four centuries of conflict, Latin America finds itself once more linked to Spain as a single identity and ethnicity—under their common difference from Anglos in the United States. The situation of Latin Americans in the United States is similar to that of Catalans in Spain: Both find themselves defined by a center that is *somewhere else*; an external and distant unification.

With their intersection of material citizenry and genealogical nationhood, the Hispanic American, the Chinese American, the African American, the Japanese American, all point to the fact that within "America" some are the same, some are the difference. The hyphenation already reveals the fundamental inequality of those who are supposedly equal in the face of law or society. Some are the normal body (Anglo), and some are the marker of difference (non-Anglo) within the same body (American). The "American" (without qualifications) is a specific status within the United States, the one identified with the same, the core of identity, and the mainstream.

Thus, if there is a mainstream in the United States, this mainstream is less empirical than discursive. This site of breakage (Sloterdijk [1986] would call it cynicism) between the materiality of social practices and the—disciplined—ways of speaking about them is one of the aspects that the analysis of discursive practices needs to undertake, particularly with respect to the rhetorical construction of nationalisms. There are breaks in which discourses manifest their regularities, delimitations, and rules of inclusion, exclusion, and extension. These breaks emerge out of the (incomplete) juxtaposition and confrontation of contiguous discourses. Such juxtaposition reveals vacuums despite internal logics and "interstitial spaces," despite the given completeness and complementariness of discourses within a social formation.

Discourses emerge as salient threads whose crisscrossing produces texts and whose vacuum reveals other threads, other aspects of the texture. The texture that interweaves discourses, that grounds them in *intertextuality* and *intersubjectivity*, is always more than discourse. It is a co-present excess that does not resemble, imitate, contradict, or represent, but it provides the support, coordinates, and intentionality required to construct anything. Foucault (1972) would call this excess *power* and *desire*.

Orale, Vato, Whaaas sappenin?

The invention of the "Hispanic" label by the U.S. Census Bureau in the 1970s and the more recent census legitimization of the label "Latino" point to the conventionality, positivity, and situatedness of ethnicities. No race or ethnicity is given prior to their localization within a territory, their semantization across discursive fields, and their exteriorization through semiotic codes. These designs imply a framework, a style, and a rhetoric.

According to a Tijuana local in "Born in East LA," there are two types of people are trying to cross the U.S.–Mexican border: the Mexicans and the Other-Than-Mexicans (OTMs). Rudy is asked to train five OTMs, all "Chinese, Indian or something," to pass for East L.A. natives. Rudy trains them in the art of being *vatos*, including the proper swagger and the Spanglish diction: "Orale, vato!! Whaaas sappenin?" is the proper greeting manner, followed by a festive and arduous five-step hand-shake and the mandatory whistling at female passersby. The OTMs follow the directions rather clumsily, but more and more joyfully. They are being trained into the language and traditions of an emergent culture, for which neither Mexico nor "America" could have given appropriate or sufficient direction (see Figures 3.1 and 3.2). As funny as this categorization appears, its humor resides less in being absurd than in pointing out the absurdity of naturalized conventions. Categories are productive not because they are true but because they are effective sense-making devices. Their power comes from the distillation of unlimited semantic possibilities into sedimented, binary oppositions that become common sense. If one looks closely, one could start noticing commonalities among the OTMs: similar physical features, similar dreams, common ignorance of the English or Spanish languages. Against a given background, things acquire features and shapes that can be empirically verified and studied. The qualities of the thing emerge as inseparable from the field, from the intentionality of the situation, the background and the horizon. When the intentionality of the thing and the field is read as manifestation of a "deeper" truth, a "metaphysical leap" appears. This leap attempts to find the true core of the thing by undressing it, by taking it apart from the field, suspending it in the neutrality of air, and demanding that it performs in the whole fullness of its being. But to do so is to miss the depth field in which the thing appears.

In U.S. video stores, films are categorized according to a basic dichotomy: American genres and international films (or foreign). Thus, movies have genres unless they are international, in which case "foreign" becomes the genre. The "foreign" is characterized by the eccentricity of subtitles and recognized, given this reference, in the now naturalized similarities between an Indian melodrama and a Japanese horror story; a German epic and a

Figure 3.2. OTMs being instructed by Rudy on the ways of East L.A.

Spanish comedy. Weird languages, bizarre topics, odd paces, and strange faces may become the characteristics of this genre. This generic categorization is neither just an imposition from the outside nor a fair description of a state of affairs. It is a convention—an element in a classificatory system that facilitates identification, analysis, and control. As an element in a legitimized system of classification and as participant in a discourse of identities and differences, the categorical name is the expression and the source of a power that can be oppressive or liberating, active or reactive. Such is the case of the "Hispanic-Latino" categories, for they create a nominal difference that social practices might deny, and, in turn, they may transform those social practices and assign them new significance. For example, a Chilean who has been residing in the United States for five years is a Latina (she has a green card). Her brother, who has been studying in the United States for those same five years, is a Latin American with a student visa. The siblings are seen as belonging to two different ethnicities. Even more clearly, the sister belongs to an ethnic minority, and, as such, she has acquired a specific social profile, whereas the brother is an undistinguishable foreigner, a non-ethnic person, with more in common with other students than with Latinos or Chileans.

The cohabitation of simultaneous and contradicting logics in our daily writing, speaking, and acting announces an interstitial space, a territory that allows us to see the limits of our own discourse, while it is itself framed by discursive practices. The non-discursive appears in discourse and through discourse, in the necessary contradiction of the countless logics to which we have pledged allegiance. The material struggle and the rhetorical struggle are never too distant from one another. One fights back the power of names with alternative names, the power of discourse with counter-discourse, and the power of the state apparatus with a political body (to borrow from Deleuze & Guattari, 1987).

Let us end by inviting Chicana poet Margarita Cota-Cárdenas to evoke this power and this struggle in her celebrated poem "Nocturno Chicano" (1977):

Cuando éramos niños
el ploquito y yo
  no había
    sirenas
      por la noche
      por el dia
      de bomberos
      de ambulancia
      de la policía

aterrorizando asustando
  a los grandes
    a los jóvenes
    y a los hermanitos
sólo había   bastaba
    "la migra"

    When we were children
      my little brother and I
        there were no
          sirens
             all night
             all day
             of firemen
             of ambulances
             of the police
   terrorizing   frightening
     big people
      young people
        and little brothers and sisters
there was only   it more than
              sufficed
    "THE IMMIGRATION PATROL"[6]

Notes

1. The term *African American*, a U.S. national of African descent, loses its liberating power and becomes another instance of U.S. rhetorical power when it crosses the border. Any Black in the American continent is, strictly speaking, an African American. This label, therefore, institutes an interesting couplet: There are African Americans and there are people of African descent in the Americas. What does one call a Black Colombian who is a U.S. resident? A non-African-American African American?

2. "Vato" means man or "dude" in Mexico, and it is a Chicano slang term meaning a Mexican or Latino male.

3. The label *Hispanic* excludes Brazilians and includes Spaniards, both of which are extraordinarily difficult moves. Although *Latino* could provide a better sense of "ethnicity," it also carries its own ambiguity because, in principle, it should include Latin European peoples such as the French, Italian, Romanian, and Portuguese. Cultural experience and practice slip beyond binary structures of signification.

4. By "master practice" I am referring to a pervasive pragmatics of life, an overarching sense of "how to go about business." In the case of the United States, this is

a performative and public code of action whose mastery is required of anyone who aspires to be a successful "speaker" or "actor." Such "master practice" is fundamental for the maintenance and continuous rebirth of the "American identity."

5. Homogeneity does not presuppose in this case the absence of contrasts or variety, but the uniformity of varieties and contrasts under commonly understood rules of division, segmentation, and affiliation (i.e., the homogenous follows an *arboreal* logic). They are evenly oppositional and as easily traced on tables and demographic charts.

6. Cited in Rebolledo (1980, p. 32).

II

THE EXPLORATORY TOOLS

Textual Analysis

4

Three Issues on Television Studies

Banality, Universality, and the Text

The Banality of (Hispanic) Television

The relative invisibility of Hispanic television within critical media and television studies parallels the invisibility that television once experienced within the humanities and the scorn that its study still attracts in many circles. In 1990, Mellencamp observed that "for many intellectuals historically leery of entertaining machines of pleasure, TV is just too banal an object" (p. 13). Fourteen years later, Jeffrey Sconce (2004) made a similar observation: "Gather a roomful of intellectuals of almost any stripe and their point of agreement will be that television is the sewer of national and global culture" (p. 93). After all, isn't television by definition formulaic, repetitive, and trivially domestic? Doesn't it strive to avoid intellectual challenges, formal experiments, or aesthetic surprises? Isn't it guided by the principles of profit, predictability, and low creative risk? So, what could possibly be said about television that is not already plain and obvious?

From this perspective, it would follow that to produce theories about television, study its "logics," or analyze its texts is to force complexity out of shallowness, to search for value in a "vast wasteland." Therefore, and to paraphrase Newcomb (2005), if it is necessary to study television (say, to measure its effects), it is, on the other hand, superfluous to perform television studies (i.e., to consider the medium as such).

That there are cultural phenomena or productions considered "banal" (thus unworthy of critical consideration) is an issue of interest in its own right, for it invites us to interrogate the aesthetic and ideological grounds on which taste (and other) judgments are passed over cultural products.[1] In this sense, television studies are not only important in what they "uncover" about television, but also in what they reveal about cultural discourses on taste, class, identity, and culture itself. That which is included in these studies is as important as that which is excluded.

47

Discourses on television, academic or otherwise, are as revelatory as the televisual discourses themselves; their terms and conditions; inclusions and exclusions; chiasms and breakages as compelling as that which is on screen. In her introduction to *Logics of Television*, Mellencamp (1990) states, paraphrasing Barthes, that the aim of her book is to "change the object itself," "transforming TV into a theoretical object" (p. 12).[2] It is important that we address the ways in which television becomes such an object, calling into question the assumptions that inform our understanding of television. Failing to do so would imply granting invisibility to that which is irregular and granting *transparency* to that which is regular and generalizable.

The scholarly legitimacy of television studies was fought and gained over decades of debate against a powerful and dominant positivist paradigm that saw television as inconsequential in any other way than as a black box of causes and effects. Television studies experienced in the late 1970s and early 1980s a "turning point" in the United States, marked by the emergence of highly influential studies that moved away from the traditional "administrative/effects" model and examined television in relation to production, programming, and consumption (D'Acci, 2004). Cultural and television studies attempt to study television within the context of its social processes of "encoding and decoding," to borrow S. Hall's (1980) influential concept; that is, in relation to the specificity of televisual industrial production practices, socially hegemonic discourses, televisual aesthetics, and everyday life rhythms.[3] Because of this interest in context, history, and materiality, television studies face an unstable object of research whose specific contents may age rapidly and whose varying contexts of use and production constantly challenge our ability to produce theory and analyses that do not expire seasonally.

The emergence of new technologies and social media have transformed the practices of watching and studying television, bringing into question the validity or meaning of concepts such as flow and immediacy (D'Acci, 2004; Uriccio, 2004). That transformed object of study invites Lynn Spigel, Jan Olsson, and their colleagues to ponder in *Television after TV* how "television" (the object of investigation) needs to be studied and understood "after TV," that almost defunct three-network mass medium (Spigel & Olsson, 2004).

As D'Acci (2004) suggests, in the theoretical crisis generated by new technological developments and communication practices, some theoretical paths are abandoned, some approaches fall out of favor, and some questions and issues may be dismissed or left unexamined.

Uriccio (2004) reminds us that when Raymond Williams proposed his groundbreaking concept of "flow," it was 1973, and he had been mesmerized by the uninterrupted flow of TV programming he saw from his hotel while visiting the United States. This seamless flow, proposes Uriccio, was a particular generation of TV technology, soon to be transformed by the popularization of the remote control and cable television and subsequent forms of program–viewer "interface." Those technological changes and many more to come transformed the flow of programming into several forms of interruption controlled by the viewer, which, in turn, can be said to have produced another sort of flow, this one created by the viewer's actions of channel-surfing, taping, and mixing media (Uriccio, 2004). When I first encountered Univision and Telemundo in 1989, I was a graduate student in Athens, Ohio, one of two Latin Americans then studying in the School of Interpersonal Communication. Needless to say, there was no Spanish-language television accessible on cable or broadcast in the area. My attraction to Hispanic television was not based on its *immediacy* but on the singularity of its remoteness yet familiarity. I found that the Hispanic TV programming, which Dávila and others later critiqued as being too Latin American (therefore alien to the U.S. Latino experience), was intriguingly foreign to my own (Latin American) televisual experience and deeply "United Statian," in ways that I thought were worth exploring.[4]

I had the programming taped for me via satellite from stations in Miami and L.A. I wanted to study Hispanic television, and I watched a perfect flow. When I moved to Chicago in 1993, I continued to tape the programming for the purpose of studying it, freezing, if you will, an endless stream to fit the boundaries of tapes; transforming an unlimited semiosis into the recorded boundaries of a readable *textuality*. Indeed, that textuality is the focus of my attention, and it is the *archival* nature of both television and of my own action that I wish to explore. Before turning to the issue of television as mediated social archive, I would like to explore that "intimate foreignness" to which I referred above.

"Typical Television"

In the introductory pages to his influential work on television, Fiske (1987) explained that his analysis focused on "typical television," that is, "the most popular, mainstream, internationally distributed programs, for these are the ones of greatest importance in popular culture" (p. 13). Fiske's book studied television as a site of cultural production and consumption. Its argument that television was a cultural site from which audiences derived "meanings and pleasures" with ample room for negotiation of, and opposition to dominant readings, was a rebuttal of the "hypodermic needle" approach to the understanding of the mass media. Fiske joined other cultural studies scholars in the United States, Latin America, and Europe in arguing that television's power over social consciousness was not all encompassing, and that power itself was not merely vertical or one-directional. Fiske's argument regarding the participatory engagement of audiences was discussed in subsequent studies and its "optimistic" nature questioned (D'Acci, 2004; see Spigel, 2004), or even subject to "vehement denunciation" by what Hartley (1999) calls the "Fear School" of television studies (p. 133).[5]

I would like to call attention to the definition of "typical television," for it is illuminating in both what it uncovers and what it covers up. Although not stated explicitly, it would appear that Fiske had the United States as the implicit point of reference. Otherwise one would have to assume that there is one, universal, televisual medium whose transnational standards are the same whether in China or Germany; whether it is state-owned or a private enterprise; whether it broadcasts 3 or 200 channels; whether it carries mostly national or mostly imported programs; and whether these are dubbed or subtitled. Defining "typical television" is much more problematic than what may have appeared to Fiske, but just as compelling a conceptual exercise in the 21st century. Globalization, transnationalization, homogenization, media convergence, and other technological transformations have helped make "television" a plurality for which single descriptions are more, not less, elusive. And yet, we still tend to think of it as "one" (Caldwell, 2004) and of that one as "American." A critic could not have characterized "typical" Colombian television in 1987 as that which was "internationally" distributed. She could have not argued that in 1980, 1990, or 2015. Most popular Colombian programs were never exported while many others were imported from neighboring countries, the United States, Japan, and the United Kingdom.

But when living, thinking, and analyzing television from our living quarters in Madison, L.A., or Chicago, we may turn the U.S. particular into a particular universal. It is often difficult to not do so, for the United States does in fact stand for the world on occasion (see Chapter 3). Thus, often we refer to "television" when we intend to say *U.S. mainstream television.* Otherwise, we may say "ethnic," "international," or "specific case" television. In speaking about television, we may replicate the same representational rules we use to differentiate the same from the Other—the transparent standard from the anomalous multicolored others.

We should ponder whether it is possible to speak of national television systems, such as Brazilian, British, or Mexican. But more often than not, we refer to "television" as the all-encompassing cultural category, subsuming national or regional differences into a common experience (a situation that would not occur in film studies, in which the distinctions between "cinema" and "film" are as important as those between the *apparatus* and the *text*).[6] We would be hard pressed to take seriously the premise that there is one "film culture" that is fundamentally the same in India and Brazil, Egypt or England—unless by "culture" we are referring to basic, technical conditions of production and reception. The same assumption made about television does not appear so implausible. In fact, there seems to be a full identification of television as a technology with television as a cultural practice. Television is *the television*; the televisual is the set. We "watch television," whether it is the news or soap operas, the Super Bowl or Oprah, MTV or the Discovery Channel. Television's specific *mode of address*, its forms of bodily interpellation and material engagement, seems to supersede the specificity of types of programming, formats, or content. Television is defined by its being "watched."[7] If that is the case, it follows that it is more relevant, from the perspective of cultural critique and research, to study the ways in which audiences watch television than to pursue textual analyses of television or inquire on the nature of television's aesthetics (Brunsdon, 1990; Sconce, 2004). It is extraordinarily important to explore audiences' "uses of television," and claims regarding the *meaning* of texts should be suspect without ethnographic explorations (see Dávila, 2000; Martín-Barbero, 1993, 1996). However, this does not mean that textual analysis may be forfeited, replaced, or proved unnecessary by audience or production analysis, as they are different and equally important aspects of meaning production.

Text and Intertextuality

Television is not only "programs" but also an *articulation* of programs. Thus, "typical" television is also a form of structuring narratives; a play of syntagmatic and paradigmatic interconnections among programs. An "atypical" program (e.g., a special live report) can become part of typical television once it is located and inscribed within the normal flow. "Typical" programming, in contrast, can become fully atypical, an unrepeatable performance when an expected articulation of programs is broken. We witnessed such a situation for the first few hours following the September 11, 2001, attacks on U.S. soil. Advertising was stopped, and networks and newscasters struggled to find the right form of address to communicate tactfully a multiplicity of discourses and emotions. For a few hours, newscasts were the only legitimate TV content, and TV programming gained a sense of immediacy and urgency generally absent from the medium in the new millennium.

A typical program can be seen as "anomalous" or atypical if it is taken apart from the TV flow and incorporated within other televisual or audiovisual structures or systems (e.g., a typical Brazilian commercial would be an anomalous presence in U.S. mainstream television; a typical Super Bowl game would be an interesting aberration in a regional Colombian channel). In other words, "television" is defined not only by programs but also by *intertextuality* (as Fiske and others have pointed out).

A second issue with Fiske's definition of typical television is that it may lead us to conclude that, for most countries, popular television is *imported* television. In other words, either one assumes that every country internationally distributes programs—and that this is its most representative television—or that typical television is "best-seller" television (i.e., the programs consumed or aired by most countries). According to this reasoning, both programs and (popular) culture are defined in terms of international distribution. Thus, the more distributed a program is, the more "typical" it proves to be, and, conversely, the less distributed programs are less typical.

There is some relevance in explaining "typical" television as that represented by the most widespread programs worldwide. However, national televisual systems do not rely exclusively on the international buying and selling of programs (Havens, 2002). Many programs are produced "at home" exclusively for the home audiences and may be as typical as those imported and exported. Typical Mexican television is not typical French television despite the fact that *Dallas* was broadcast in both countries.[8]

It is clear that for the country which produces them, internationally distributed programs can be *both* the most popular (they are not only liked at home) and the ones that are typical (i.e., they represent mainstream televisual production). But typical television is simultaneously a transnational and a regional phenomenon. As much as it contains international "best sellers," a televisual system also includes domestic programs for the "home" audiences, specific daytime/primetime arrangements, and intertextual connections among programs and between TV programs and other mass-mediated and cultural forms. The "typical" television of the United States is not only that which is best-selling or "internationally distributed." It also includes talk shows, commercials, and local news shows that might not be exported and yet still are quite typical of U.S. commercial television. Let us take the case of U.S. Spanish-language television. Is this typical U.S. television? Does it contain typical TV programming? If so, are those programs typical in terms of *which* system of reference? The Mexican? The Latin American? The *United Statian*?[9]

It is necessary, and in fact unavoidable, to speak of television as a generality. As such, television can be said to be a "bearer/provoker of meanings and pleasures" (Fiske, 1987, p. 1), as well as "a part and a promoter of historical changes of very long duration" (Hartley, 1999, p. 25) and a teaching device of superb influence. Other claims about television may suggest both the limits and validity of the generalization. Thus, TV is indeed "a profit-making producer of commodities" (Fiske, 1987, p. 13), but this description is complicated by television in Cuba, China, or North Korea. Television is also a domestic medium, whose main site of reception remains "home," but it has encroached more and more into other social spaces and "no-places" such as bars, lounges, supermarkets, airports, and reception offices. If, as a technology, an apparatus, and an industrial practice, TV may be addressed in the singular, as a cultural phenomenon, television requires the plural. Because television is "situated and historical" (Fiske & Hartley, 1978, pp. 17–18), we may need to refer to "television systems" instead of "television," inflected by national, regional, and international policies, social contexts, cultural mores, and political structures. Structurally speaking, television is not only an (abstract) grammar but also a (particular and actualized) speaking—a performed language and aesthetics. Therefore, one may study the post-Apartheid South African three-channel television landscape (Teer-Tomaselli, 2005) or "one commercial week" in Sweden's public service television system of the 1950s (Olsson, 2004) or the evolution of Chinese television from a "propaganda instrument of the Communist party" to a commercially oriented mass medium (Zhao & Guo, 2005). One may also ponder the cultural implications of the Pan-Arab satellite channels in the Arab East or the destruction and subsequent transformation of Iraqi television after the 2003 U.S. occupation (Dajani, 2005). Geopolitical boundaries become the natural limits of national and regional televisions, which speak, therefore, with the accents of specific "nationalities" and identities.

National televisions negotiate the "national" and the "universal," voicing identity and regulating differences, omitting dialects and inventing "home," the Dome(stic) and the Polis. In the process of "bringing the world home," both *home* and the *world* are invented; defined in visions of familiarity and foreign exoticism; immediacy and distance; nationalism and regionalism; legitimate voices and silence.

The Question of the Text

In order to discuss the concept of television as a site for the *production of meanings and pleasures*, Fiske (1987) made reference to the theoretical distinction between "work" and "text." While the former, the *program*, is a "stable" and "fixed" entity "produced, distributed and defined by the industry," the latter is the "product of [its] readers" (p. 14). Thus, explains Fiske, a televisual *program* remains the same regardless of the place in which it is broadcast. What changes is the *text*, that is, the meanings extracted from or assigned to the program. Therefore, "*Dallas* is the same program whether it is broadcast in the USA, North Africa, or Australia" (p. 14).

It is basic to establish the difference between the text (that being read) and the physical entity (i.e., the signifying artifact). However, one cannot disregard that "physical entities" may change in their very physical (and semiotic) properties when removed from their original settings and contexts. One would have to assume either that Moroccans, Egyptians, or Colombians watch *Dallas* in its original English-language version or that translation does not affect discourse.

In "Las versiones homéricas," the Argentine writer Jorge Luis Borges (1932/1996) suggests that we do not have one *Odyssey*. We have as many versions of the Greek epic as there are translations. Says Borges (using Levine's translation),

> The Odyssey, thanks to my opportune ignorance of Greek, is a library of works in prose and verse, from Chapman's couplets, to Andrew Lang's "authorized version" or from Berard's classic French drama and Morris's lively saga to Samuel Butler's ironic bourgeois novel. (Borges, 1992, p. 1136)

Thus, we might have a romantic, a classic, and a high-modernist *Odyssey*; one may be bucolic whereas another is ironic. A Chinese *Hamlet* is not a duplicate of the Elizabethan version; the "Old Man and the Sea" is much longer and descriptive in Spanish than it is in English. Borges pushes this intertextual insight to its limit in his "Pierre Menard, Author of the Quixote" (1941/1981c). Pierre Menard, a 20th-century French writer, decides to write the 17th-century Cervantes' Don Quixote. He does not want to write a version of Don Quixote but the Quixote itself. Thus, Menard vows to "know Spanish well, to reembrace the Catholic faith, to fight against Moors and Turks, to forget European history between 1602 and 1918, and to *be* Miguel de Cervantes" (p. 99). Borges proceeds to analyze and compare Cervantes' and Menard's Quixote. Whereas Cervantes' Quixote manifests the dreams and doubts of a Spaniard in the 17th century, Menard's shows the doubts and tensions of a modern man. One Quixote is a nobleman who dreams himself a knight; the other is an isolated individual in the modern world. And yet, they correspond to one another word by word. As de Lailhacar (1990) puts it, Cervantes' Don Quixote is different from Menard's "because the latter [is read] through the prism of all those texts that came to superpose themselves on [the original text] like new inscriptions on a palimpsest" (p. 155).

The translated text, even if that translation borders a utopian "degree zero," is already another text, a work in another intertextual web. A work "authored" by a 17th-century Spaniard is not the same "authored" by a 20th-century Frenchman. The contextual "presentation" already inflects reading, announcing interconnections, dialogues, complicities, and semiotic webs. In order for *Dallas*, the program, to "remain the same" throughout the world (i.e., not to undergo material or semantic transformations), it would need to be absent from *trans-lations*: *trans*-portation, *trans*-literation, and *trans*-formation. Unless the whole global village already speaks English, *Dallas*, the industry product, undergoes several adaptations; several *interpretations*, one could say, of an original "score."

Translations inflect in diverse ways the works translated. A thing acquires different properties as it is reframed within a new context, against a new horizon of expectations. Each new translation—or recontextualization—is a "variation" on the original, an opening up of the otherwise "closed" work; a renewed play on the possible ways of "staging" the otherwise fixed product. Following this reflection, one may suggest that *Dallas* (or *The Simpsons*) is not one but all of its versions in intertextuality. The work—the product, the materiality of the text—is itself transformed in the process of "reaching audiences"; of becoming available for global consumption. In its global broadcasting, *Dallas* is translated in the different meanings of the word: moved, relocated, and reinscribed within other televisual flows and lineups of programming, other logics of market segmentation and forms of commercial rhetoric, and other performed languages. What are the limits of the "fixed" program? The TV show is also an industrial product, a P.R. and marketing strategy, a presentational rhetoric (credits, music, announcements), and a web of direct and indirect references by other TV shows or programs. Between the interpretive task of audiences and a "fixed" industrial product, material transformations are semantic and semiotic phenomena in their own right.

The (Colombian/Mexican) Voice of McGarret

The phenomenon of translation has interesting implications for television in a global context. A percentage of Latin American TV programming is made of U.S. shows dubbed in Spanish by professional actors, mostly Mexican.[10] Growing up in Bogotá, Colombia, my favorite show was *Hawaii 5-0*, one of the most popular "Colombian" television shows of the 1970s. The voice of McGarrett also "starred" in other U.S. dubbed shows, so that McGarret's *Hispanic* voice incarnated detectives, soldiers, war heroes, spies, lovers, and executives. Mexican José Maynardo Zavala, the voice of McGarrett, is as much a part of *Hawaii Cinco-Cero* as Jack Lord. In turn, that syncretic character, McGarret, was "vicariously" present in many more Latin American TV roles than Jack Lord could have ever dreamed of. His voice was an aural icon that carried signification by itself, able to represent and be read in its own right (Lozano, 1990). His was a "hero" voice, a self-determined, masculine, pragmatic voice. If someone held "McGarret's voice," one could assume that he was in command of the situation; he would probably solve the mystery and defeat the enemies—and, occasionally, play on the dark side. Zapata was also Bill Cosby in *The Bill Cosby Show*, chauffeur Hoke/Morgan Freeman in *Driving Miss Daisy*, King Harold in *Shrek2*, and The Bad/Lee van Cleef in the *Good, the Bad, and the Ugly*.

Similarly, BBC productions can be recognized in Colombia not only because of the special quality of the acting, lighting, camera work, and settings, but also because of the quality of the characters' voices. BBC characters speak an overall "British-like" Spanish language; a refined, slow, proper, thoughtful Spanish, one that dramatically differs from *Married: With Children* or *The Simpsons*.

From the voice of the *character* (which is not that of the actor), audiences can expect certain dramatic features and role patterns. There is the voice of the bad guy and that of the *femme fatale*. The dubbed voices become rhetorical and theatrical, expressive and significant by themselves. They are much more "significative" (i.e., coded) than the original ones, which are, basically, uncodified voice registers: "arbitrary" variations. It is not possible to read the American character in her American voice (she does not make up her voice as she does her face; she does not impersonate a voice as she does a body). The spectator can read her, however, over her Spanish voice, carefully selected to match her role and her moral attributes. Television is situated and rhetorical and must be studied as such.

A second, equally compelling outcome of translation is the transformation of that which appears immediate and realistic. One of the ways in which TV programming has traditionally provoked a sense of "immediacy" (Flitterman-Lewis, 1987, p. 189) is by its imitation of lived time; of the daily and seasonal temporality off-camera (i.e., one that demarks day from night, spring from winter, Christmas time from Summer solstice). However, programs that in a given context appear to "mimic" lived time will be, for the same reason, plainly exotic in other contexts. For example, the televisual presence of snowy winter, a relished yet mundane image of U.S. shows, acquires fantastic undertones when broadcast in equatorial Latin America.

Television can be as direct and immediate as it can be a bearer of distant and implausible stories. It can turn to be a magic-realistic storytelling machine, in which *Las Vegas* (the hyper-modern U.S. city) is as exotic as *La Vorágine* (the famous Colombian novel about rubber exploitation in the Amazon) and *Simplemente María* (the famous 1960's *telenovela* of a peasant maid turned rich sewing clothes) is as realistic as *Murphy Brown*. In its magic-realist flow, the Colombian national TV news may include the political ordeals of the current Colombian president, the latest installment on the Clinton–Obama–McCain–Palin drama (the "most compelling show of 2008"),[11] as well as interviews with telenovelas' *characters* (and their actors). Fiction enters daily life, and life becomes fictive.

Where Is the Text?

The phenomenon of translation reminds us that what we call "the program" has already been subject to *readings* and interpretations before it officially becomes a "text" in Fiske's sense (i.e., before it reaches mass audiences). The program is already a text, even if considered only as a material assemblage of parts not yet endowed with meaning by its broadcast reception. That assemblage of parts is already significant; it has already been, in its production, a site of social reading. To produce the program is not only to write it, but also to read it—against a background of expectations, constraints, and possibilities.

There is no text without a materiality (the canvas, the paper, the stage, the building), and there is no cultural material without an inscription in text (i.e., it is already written, composed, and organized across and through discourses and practices). To say that *one* is the program and *another* is the text is to propose a clean split between *signifier* and *signified*, in which the latter would be the open recreation of wandering audiences and the former the closed creation of hegemonic producers. Given such a split text/ program, textual analysis cannot but be irrelevant, as it cannot access the text (it has already been dispersed across countless readers) and cannot read the program (i.e., the program can only be seen, not *read*, as it is a self-explanatory object).

Unless the program is already textual, one would have to conclude that *between* programs and texts there is a space in which hermetically closed programs start a process of semantic undressing (or dressing up?), now investing themselves with codes and clues to be opened by polysemic decoding. In this case, audiences' work would be to "invest" programs with meaning, for the former would be expected to be semantically empty. Without the existence of such a link, no connection would exist between the closed product and the open reading text.

If the text is the polysemic reading of audiences and the audience is positively different from the producer of programs, the program (and the critic) might reveal itself to be culturally and socially irrelevant. For, regardless of what the program states, we do not know what it says until we reach the text, we do not know the text until we ask audiences, and we cannot reach it through audiences for it has already been dispersed in endless polysemy. The program is transparent and the text is unreachable. If the text is in the hands of audiences, the program cannot be studied textually. If this is the case, we face the paradox that the only text that can be considered a text would be one that is not a text, at least in Ricoeur's (1991) sense of the concept: a record, an inscription, and a delimited and framed discourse. The critic could do no more in this situation than uncover the intentions of producers and try to recover the wanderings of audiences. As such, she would be positioned away from both producers and consumers, as a professional interpreter who remains "outside" the social conditions that drive the dialogue of the parties whose exchanges she translates.

Although the above scenario is a possibility, semiotics and hermeneutics suggest that the assemblage of a product is already an active textualization. Following an insight that permeates much of Borges' writing, one can say that a writer is first and foremost a reader of his or her own and other texts (Rodríguez Monegal & Reid, 1981). The writer, the producer of the cultural artifact, is also one of its readers. Between audiences and producers, there is no clear-cut opposition. If audiences produce meaning, producers are certainly active audience members—the ones with the guaranteed access and participation. The relationship between writing and reading, producing and consuming, authoring and using is not one of complementing opposites but of overlapping, dialogical moments in an ongoing process of semantic unfolding.

Textual Meaning

Cultural and critical studies have transformed the traditional ways of studying television by proposing the centrality of interpretive and critical approaches to the study of mass media. Instead of conceptualizing the media in terms of transmission, message, contents, and effects, cultural and critical studies address the media in terms of symbolic, performative, rhetorical, and interpretive dimensions.[12]

As a cluster of terms, "meanings and pleasures" seem to synthesize the cultural dimension of television as it expresses the complexity of "reading" television: a polysemic and interpretive activity informed by desire (see Allen, 1985; Ang, 1985; Fiske, 1987; Hartley, 1999; Modleski, 1982). As such, the question of the production of "meanings and pleasures" is a central problematic for cultural/critical studies. Such a question makes evident the difficulties that television offers to traditional ways of looking at texts, as well as to traditional ways of understanding reading, interpreting, or meaning production. The "meaning of meaning" becomes an issue at the forefront of the understanding of television as a cultural form. Should I consider translations of the kind highlighted earlier a matter of meaning production? Should I consider the scheduling of *Dallas* as a prime-time program (in the 1980s) and a daytime program (in the 1990s) two "interpretations" of Dallas? Is the fact that in its prime the long-defunct daytime *Santa Barbara* was scheduled as a prime-time show outside the United States a rhetorical statement?[13] Or are these decisions without consequence to our understanding of television as a social practice?

Unfortunately, "meaning" is often used as a self-explanatory term, a floating signifier that can be fulfilled in numerous ways and play a multitude of roles, as an "unmediated mediation" that cannot be defined in terms of anything else, but that mediates everything else.[14] Thus, it has been argued that different subcultures read differently the same programs, so that they *make meanings* that satisfy the needs of their own "identity" (Fiske, 1991; Steiner, 1991). It is fundamental to acknowledge the importance of subject positioning in the production of meaning. However, one needs to be careful not to assume that "meaning" is a sort of item in a free market place where everyone can become her or his own producer and consumer. Meaning is not a thing, an object, or an entity, so that I could have "a lot of meanings," exchange some of them at my convenience, or keep them at home as collectors' items.

The interrogation of "meaning" is central to the fate of concepts such as text, intertextuality, and discourse. These concepts are grounded in an examination of processes of signification, sense-making, intentionality, coding, transcoding, interpretation, and reading.[15] The strong resonance of "meaning" within TV critical studies could be seen, to a great extent, as a form of reaction against a critical tradition that denied the popular or the mass-mediated that which was granted to high culture and art (i.e., aesthetic pleasure and polysemic depth). Thus, to speak of television as the "production of meanings and pleasures" is to reclaim for the "people" an ability that the positivistic and Marxist criticism of the cultural industry denied them—that is, the ability to read, to choose, to resist, to negotiate, and to enjoy something critically. However, as fruitful as this position is for contesting the tradition of mass communication and the model of the passive receiver and overpowering sender, its productivity might become restricted in the case of the study of the textual dynamics of particular televisual systems. To study this dynamic, it would be particularly relevant to interrogate the *conditions for the possibility* of those "meanings and pleasures." In the present case, I study Hispanic television as a discursive apparatus in which visions of reality and imaginaries are presented, represented, and legitimized. I pursue this study by taking an "archaeological" orientation and proposing *textuality* as a central concept.

Notes

1. In her *Banality in Cultural Studies*, Morris (1990) captures brilliantly the dual valence of "banality," as the question of "the banal" and the banal question. Morris juxtaposes television discourses and discourses on television and refers particularly to De Certeau's and Baudrillard's approaches to the issue.

2. Meehan (1990) discusses the ways in which "audience," "representation," and television's "cultural democracy" become concepts as accepted by scholars as they are defended by the networks. As television becomes an object of study, television studies draw scholarly conceptualizations from television's own discourses.

3. S. Hall's (1980) term, *encoding/decoding*, is compelling in its elegant simplicity. It seems to capture complexity in a binary term (*encoding/decoding*), which is opened "from within" with a slash that divides and unites, suggesting process rather than opposition. However, that same simplicity may suggest that interpretation is mainly a manner of placing into code or deciphering code. Hall himself would question this "error" as he proposes the existence of different social forms of read-

ing or understanding media texts (for a careful analysis of Hall's work, see Rojek, 2003).

4. I use the adjective *United Statian*, a rough translation of the Spanish "Estadounidense," that is, "of the United States." The adjective is needed to make explicit the difference between things American and U.S. things, a matter that becomes quite fundamental to make sense of any discussion of culture in the Americas.

5. Hartley (1999, Chapter 10) considers that Fiske (and himself) belongs to the "Desire School" of television studies.

6. Film studies make the difference between *film* and *cinematic apparatus*. Thus, we speak not only about the cinematic "gaze" and of cinema's subject positioning, but also about film as a specific industrial production. As the former, film is inflected by local conditions of production, state regulations, material constraints and social contexts, language, genre, style, and school. On television, the latter seems to collapse into the former.

7. It is important to note, incidentally, that "watching" is not an activity of the eyes only. It includes a posture, a form of engagement, and a logic of interaction—a "procedure," Caughie (1990) might say.

8. It might be worth noting that *Dallas* and *Dynasty*, two of the most popular U.S. TV shows of the 1980s, were still broadcast in some countries ten or more years after they went off the air in the United States.

9. The compelling yet at times subtle differences between the United States and America are discussed in Chapter 3.

10. According to Martínez Garza (2005), Brazil and Mexico are the Latin American countries with the highest amount of U.S. TV imports (one fourth and one third of their TV programming, respectively). In average terms, U.S. TV shows constitute 18% of the Latin American programming.

11. *Entertainment Weekly* called the U.S. presidential primaries of 2008 the "most entertaining TV show of 2008" (Svetkey, 2008, p. 1).

12. Especially influential in television criticism have been the concepts of polysemy, subject positionings, and open/closed texts (see especially Fiske, 1987; Grossberg, 1988; Hall, 1980; Morley, 1980; Radway, 1984). Together with these conceptualizations, TV criticism has been nurtured by theories and research strategies developed in *structuralist semiotics* (i.e., signs, structures of signification; aesthetic, ideological, cultural codes), *hermeneutics* (i.e., text and context, interpretation and understanding), *phenomenology* (i.e., lived experience, intersubjectivity, pre-discursive awareness), *poststructuralism* (i.e., intertextuality, desire, subject positionings), and *postmodern theories* (i.e., segmentation, dispersion, deconstruction, nomadism).

13. U.S. daytime soap operas have been, occasionally, successful prime-time programming outside of the United States. In the late 1980s, for example, *Santa Barbara* became "the most popular show" France "has seen in years," whereas in 1988, *Loving* and *Capitol* enjoyed more popularity in Italy than *Dallas* in 1988 (Butler & Logan, 1988, p. 99). *Santa Barbara* was canceled in the United States in 1993, but continued to be broadcast in several countries after that date (Armstrong, 1999).

14. See the debate between Fiske (1991) and Condit (1991). See also C. Hall (1992) for a discussion on the risks of reifying concepts within cultural studies. She refers in particular to the triad "race, gender, class" (pp. 240–241).

15. See the works of Barthes (1977), Deleuze (1988), Deleuze and Guattari (1987), Eco (1979, 1984), Foucault (1970, 1972), Gadamer (1975), Greimas (1983, 1987), Greimas and Courtés (1982), Kristeva (1969, 1987), Merleau-Ponty (1962, 1964), de Saussure (1959), and Schleifer (1987).

5

Television as Textuality

A Discursive Approach to Television

The Social Archive

Television has been described as the most important contemporary *circulator* of the social mainstream and as an *organizer* and *reinforcer* of social myths and values (Gitlin, 1986). Television plays a central role as textual enactment of the contemporary social scene, and as inscription, organization, and (re) presentation of that which is considered socially significant and legitimate. As such, the televisual text becomes a (rhetorical) document and television its globalizing archive. As a document, a televisual text participates actively in producing that which it "documents," giving it discursive shape, form, and density. As an archive, television is a site in which contemporary phenomena are categorized, sanctioned, and "cross listed" over multiple fields. Television comments, speaks, and organizes things, including itself, according to rhetorical and normative rules of which it is not only manifestation but also source. As such it not only represents (i.e., provides a vision, a signification of a second order) but also *presents* social reality. In inscribing the real, television becomes a form of the real; not a writing of a second order but "the thing itself"—that which is present and directly experienced. One might ask, in fact, whether there are not forms of the real that become so *on TV*; events, facts, and phenomena whose "authentic" nature is pop-mediated, tele-envisioned, and video-experienced. Hartley (1992) has suggested that the "public" is one of such instances—a social figure whose contemporary existence only becomes "real" in the televisual or mass-mediated text. Says Hartley (1992) in his introduction,

> Neither the public domain nor the public itself can be found in contem-
> porary states; they've literally disappeared. However, both of them are
> very familiar figures, figures of speech, in which everyone spends quite

a bit of time. So while they don't exist as spaces and assemblies, the public realm and the public are still to be found, large as life, in media. Television, popular newspapers, magazines and photography, the popular media of the modern period, are the public domain, the place where and by which the public is created and has its being. (p. 1)

One of the implications of Hartley's insight is that one can—or even should— study the public (e.g., TV audiences) through its inscription on the mass-mediated text (e.g., televisual genres or programs). The public of television is a televisual construction. As such, it is already in the text, named, positioned, defined, and materialized by the act of enunciation; by the diverse forms of televisual rhetorical address.

By the same token, one can say that the televisual text already proposes, implies, and exercises an order—a textual organization—of "things" (to paraphrase Foucault). Therefore, television *presents*, *represents*, and *enacts the rules* by which (re)presentation is possible. In the enactment of these rules, television becomes document and archive—a discourse and its field, or better yet, a discursive field.

Textuality: The Materiality of the Archive

An archive is a gathering of selected and organized information, both a material form and a structuring principle. The archive is an intertextual mapping—a document on how to organize documents—and it implies a site, a design, and a reader—who is inscribed by the archive's material conditions. It is a place in which knowledge and the material of official memory is kept and a space that is structured according to an understanding of time, space, movement, interiority, and exteriority. As much as an archive does not make sense without the documents it contains, it cannot be understood in the absence of its material constitution.

To study Hispanic television as an archive or *an archival formation* implies a focus on the very materiality of its televisual inscription; its textuality. Thus, its programs and genres are studied as intertextual components of an overall writing, one whose rhythms, repetitions, and presentational styles constitute Hispanic television as a textual flow. To study such a televisual textuality implies making visible the programmatic limits and (re)presentational boundaries of the televisual flow. That is, not only its discursive and rhetorical patterns, but also its diverse *forms of exteriority*—that which is excluded, silent, or absent. This, in turn, requires specific programs, shows, and genres to be considered not as the foreground or substance of the flow, but as its *background*. In this way, I am shifting the reading of television, from programs and genres to the televisual weaving from which and in which texts emerge. It is this textual fabric as a whole that establishes Hispanic television in relation to Latin and Anglo American television, as similar to and different from both. Hispanic television may emerge as a sort of *"third text,"* whose signifying relation to the preceding televisual systems goes well beyond a play of differences to propose a new set of rules of inclusion and exclusion. Thus, my interest is the continuous interpenetrations of the Latin American and the Anglo American discursive fields into a Spanish archive that reframes both.

Discourse and Archaeology

My aim in investigating U.S. Hispanic television is to explore the recurring motifs, common themes, and narratives that pervade this televisual programming, constituting common discursive threads. These threads cut across what otherwise could be seen as a number of sequential units, discrete programs, and separate genres. Foucault's conceptualization of "archaeology" appears especially fruitful in this context, as he saw the archaeological investigation as a way of exploring discourse and approaching cultural materials as "documents" rather than texts (as they are understood by hermeneutics).

An archaeological search can be understood in at least four ways. It can be seen as a digging up of the (underground) monuments and material designs of a culture in reference to which discourses have been produced, established, and sanctioned (i.e., a critique of history, as that of *The Order of Things* [Foucault, 1970]). Second, we can understand archaeology as an exploration of the *archives* and documents of a time and culture so as to unfold the rules of production, territorialization, and regulation of epistemic, social, and discursive practices (i.e., a critique of Modern Reason, as that of *Discipline and Punish* [Foucault, 1977]).

Third, an archaeological search can be likened to a study of cultural *architectures* that could advance an understanding of the logics by which monuments are erected, rooted, designed, rejected, or destroyed (i.e., a study of the contemporary discursive practices, as suggested by the *Archaeology of Knowledge* [Foucault, 1972]). Finally, this search can be understood as the study of the multiplicity of layers of strata that constitute a (discursive) formation, as well as its process of sedimentation, densification, and transformation. This would be an exploration and mapping of cultures, as suggested by Foucault's *cartographies* (Deleuze, 1988; Foucault, 1977), and Deleuze and Guattari's (1987) *geologies*.

It might appear contradictory to study architectures in the pursuit of archaeology. After all, the latter suggests an underground and the former an over-the-ground exploration of cultural materials. And yet, *both* archaeology and architecture deal with materials that can be considered external even if they are not immediately visible. They entail the description, tracing, and reconstructing of external, even though implied, connections of that which is materially given.

At this level, then, architecture and archaeology not only cease to oppose one another but become complementary aspects of a single task. One is the strategy of investigation (archaeology), and the other is the material to be investigated (architecture).[1] The architecture of the past becomes visible in the archaeological investigation of the present, as much as the documents and monuments of the present can reveal their architectonic designs when they are explored archaeologically. Indeed, Foucault asserted that his work was less a new history of the past than an archaeology of the present as it revealed our cultural specificity, our designs, and our epistemic presuppositions.

Documents and Monuments

In his *Archaeology of Knowledge,* Foucault (1972) argued that a document, *any* document, not only represents or signifies a social "reality" but enacts discursive hierarchies, valuations, and orderings. This engagement of the document in the discourses of its time, place, and culture has prompted Foucault to refer to the documents he investigates as *monuments.* That is, documents are architectonic materiality, "positive" edifices in the field of knowledge or in the field of an era's common sense.

Because the monumental dimension of documents cannot be explored with the traditional tools of formalization and interpretation (as embodied by history or anthropology), Foucault proposed archaeology as a different strategy. The latter can be seen as the activity of digging and tracing the interstitial connectivity of cultural documents and monuments. Although archaeology appears to suggest a vertical search (i.e., a search for roots, grounds, or origins), its task requires, more likely, a *transversal* or *diagonal* exploration. The archaeological digging does not reveal the essence of a culture or its totalizing model, but traces, pieces, and materials whose mapping and reconstruction is the archaeologist's task. Thus, she works from within, following the logics offered to her by the uncovered strata, instead of applying to the found material the already given logic of an official history or interpretation.[2]

A Discursive Approach to Television

I propose to do a discursive study of Hispanic television by appropriating some of the insights of Foucault's (1972) archaeological investigation of discourse.

For the purposes of such a study, I recover something that is *there* but not yet *visible*—those narrative, rhetorical, and ideological elements that permeate the TV flow, supersede the programming, underlie or exceed the organized schedule, and emerge as expression or style.[3] Elements, one might say, that are less akin to identifiable texts than to a *videoscape*, to use Williams' (2003) term. These elements constitute, as they unfold, the discursive textuality of (Spanish-speaking) television, a "writing" that provides a sense of *archival logic* to what otherwise can be considered as a mere accumulation of discrete programs, isolated shows, or individual commercials. Thus, an archaeological investigation of television would study the modalities of interconnection and the rules of writing by which experiential, expressive, and intentional "matter" become cultural materiality (rituals, narratives, mythologies) and social material (documents, monuments).[4]

The archaeological study of television has four motivations or interests: (a) the methodological interest of imagining an archeological exploration, and possibly opening new paths to the study of television; (b) the theoretical interest of exploring the signifying materiality of television, which is central to the construction of contemporary social narratives; (c) the critical interest of exploring a mass-mediated "archive" that is constituted at the crossroads of two cultural spaces; and (d) the possibility of grasping and understanding the ways in which a televisual "border" illuminates, transforms, and redefines cultural systems.

Consulting a Televisual Archive

A discursive approach to the study of Hispanic television implies that I examine it as an archival formation, performing, therefore, three operations. First, I move singular programs to the background so that their common discourses can be foregrounded. In doing so, I bracket various layers or levels of the televisual composition in order to focus on what I call the *televisual textuality*. In particular, I am bracketing questions that assume either the program or the genre as the focus of analysis, such as narrative morphologies, semantic typologies, and semiotics of televisual genres. Third, in this process, I *deconstruct* or untie the delimitations and specifications of generic classifications (the serial, the talk show, the news) and *reconstruct* them according to their intertextual threads. My focus, therefore, is not on the programs themselves but on the flow that articulates and supersedes them.

In the process of highlighting interconnections and bracketing genres, I risk losing the very object I pursue, and I indeed get lost a few times. In this process of "loss," however, I happen into unexpected materials I would have not otherwise seen, and I gain insights I would have not otherwise reached.

Archaeology and Semiotics

From Linguistics to Semiotics

To study the textuality of Hispanic television is to make visible the textual weaving that emerges in the interconnections among texts. In order to investigate this televisual textuality, it is important to address questions of signification and discourse. Many semiotic analyses of the media refer to the Saussurian duality signifier/signified as the principle of sign and text constitution. In the name of semiotics, television may be assumed to be a collection of simple words or sentences (tied down within a text), which are then analyzed as uttered (the signified) and transcribed (the signifier). However, this approach cannot successfully deal with anything more complex than a sentence (i.e., a clip, an episode, a genre), for its purpose and object are syntax and the binary organization of grammar.

It is pedagogically sound to propose this dichotomy as a way of introducing the problematics of signification, but it is important not to stop there, for the mass-mediated text cannot be reduced to a linguistic object constituted by binary oppositions. The signifier/signified relationship is indeed a specific form of *semiosis*, that of linguistic grammar. But the purpose of semiotics is wider than the study of this particular form of semiosis, for it aims to study *signification*—which can have diverse dynamics, processes, and logics. In fact, more than 30 years ago, the duality signifier/signified was contested, problematized, and rejected by semioticians or theorists such as Umberto Eco, Christian Metz, Julien Greimas, Julia Kristeva, and Jacques Derrida.

Language cannot be fully studied based on these structural rudiments, let alone textual compositions that include the articulation of more than one language. Beyond phonetics, syntax, and grammar, language posits the problem of enunciation, which requires a different conceptualization of signification.

From Sign to Text

One of the most important and earlier alternatives to the Saussurian tradition of *semiology* described above is that of Louis Hjelmslev (1943/1969), who saw the opposition signified/signifier as diffused and multiplied to the point of indeterminacy. Whereas for traditional structural semiology a sign is a form (which organizes two substances), for Hjelmslev a sign is an intersection—of form and substance, across two planes. A sign is, in other words, the conventional and temporal intersection of forms and substances across planes—the expressive and the semantic strata. Signification, therefore, occurs in the plural relationship of two planes, themselves composed of diverse layers.

According to Hjelmslev (1943/1969), Greimas (1983), and Eco (1979), signification does not reside in the necessary connection of the two sides of a coin (Saussure's analogy). It is already, and from the beginning, a field matter, the spatial and temporal encounter of a multiplicity of multilayered phenomena. Thus, instead of binary oppositions, one can think of signification as organized in a coeternal arrangement (Greimas, 1983, 1987), in *geological strata* or rhizomatic proliferation (Deleuze & Guattari, 1987), and according to the intrinsic rules of discursive formations and their *topographic dissemination* (Foucault, 1972). To paraphrase Deleuze and Guattari, *expression* (the folding strata) and *content* (the sedimented strata) have both substance (rules for the combination of units) and form (codes for the selection of units).[5]

Foucault's archaeological analysis seems sustained, at least partially, by a similar concern with the study of semiotic practices that do not necessarily obey a *discipline of signs* (e.g., the study of the structural "behavior" of signs and their codes). Thus, to study discursive formations is to examine the sedimented and folding strata of cultures. In terms of Hjelmslev, later recovered by Deleuze and Guattari, the study of discursive formations is an attempt to contrast the *plane of consistency*, the topography of a place, with the codes and arrangements of the *plane of expression* (the monuments) and the *plane of the content* (the segmented and territorialized field) of particular cultures (see Figure 5.1).

In terms of Hjelmslev and Greimas, Foucault could be seen as dealing specifically with one layer of the constitution of signification, the form of

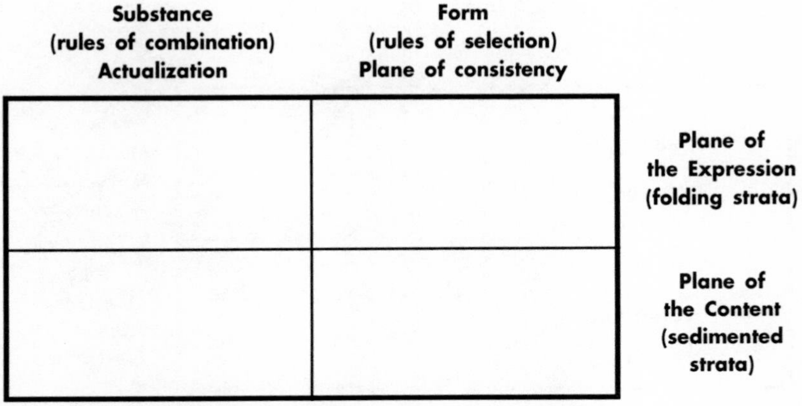

Substance (rules of combination) Actualization	Form (rules of selection) Plane of consistency	
		Plane of the Expression (folding strata)
		Plane of the Content (sedimented strata)

Figure 5.1. Hjelmslev's model as read by Deleuze and Guattari (1987). My visualization.

the expression, and the form of the content. First, the Foucaultian *discursive formation* (or form of discourse) would correspond to the Greimassian *form of the content*. Second, Foucault's *form of the nondiscursive* (institutions, social practices, power exercises) would correspond to the Greimassian *form of the expression*.

However, one could argue that Foucault's investigations are less concerned with the study of signification than with the study of *signifying practices*, the social, institutional, and discursive practices of specific cultures in a space and a time. Thus, from the Greimassian perspective, Foucault would be dealing with these aspects of cultural signification (see Figure 5.2).

The substance might be seen as the level that has preoccupied historians, as they focus on the substance of the documents to interpret their meaning. Thus, for the traditional historian, philosopher, or linguist, the form of the historical systems is either to be induced from the documents (as if the form copied the substance or repeated it at a higher level of abstraction) or from our own system (assuming that history follows a logical plan, and that historical differences are no more than a matter of lesser or higher development). In fact, Foucault could well point to Greimas' *Actantial Model* as a sound and effective model to describe discursive processes in the modern age, but not to describe the discursive specificity of other ages. For Greimas, the form of the content can be visualized and formalized in the Actantial Model (see Figure 5.3).

The Actantial Model expresses the fundamental narrative structure of language and discourse, as one constituted by the three intersecting planes of communication, desire, and action (i.e., the *form of the content* of any discourse). However, these levels and emphases can be read as a modernist description of sense-making processes. This does not discredit Greimas, but

Monuments **Architecture**	**Institutions**	**Plane of the Expression** (Non-discoursive practices)
Utterances, **Statements,** **Documents**	**Knowledge production** **Discursive formation**	**Plane of the Content** (Discoursive practices)

Figure 5.2. Foucault's archaeology of discourse, seen from the standpoint of the Hjelmslevian/Greimassian conceptualization of signification. My visualization.

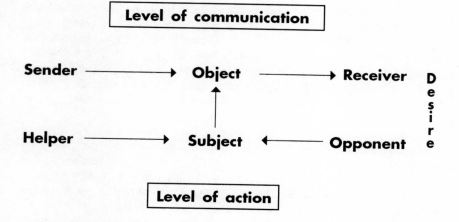

Figure 5.3. The Actantial Model (Greimas, 1983). For Greimas this is the basic semantic structure that underlies any human discourse. It can be traced in the structure of the sentence, the syntactical structure of language, and the narrative patterns of folk tales. According to the model, human discourse will be structurally defined as a relationship among "actants" established on the basis of desire (for an object), communication (about that object), and action (toward the object).

instead points out that models are offspring of the systems they are analyzing. This is not their shortcoming but their value and their capacity. To paraphrase Nietzsche (1966), no model is more than an excuse for thought to continue its activity (I return to Actantial Model in Chapter 6).

It is important to remember that the form of the content was traditionally understood as a concern external to the sciences of language and proper to anthropology or the social sciences (Eco, 1979; Greimas, 1983).[6] Hjelmslev and Greimas argued for the possibility of studying meaning from a structural perspective, as an essential part of signification, and not as an external aggregate. With Greimas it is understood that the form of the content is not a matter of a primordial will or a free consciousness, but a matter of constitutive logics, discursive structures, sedimented patterns, and organized choices. In this way, the semantic plane itself (not only the expressive or communicative) enters the realm of rhetoric. No discourse, regardless of its scientific or formalist status, can escape narrative structures and patterning motives.

The aim of the Greimassian proposition is to reach an understanding of the *semiotic structuring of meaning* and, conversely, of the semantic structuring of social discourses. It should not be surprising, in light of its intertwining of semantics and semiotics, to find out that the Greimassian "form of the content" is one of the structural conceptualizations that more clearly interests poststructuralists such as Foucault, Derrida, or Kristeva. Particularly, the Greimassian project appears quite illuminating for an *archaeology* of knowledge. The former as well as the latter point out that discourses are not mechanical translations of internal psychological states or external realities, but social practices grounded on presuppositions of direction, order, logic, and connection.

Thus, what Greimas calls the "form of the content" would be akin to what Foucault calls the "discursive formation," the form or order that positive knowledge has within specific eras, cultural epochs, or epistemes. For Foucault, discourse is not only a system of differences without "positive" value (as language is for de Saussure) but also a system of rules of exclusion and inclusion, which is arranged according to a given rationale or episteme. In *The Order of Things*, Foucault (1970) suggests that the table, the sphere, and the tetrahedron, as well as representation, resemblance, and the replica, have been at different times *forms of the content* of epistemic systems that otherwise may appear to be "using" language as a neutral tool for the sake of truth seeking.

This argument has important implications for the cultural analysis of texts. When two semiotic fields collide or overlap, the form of the content becomes visible, externalized, and problematic, losing its uncontested merits and given legitimacy. The clash, intersection, or mixing of two semiotic systems or two cultural matrices rearranges structures, logics, and surfaces in ways that could not have been averted or envisioned prior to the event. The form of the content, the *sedimented cultural strata*, becomes apparent when one brackets expressivity as the organized presence of "meaning" and understands it as the territory in which "sense" is culturally enacted. To study a text from this perspective is to explore its expressive arrangements and intrinsic logic. Thus, the issue becomes less one of interpretation than one of intertextuality, the interconnection among texts, discourses, and practices.

From Structure to Enunciation

Eco (1979) has asserted that semiotics is a discipline concerned with the double task of investigating codes and communication in order to understand cultures. Greimas (1983, 1987) understands semiotics as a discipline dealing with the doublet semiology/semantics that seeks to understand the (narrative/cognitive/ideological) regulations of the production of *meaning*.[7] Both, then, propose that semiotics should be concerned not only with the study of structures of signification and the social processes that transform them, but also with the cultural intertextuality by which enunciations not only signify but make sense.[8] In this latter concern, Greimas and Eco might coincide with Foucault's interest on the study of *discourse*.

Generally speaking, discourse can be understood as *enunciation*, the actualization of (the indefinite possibilities of) language in a particular speech that selects and combines units of signification from the given repertoire or cultural code. This approach to discourse is adequate if one's main concern is the study of language, but it proves to be inadequate if the focus is discourse itself.

The study of discourse, in a Foucaultian sense, requires one to invert—or better, question—this structuralist relationship between matrix and manifestation, code and enunciation, language and speech, structure and discourse. The latter is not the manifestation of a structure, but a structuring activity. Thus, one should not study discourse as a detective—searching for the hidden and secret meaning of traces—but as an explorer would, taking it as it comes.[9]

> We must be ready to receive every moment of discourse in its sudden irruption; in that punctuality in which it appears, and in that temporal dispersion that enables it to be repeated, known, forgotten, transformed, utterly erased. . . . Discourse must not be referred to the distant presence of the origin, but treated as, and when, it occurs. (Foucault, 1972, p. 25)

Thus, to define signs (and therefore discourse) as the presence of an absence, or as that which stands for something else, is either a tautology or a metaphysical claim. It is a tautology within modern semiotics, as it is understood that signs can only point to signs (i.e., they only work within a system of interconnections and differences). To say that a sign is that which replaces a sign is an unnecessary redundancy that leaves the question unanswered. This is a metaphysical claim within contemporary philosophy, as it supposes an (absent) identity of which the sign is a mark and, therefore, a presence. It also assumes the primacy of Being, and with it, the existence of various levels of representational proximity to the real, so that what I think is closer to the real than what I say; what I write is more removed from untamed reality than what I say; and what I see is the fundamental linkage between thought and truth.

In both of these cases, "reality" will be something that always escapes us because it "exists" away from the actions and words of humans. That nothing ever said, written, or expressed is really there because it is only a manifestation of something deeper or truer, is what Derrida (1976) calls the *metaphysics of presence*. In the last analysis, such a "reality" would be irrelevant for the study of social practices, for as that which is never grasped, seen, or heard, it is well beyond the realm of sense-making processes or discursive practices.

Because reality will always be deferred by this endless play of re-presentations, one could very well "ignore" the real and deal exclusively with the experienced.

Baudrillard (1988) would radicalize this proposition, both raising strong criticisms and suggesting important ways of dealing with the nature of a new, postmodern "instauration" (Ulmer, 1989). Baudrillard suggests that in the age of mass media and the communication explosion, there is no longer a difference between reality and discourse, presence and representation, original and replica. Thus, the cultural realm is a simulacrum in whose realm it is impossible to "lie" because there is no truth.

The Archaeological Strategy

To invert a familiar saying, Foucault (1972) requires us to "suspend belief" in our conditions of truth (i.e., the categories, divisions, and continuities that we take for granted) so that the field grounding them could be set free. Such a field is not a hidden structure or a latent code, but "the totality of all effective statements (whether spoken or written), in their dispersion as events and in the occurrence that is proper to them" (Foucault, 1972, p. 27). As Foucault envisions it, the purpose of archaeology is more descriptive than analytical; closer, one might say, to the task of phenomenology than to that of hermeneutics.

Within archaeology, the study of discourse and "ways of speaking" about things takes precedence over the study of sign systems or language structures. Discourse structures and is structured by social practices, without preceding them or proceeding from them. My "speaking" is not the manifestation of an inner awareness or an inner thinking, but is coextensive with thinking or awareness. Thus, it is not that language houses being, the very awareness of essence or of authentic identity (as Heidegger would have it). More likely, discourse, the social and legitimate practices of semiosis, is the temporal sedimentation of identities and differences, orders and resemblances, objects, subjects, and representations. Discourse, therefore, is the site of knowledge, the site of power, and the site of communication.

From Text to Textuality

To attempt an archaeology of television is to focus on an *interstitial writing*, that is, on the discourses that pervade diverse texts and that provide them with a sense of regularity. Because these discourses remain on an intertextual "background," they do not constitute recognizable texts or documents in themselves. An archive, in a similar manner, implies a discourse about history, knowledge, and truth, although such a discourse might not be written in any of its texts or documents. To trace this interstitial writing or *textuality* is an attempt to recognize the emergent *form of the content* of the (Hispanic) archive. This would imply investigating, structurally speaking, the ways in which "content," a universal or structural semantic field, is inscribed, inflected, and transformed by archival principles and semiotic orderings.

However, the very relation between archive and document allows one to see that the form of the content is, in fact, *the content as expression* (i.e., there is no such thing as a pure content on which the demands of the archive have forced an official form). The content of the document is already a material form that prefigures the archive. This is why Foucault proposes to speak about discursive formations and why Hjelmslev points out that what functions as expression at one level may become content at another level, in a play of *unlimited semiosis* (Eco, 1979) or connotative semiotics (Barthes, 1968; Hjelmslev, 1969).

This discursive formation is similar to what Greimas (1983, 1987) calls the "content form," following Hjelmslev's (1943/1969) classification (see, among others, Greimas & Courtés, 1982, pp. 57, 121–122). For Greimas, such a form is universal (thus, it can be expressed in a single, Actantial Model.[10] For Foucault, in contrast, the discursive formation is an *episteme*, a specific understanding of knowledge, truth, and world. Thus, there is no universal form of the content, and in consequence, there is no content that can be studied in the absence of its *formation* in an epoch and place.

The Televisual Archive

As an ongoing flow, television is less an ordering and a sequentiality of discrete programs than a fabric that grows in knots, intersections, and patterns. Thus, television is simultaneously a collection of texts and a site in which texts extend into one another, weaving threads that can be followed vertically, horizontally, and transversely. Television is an archive in which discourses are inscribed along with an arch-texture (or a writing) that extends texts through intertextuality and palimpsest.[11]

Ulmer (1989) argues that television has transformed the "simple forms" of anecdote, joke, proverb, riddle, and legend into new functions of classification and evaluation. Television, therefore, orders "the complex interaction of sound and image through time by a combination of oral and pop culture forms" (p. ix). Ulmer has hinted here at a semiotic capacity of television that is not particular to specific programs or genres: that of weaving the most distant topics or concerns into a common writing or inscription. Such capacity is what

I describe as textuality, although it would differ from Ulmer's conceptualization in at least two ways. First, Ulmer assumes that the forms of television are either oral or "pop," an assertion that assumes these two as oppositional and distinct categories. Second, Ulmer may be granting universality to the "forms of television," a move that cannot be warranted prior to the examination of different televisual systems, as discussed in Chapter 4.

Televisual Textuality

If a text is a node of discourse, textuality is the fabric in which the node appears. It is, to use a metaphor, the thick texture of a tapestry in which figures and shapes densify, thicken, and spread into other shapes and figures, forming a texture that is simultaneously plural and interconnected. To examine textuality is to approach the materiality of television, that *in-between* realm, the territory that grounds meaning and signification and that escapes both.[12] The exploration of textuality thus posited is more an archaeological than a structuralist or hermeneutical task, which is to propose that "that which is there, *is there*."[13] The question is not, then, what lies hidden beneath this surface, this mask of lies, but what is the texture of this surface, what is its specificity and its edges, and, indeed, why we encounter this texture and not others (see Foucault, 1970)? This does not imply that surfaces become more important than depths, so that somehow one is forced to deal with the trivial and let the transcendental go, but that the opposition (depth/surface) is unwarranted.

For, indeed, can we ever leave the surface? Can we ever say that we have left behind the surface and that we are now surrounded by the deep—on top, around us, behind, and below? Surface and depth are always relational, as one is seen through the other's articulation. We cannot leave the surface and enter pure depth—except, perhaps, in the silence of death. Conversely, we cannot *inhabit* surfaces without depth (how can we inhabit something that lacks depth?). The relationship between one and the other is not that of the (false) mask that hides the (true) face, but of the mask and face that are coextensive and co-constituted, as both are surfaces and both have a depth.

To say that one cannot leave the surface is not to say that one is condemned to alienation or denied the contemplation of the truly profound (as the Marxist or Platonic tradition would have it). It is rather to say that depth is not somewhere else but here, in the thickness of a field in which proximity and distance are equally present. Thus, to reject formalization or interpretation (as Foucault does) is to reject the epistemic hierarchy and ordering on which they are based, not their intentional or experiential positivity. Because archaeology focuses on the study of materiality, it has bracketed depth as a transcending realm of scientific investigation.

Notes

1. In fact, one of the tasks of archaeology is the exploration of the architectural as both the buildings that host daily life and the cultural logics that inform those buildings.

2. One might add that archaeology is an attempt to "bracket" current discourses to unfold their own discursive grounding. It is an irreverent attempt because it suggests the circumvention of normalized formalization or interpretation, an arguably futile enterprise.

3. It may be tempting to call this textuality a "mega-text," as Allen (1985) does in order to define soap operas. That is, a text that lasts a formidable amount of time and that nobody can fully read (i.e., soap operas can last as long as 30 years). Given the difficulties of calling a text something that lacks definite boundaries, it is more appropriate to call this flow a *textuality*, a *writing* that supersedes documents and traces their intertextuality. Perhaps no other work has so explicitly acknowledged this dimension of television than Ulmer's (1989) *Teletheory*. I find that these pages echo and resonate with Ulmer's work, although I do not follow any particular postulate of his (tele)theory, and my scope is certainly much more limited.

4. Deleuze and Guattari (1987) suggest the use of *matter, materiality,* and *material* in a way similar to the Hjelmslevian *purport, expression,* and *content* (i.e., the three planes that constitute the space of signification) (see Deleuze & Guattari, 1987; Eco, 1979; Greimas, 1987; Hjelmslev, 1943/1969). It is important, nonetheless, to use carefully the spatial metaphors in their application to television. If television functions as an "archival" contemporary memory, it does so defined by the bounds of time and movement rather than those of space and place. Its architecture is temporal; its location, virtual; its documents, ever-flowing.

5. Greimas (1983; Greimas & Courtés, 1982) explained the form as an established and immanent system that is able to generate units—a background from which elements are selected to be actualized in a specific way. The substance, in contrast, is the actualization of the form; that is, the cultural *units* that are generated by the expressive or semantic *system*.

6. "The problem of the form of the content remained at so imprecise a level that it led many authors to think that linguistics (and therefore semiotics in general) could not be concerned with the problem of meaning; they dealt rather with the universe of objective referents, the universe of psychic events, and the social universe of uses" (Eco, 1979, p. 75).

7. Even though semiotics and semiology designate to some extent the same discipline, they entail different approaches to the study of signification. The difference, which for Eco and Greimas is important, refers back to the history of the terms. Semiotics, a term coined by the U.S. philosopher Peirce, is seen as a general science of signs, natural and cultural. Semiology, a term coined by the French linguist de Saussure, is understood as a science of the social life of signs. If the former studies any kind of coded information and avoids the privilege of verbal structures over nonverbal, the latter gives primacy to language, having linguistics as its preeminent model (Eco, 1979; Greimas & Courtés, 1982).

8. Understood as such, a poststructuralist semiotics would be concerned with rules and disruption; the coded and the *uncoded*; the unpredictable, the unclassifiable, and the "floating" signifiers of which Eco (1986), Baudrillard (1988), and Kristeva (1984; Moi, 1987) speak.

9. Grossberg (1988) proposes that the cultural critic can be understood as a detective, a guide, a tourist, or a wanderer. His reflection, based on de Certeau's (1984) and Deleuze and Guattari's (1987) work, carries important implications for the exercise of a critical practice in the postmodern age.

10. In Greimassian terms, the form of the content alludes to the semantic structure that any text or discourse articulate. This implies a narrative in which specific relationships, actions, and conflicts sustain a "drama" that embodies ideological and cultural constructions.

11. For Derrida (1976, 1978), *writing* is the very task of inscription that transverses texts and extends into all activities of signification and symbolic play.

12. It seems quite speculative to speak, within the realm of culture, of a space that is neither meaningful nor signifying. Let us say that such a space is the one that Stroeker (1987) calls "attuned" or expressive. It is the space of awareness *prior to intentionality* in which there is no direction, no focus, and, indeed, no meaning constitution. Investigation of this prereflective realm can be seen in the work of phenomenologists and poststructuralists, in the *semiotic realm* of Kristeva (1987), the *smooth space* of Deleuze and Guattari (1987), the *purport* in Hjelmslev (1943/1969), the *in-between* space of Foucault (1970), and the *world* in Mickunas (1983).

13. Foucault envisions archaeology as a response to the hermeneutical/structuralist logic of cultural deciphering, in that it studies historical documents without (a) asking what they mean (so to avoid the hermeneutical circle), or (b) asking how they signify (so to avoid the structural presumption of a universal order of signification).

6

Semiotics, Discourse, and Archaeology

Semiotics studies culture from the perspective of signification and focuses on the codes that generate signs, as well as on the social processes that produce, enhance, subvert, and transform them. A semiotic approach is a study of the processes of *production* of meaning (the economy of signification) as well as of the systems of codification (the structure of signification). It is concerned with permanence and change, rules and disruption, the coded and the *uncoded*—the unpredictable, the new, the unclassifiable, the "floating" (Eco, 1979).

Semiotics allows us to understand that we construct the world rhetorically by means of languages that work through selecting, opposing, and ranking. Eco (1979) has asserted, not without irony, that a sign is a "lie," a metaphoric substitution; something that stands *as if* something else; the mask of an absent body. A theory of signs, then, could be defined as the study of everything that "can be used to lie" and, paradoxically, of everything that can be used to tell the truth (p. 7). Such an apparent contradiction points out lucidly to the rhetorical nature of human communication and human action.

It is because it is a "lie" that a metaphor has power of illumination and insight (I'm looking for a man—said Diogenes to Caesar—I don't see any). Such capacity makes metaphor an articulating principle of scientific thinking and led Aristotle to assert that there is nothing greater than a good command of metaphor. It is rhetorical (i.e., not literal or transparent), which is what makes human language a source of knowledge in itself and not a mischievous translator of an external reality (as in the Platonic conception) or of a purer, self-sufficient thinking (as for Descartes).

The Nature of the Sign

In general terms, a sign is, as French linguist Ferdinand de Saussure explained it, a form that gathers two substances (Sebeok, 1986). That is, a unit composed by the *conventional* relation of two entities: the *signifier* or "sound image" and the *signified* or "concept" (Sebeok, 1986). A red light is a sign insofar as its color and physical shape is the vehicle for the message "/Stop/." The red light, however, does not mean anything by itself (or it could mean anything). Its meaning—as that of any sign—is not an intrinsic or a substantive property.

It is only by contrast to other signs (e.g., by opposition to the green light) and in relation to an established system of *differences* (stop/go, slow/fast) that it can be read as /stop/ that signification will take place. In other contexts and in reference to other systems or codes, the red light could mean /danger/, /exit/, /bordello/, or /airport/. It can also provoke richer and ambiguous readings (e.g., if placed in an unexpected context, such as a museum) or be empty of meaning (if it cannot be distinguished from other lights, colors, or shapes). The sign does not mean anything (it does not have a positive value). What makes it meaningful is its relational value; its position in a system of differences. In Eco's (1979) terms, "A cultural unit cannot be isolated merely by the sequence of its interpretants. It is defined inasmuch as it is *placed* in a system of other cultural units which are opposed to it and circumscribe it" (p. 79).

The Saussurian is an adequate explanation of the functional capacity of the sign (it is a form that *communicates*, that carries a meaning). However, such explanation is unsatisfactory as an account of *the economy* of the sign—that is, as an explanation of the *production* of meaning; of the sign's historical, ideological, and aesthetic processes (Eco, 1979). As fruitful as the duality signifier/signified is to understand the basic working of language (as a grammar), it becomes problematic if applied to the analysis of the semantics or pragmatics of texts or complex signs.

This situation has led scholars such as Umberto Eco and Algirdas Julien Greimas to reconsider the nature of the sign and to shift attention from the sign to the *processes of signification.* As different as they are (Eco focuses mainly on the semiotics of communication, Greimas focuses on the semiotics of language), both semioticians have appropriated the concepts of the Danish linguist Hjelmslev and accordingly formulated the sign as a space of signification more than as an entity.

The Hjelmslevian Model

Louis Hjelmslev (1899–1965) proposed that the Saussurian opposition signified/signifier could be better explained as two planes, the *expression* (i.e., the signifier) and the *content* (i.e., the signified), which are articulated vertically with their own codified systems (the expression with the form of the expression, the content with the form of the content) and horizontally with each other (the expression and the content). The vertical axis points to the systemic aspect of the sign, the horizontal axis to its signifying aspect (Eco,

1979). While the content plane is the semantic level, the expression plane is the communicative level.

Signifier and signified, then, must be thought of as having their own *form* (i.e., a system, a code) and their own *substance* (i.e., units, actualized elements of the system). According to Hjelmslev, then, instead of a form that organizes two substances (as in de Saussure), the sign has *two* forms that organize substance (Eco, 1979; Sebeok, 1986). While this proposition sounds almost esoteric in the case of the linguistic sign (and, one may add, it is an unnecessary complication), it is of greatest interest and pertinence in the study of nonverbal or "multidimensional" signs (i.e., signs that articulate more than one continuum or purport). One can inversely allege the inappropriateness of the Saussurian definition of sign while dealing with nonlinguistic or extra-linguistic systems. It is esoteric to approach an advertisement as if it were *only* a linguistic utterance (linear, syntagmatic, digital, and noniconic). Because of the fact that images (visual or otherwise) are not discrete signs (i.e., organized in binary oppositions), the search for the duality signified/signifier can be problematic. Eco (1979) insinuates this difficulty when he asserts that:

> Nearly all the non-verbal signs usually rely on more than one parameter; a pointing finger has to be described by means of three-dimensional spatial parameters, vectorial or directional elements, and so on. . . . It is only in recognizing such a range of parameters that it is possible to speak of many visual phenomena as coded signs; otherwise semiotics will be obliged to distinguish between signs which are signs (because their parameters correspond to those of verbal signs, or can be metaphorically analogous to them) and *signs which are not signs at all*. Which may sound paradoxical, even though it is upon such a paradox that many distinguished semiotic theories have been established. (p. 177, emphasis added)

It was in part this debate that moved scholars (surprisingly led by Margaret Mead in 1967) to opt for a "semiotics" of sign systems (the pragmatic tradition) instead of a "semiology" of signification—the linguistic tradition (Eco, 1979; Sebeok, 1986). The point in question is one of epistemological and methodological concern. That is, whether language is one among other semiotic systems or the most important one and the only one that can reflect on itself. The latter position has been held by scholars such as Jakobson, Benveniste, Todorov, and Levy-Strauss and questioned by Eco and Sebeok (see Ducrot & Todorov, 1979; Eco, 1979; Hawkes, 1977; Sebeok, 1986). More important, however, is the questioning of linguistics as the only science of language (are the complex problematics of language exhausted by linguistics?) and its role as an "archetype" of semiotic investigation (Sebeok, 1986, p. 913). Other scholars, following a Hjelmslevian proposition, have found it more useful to keep "semiotics" and "semiology" as concepts alluding to different theoretical realms (Eco, 1979; Greimas, 1987; Sebeok, 1986). Semiology according to such a proposition is a meta-semiotics: its object of study is semiotics itself, its procedures, practices, contradictions, limitations, and internal logic.

The Sign-Function

According to the aforementioned proposition, the sign is not an entity but a point of encounter, more a "sign-function" (it is unstable and flexible) than a "sign," which suggests a fixed nature and identity (Eco, 1979). The sign does not exist physically but as the cultural point in which the four mentioned dimensions converge. The same expression, in consequence, can correspond to different contents; a content can be associated with different expressions, and both content and expression can be read (i.e., decoded) with the use of different codes (Eco, 1979; Sebeok, 1986). Therefore, what a sign communicates depends on: (a) the cultural codes used to decipher the content, (b) the cultural codes used to decipher the expression, and (c) the particular way in which these deciphered expressions and contents are associated.

It is important to note that Eco and Greimas have appropriated the Hjelmslevian model in ways that at times seem to be even contradictory. This points to both the richness and complexity of the model, and to the differing perspectives of both semioticians. One could even say that this model has not been *used*, but translated, transcreated, and inscribed in the context of new problems and semiotic inquiries.

Greimas (1983) explains the *substance* as being the manifestation (surface level) of an immanent *form* or system (deep level), and the *content* as the semantic plane communicated through the *expression*. The relation between substance and form is, therefore, similar to the one existent between *langue* and *parole*. It is a *vertical* relation in which a fundamental syntax generates specific languages, which in turn are actualized in discursive practices and situated performances (Greimas, 1983). These three structural levels closely resemble what Morris (cited by Eco, 1979; Sebeok, 1986) calls the three domains of semiotics: syntactics, semantics, and pragmatics. The relation between content and expression, in contrast, is a *horizontal* one, which presents among a signal, an object, a graphic shape, and the cultural content that it conveys (Eco, 1979; Sebeok, 1986). The way the Hjelmslevian model visualizes this horizontal axis (the processes of signification) places special emphasis on the mobile, continuous, conventional, and cultural nature of signs.

Form and Substance

The form is an established and immanent system that is able to generate units; a background from which elements are selected to be actualized in a specific way. The substance, in contrast, is the actualization of the form; that is, the cultural *units* that are generated by the expressive or semantic *system* (Eco, 1979). To use a rhetorical analogy, the form is a repertoire, and the substance is the selected and combined motifs from this repertoire. While the substance points to the actual, specific configuration of the sign, the form calls attention to its systematic, structural nature.

Traditionally, linguistics studied both the form and substance of the expression, but saw the content only as a substance (Greimas, 1983; Greimas & Courtés, 1982; Sebeok, 1986). In other words, the content was studied only as a purely syntactic matter empty of cultural significations. Whereas the form of the expression was studied by phonology and the expression-substance was addressed by phonetics, the content was studied as a linguistic syntax (Greimas, 1983; Greimas & Courtés, 1982). That is, as the formal organization that allows utterances to "make sense." The form of that "empty," purely relational content, nevertheless, was assumed to be beyond the concern of linguistics, belonging to the realm of social anthropology or related social sciences.

It was Greimas who, retaking the Hjelmslevian model, argued for the possibility of studying *meaning* from a structural perspective, as an essential part of the very constitution of the sign and not as an external aggregate. A structural semantics, as opposed to a linguistic semantics, studies the content as a *substance* that presupposes a subjacent *form* (Jameson, 1972). The aim of the Greimassian proposition, then, is to reach an understanding of that form that permeates and structures discourse but that remains invisible, immanent. Saussure did not take into consideration this aspect of signification because it fell outside of language, understood as a system of differences without "positive" value. One could even argue that the Saussurian system does not take "meaning" into consideration. That this "omission" is possible points out the fact, sometimes overlooked, that one can address questions of signification *without* necessarily exploring meaning (Eco, 1979). This situation is important while dealing with the semiotic or cultural analysis of texts (see Chapters 4 and 7). As Eco (1979) places it,

> The problem of the form of the content remained at so imprecise a level that it led many authors to think that linguistics (and therefore semiotics in general) could not be concerned with the problem of meaning; they dealt rather with the universe of objective referents, the universe of psychic events, and the social universe of uses. (p. 75)

The (Form of the) Expression

This level can be described as the way in which the content is manifested and communicated. The sign-vehicle, as Eco calls it, is more than an irrelevant or a transparent medium or channel. Being a cultural construction, the sign-vehicle can be studied aesthetically, ideologically, and rhetorically. The expression would embody what Jakobson (1960) calls the text's "poetic function" and Eco (1979) its "aesthetic labor"—dimensions that are present in any discourse, but that are usually ignored or denied in texts that do not seem to have an artistic purpose. Texts have meaning not only because of content, but also because of a presentation of the content. The expressive dimension, then, points out the rhetorical nature of human discourse and the relevance of rhetorical investigation for an understanding of meaning.

The (Form of the) Content

In Greimassian terms, the form of the content alludes to the semantic structure that any text and human discourse articulates. That is, in the case of a narrative, the specific relationships, actions, and conflicts that sustain the "drama" and that embody ideological and cultural constructions. This structure presupposes and articulates the language by which a certain culture "speaks" its world.

Refining the analysis of the Russian formalist Propp, Greimas (1983) proposed that any narrative can be structurally defined as a relationship among "actants" (i.e., the roles of the actors in the narrative) established on the basis of desire (for an object), communication (about that object), and action (toward the object).

Pointing out that the very syntactical structure of language follows the same basic narrative patterns described by Propp, Greimas goes further and proposes the actantial model as the basic semantic structure (i.e., form of the content) that underlies any human discourse (Greimas, 1987; Jameson, 1972). The very structure of the sentence, Greimas states, is a miniature drama implying a process (verbs), actors (nouns), and adverbs (circumstances) (Ricoeur, 1985). The Actantial Model is shown in Figure 6.1.

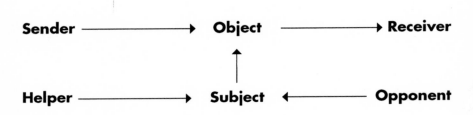

Figure 6.1. Actantial Mode.

The six actants of the model are connected in three pairs of "actantial categories," each of which constitutes a binary opposition (Ricoeur, 1985). Thus, the first category opposes subject and object (desire axis), the second opposes sender to receiver (communication axis), and the third opposes helper and opponent (pragmatic axis). In the fairy tale, the latter is constituted by the benevolent and malevolent forces that can intervene at either the level of desire or communication (Ricoeur, 1985). They can help the subject to obtain its desired object or hinder the communication between sender and receiver.

The Greimassian "Quadrature"

This model of the "elementary structure of signification" offers an interesting space to explore the "narrative" and the "cognitive" dimensions of discourse (Jameson, 1987, p. xiv). It is the dialectical linkage of these two dimensions that makes any discourse an ideological practice (Jameson, 1987). It is also this continuous "transference" and conversion from the narrative to the cognitive and vice versa that makes a text ideological and rhetorical, I would argue.

The *Quadrature* or Semiotic Square has the form shown in Figure 6.2. The "Semiotic Square" not only articulates an opposition (S1 vs. S2) or what can be called a "contrary." It proposes a set of ten possible binary oppositions between six constitutive elements (it is interesting to note that the actantial model is also paired in oppositions among six elements). It includes the "contradictory" terms (S1 vs. –S1; S2 vs. –S2), that is, not the contraries but the simple negatives of the originary terms (e.g., White vs. non-Black); the "synthetic" term S (i.e., the convergence or transcendence of S1 + S2); and the "neutral" term –S, in which "all of the privations and negations are assembled" (e.g., "colorless"). Finally, the quadrature also articulates two transversal axes that point out to oppositions that do not include the main

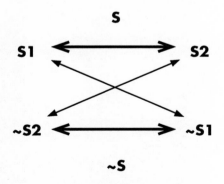

Figure 6.2. The Semiotic Square.

terms (i.e., –S2 vs. –S1) or tensions among more than two elements (i.e., S2 vs. –S2 vs. –S1).[1]

The Semiotic Square allows the critic to place in "visible" terms the ways in which a narrative discourse (e.g., *telenovelas*) presupposes an episteme, a way of knowing. It also points out the ways in which a cognitive discourse (e.g., critical studies on television) presupposes dramatization, storytelling, and "emplotment" (Frye, 1957). What makes both discourses ideological (TV discourses and discourses about television) is the very fact that they are able to take on "a cognitive and a narrative form alternately" (Jameson, 1987, p. xiv). In other words, the cognitive text not only conceptualizes a worldview but also dramatizes it, through stories, characters, plotlines, suspense, and resolutions. In contrast, the narrative text not only tells stories but *argues* them; structures them according to a certain worldview or episteme. Televisual realism, for example, is more than a style. It is a way of understanding; a legitimized way of interpreting reality (Fiske, 1987). One can argue that ideology, then, not only permeates the dimension of the content (social values, beliefs, imagery), but also the expressive form (dramatization, characterization, organization, sequentiality, and expressive structure).

Note

1. The quadrature is also discussed in Jameson (1987).

7

Television, Semiotics, and Telenovelas

Eco (1979) has asserted that "every time that there is a lie there is significa-tion" (p. 59). This definition of the sign can be understood in two different and opposite ways. First, it seems to follow the Peircean conceptualization of the sign, as something that stands for something else in some respect or capacity. Second, it suggests that *any* signification is already and from the start an activity of intentional selection, combination, and expression. The first can be considered a "modern" understanding of the sign as it asserts the positivity of representation and usefulness of substitution while acknowledging their "effectist" and deceptive nature. The second voices uneasiness with this modern conceptualization.[1]

The modern understanding of the sign has been challenged by Derrida and other postmodern critics who see in it the exercise of the metaphysics of presence. Signs cannot stand for something else unless it is another sign, which already posits the problem of why we would need another sign to sub-stitute for that which is already significant. This suggests that signs do not constitute a reality of a second or third order (i.e., they do not represent), and that instead of being the presence of an absence, they constitute an endless network of self-referentiality. Signs, then, would be constitutive of reality, not instruments of reason but the materiality of reason.

If every time there is a lie there is signification, the latter is a problem of value from which ideology and rhetoric are not excluded. The distinction between the (neutral) code and the (engaged) communication is blurred, as the code only exists in the practice of the code and language in "ways of speaking." Thus, it is not that there are structures which generate codes which generate signs, but that there is signification, which can be traced at a multiplicity of levels. Signification can be traced, among others, at the levels of expressive aesthetics, semantic fields, communicative competency, sign constitution, structural arrangements, or generation of codes. It is along the lines of this second understanding of the sign and signification that the Hjelmslevian model appears especially important for Eco.[2] Following Hjelmslev, Eco (1979) finds it necessary to establish the distinction between *sign-function* and *sign-vehicle*, the former being a coded relationship and the latter a discursive actualization. Eco asserts that:

> a single sign-vehicle, insofar as several codes make it become the function of several sign-functions . . . can become the expression of several contents, and produce a complex discourse. (p. 57)

Thus, "usually a single sign-vehicle conveys many intertwined contents and therefore what is commonly called a 'message' is in fact a *text* whose content is a multi leveled *discourse*" (p. 57). It is possible to say that at the moment of enunciation, the communicative and intentional moment of signification, there are no signs (understood as units of signification) but *semiosis* (i.e., a process of signification in which semantic fields and discursive practices intersect and transform one another).

The Hjelmslevian Model

The Hjelmslevian conceptualization of signification has been recovered by Eco and Greimas as the theoretical point of departure for their understanding of semiotics. Following Hjelmslev, Greimas (1983) asserts that language is the coincidence of two planes, expression and content, which are articulated along two axes, the immanent (the system, the *langue*, the paradigmatic level in linguistics) and the manifested (the process, *the parole*, the syntagmatic level in linguistics). The latter, the manifestation of language, requires "the reunion of two levels of language, semiological and semantic" (Greimas, 1983, p. 117). While the semantic level structures the syntagmatic plane of language, the semiological structures the paradigmatic level. The semiological level articulates the elements of the system as opposed to those of the process, and, therefore, it is related to the invariant forms of the "minimal units of signification" (Greimas, 1983, p. 117). In turn, the semantic level studies the elements of the process of language and makes possible the study of the discursive aspect of language. Together the semantic and semiological conform to a *structural semantics*, which Greimas equates to *semiotics* (see Figure 7.1).

The Hjelmslevian model has also proven extremely rich for the analysis of semiotic and textual systems that are nonlinguistic or include more than the articulation of "natural languages," as is the case of television and audio visual systems. In the case of television, the Hjelmslevian model can: (a) account for the multiplicity of languages (visual, verbal, aural, audiovisual) that constitute television; (b) interrogate the relationships among these languages; (c) provide a ground for the distinction of at least four dimensions

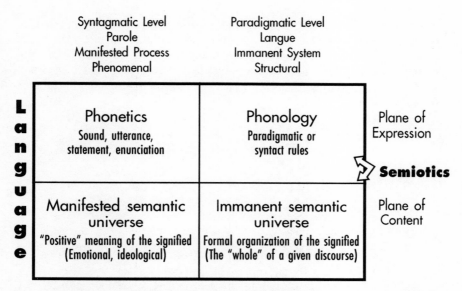

Figure 7.1. Greimas' understanding of language using Hjelmslev's model (in my visualization) (see Greimas, 1983; Greimas & Courtes, 1982; Hjelmslev, 1943/1969; Schleifer, 1987).

of signification, each of which can be studied in its own right; (d) argue, in consequence, for the equal importance of diverse signifying levels, such as the experiential "purport" (i.e., the pre-signifying matter), the expressive materiality, the cultural codes, and the systemic structures in the semiotic study of television; and (e) question, therefore, the theoretical privilege given to matters of representation in the study of television. Representation is a crucial aspect of televisual signification, but to privilege it is to reduce signification to a problem of social substance or "meaning-in-the-second degree" (e.g., television as a second-removed "interpreter of the real," to be judged as an accurate or inaccurate "reflection" of the social). To account for signification, one needs to study not only the plane of the content (via an assumed "mimetic" expression) but also the plane of the expression, with its constitutive "form" and "substance." Let us explore the model by using it to study *telenovelas*, the most important genre of Latin American television.

Reading the Model Reading Telenovelas

The Latin American communication and cultural studies theorist Jesús Martín-Barbero and his team of researchers used the Hjelmslevian model as the basis for their textual analysis of the *telenovela* genre.[3] In his adaptation of the model, Martín-Barbero identified the following dimensions to account for the processes and structures of signification in *telenovelas*: (a) the matter or substance of representation, (b) the structure of the collective imaginary, (c) the narrative form, and (d) the language of the medium. Thus, visually speaking, Martín-Barbero has articulated the Hjelmslevian model in the manner shown in Figure 7.2.

a. The *representation's matter* (the substance of the content) corresponds to the telenovela's melodramatic substance: conflicts of power, family, identity, desire, and love.

b. The *structure of the imagery* (the form of the content) is the genre's structuring of its representational substance in relation to social motives, mythical understandings, and a mass or collective imagery.

c. The *narrative form* (form of the expression) is the structure that organizes the narrative; the expressive codes by which the program acquires rhythm, pace, order, style, and coherence. In the case of telenovelas, the form of the narrative is a serial that lasts an average of a year.

d. The *language of the medium* (the substance of the expression) refers to the expressive characteristics of the televisual medium and, more concretely, to the "matter" that makes a telenovela a distinct genre, different from the news show, the sitcom,

Substance	Form	
Language of the medium	Narrative Form	Plane of Expression
Matter of representation	Structure of Imagery (social ways of seeing)	Plane of Content

Figure 7.2. A model for the textual structure of *telenovelas* according to Martín-Barbero (1986). The figure shows the main issues of signification that each semiotic level addresses.

or the talk show. These enactments are ideologically inflected and speak to us of a way of living, of understanding life. As a part of this TV language, I propose to address a *rhetoric of presentation*, which includes expressive resources such as:

1. *Nomination*, the self-presentation of the melodramatic serial (i.e., openings, closings, music, markers of identity and style).

2. *Composition*, the resources by which soap operas create space and time, construct settings, and ritualize action. This composition emphasizes continuity over closure, redundancy over economy, and suspense over resolution.

3. *Anchoring*, the ways in which soap operas are porous and anchor storylines on the happenings of the "external" world (other stories, other genres, other tales).[4]

I used the previous description of the textual composition of telenovelas as the point of departure for a comparative analysis of soap operas and telenovelas (Lozano, 1990). Such an analysis and others undertaken afterward allowed me to explore specific aspects of televisual signification and to reconsider the "capacities" and possibilities of the Hjelmslevian model. Such an exploration led me to a "minimalist" understanding of the model; an understanding that is less general and more extensive, less structural and more microscopic.

Let us now imagine that the model is not flat and bi-planar, but that it is thick, stratified, and multilayered like an onion. A geological formation or an archaeological excavation. Once imagined in this way, the semiotic model ceases to be composed of *parts or elements* arranged or located along the same plane. Instead, it can be seen as integrating diverse signifying dimensions that are simultaneous and co-constitutive as would be the layers of a geological formation. Each layer, each dimension, or each aspect could rearrange and redefine the boundaries, directions, and shapes of the text or space of signification.

The Rhetoric of Presentation

My exploration of the "language of the medium" proper of melodramatic serials revealed an aspect of televisual "writing" or inscription of singular discursive and expressive importance (Lozano, 1989). I am referring to the *rhetoric of presentation* of televisual texts; that is, the ways in which genres, programs, episodes, and segments anchor their narrative and dramatic status. Such rhetoric of presentation includes scheduling, titles, openings, televisual effects, technical resources, and setting arrangements, all of which contribute to the "identification" and valuation of a program or genre. As such, the rhetoric of presentation is not only a matter of the "language of the medium," as the bi-planar model may suggest. The rhetoric of presentation, the self-positioning of programs and genres, is not only articulated by the language of the medium, the technical, and expressive resources of television. It extends across other planes of signification and can be traced at the level of the narrative structures, the enacted representations, and the privileged imaginary of a televisual genre or program. Thus, the rhetoric of presentation is not only a matter of frames, settings, musicalization, or lights. It involves as well the presentation of the *dramatic* body; that is, of the body as a dramatic and valuative space. The rhetoric of presentation requires not only a semiotics of ideological, formal, and technical structures, but also a *semiotics of the flesh*.[5] Indeed, what could be more central to the televisual signifying materiality than the body; the enactment, ground, and mask of rhetoric, value, and signification? The body-inscribed-in-television is, it seems to me, one of the most interesting aspects of the study of the materiality of signification.

Let us visualize first the rhetoric of presentation, which, although first located as an element of the language of the medium (and the site in which it operates more openly), now reveals its extension and articulation among the four spaces of textual composition (Figure 7.3).

The semiotic body does not have a place in the Hjelmslevian model, as the latter refers fundamentally to a structural level of analysis. Nevertheless, once it becomes clear that the rhetoric of presentation crosses the model, breaking its boundaries and connecting its vertical and horizontal planes, it becomes clear, as well, that the model has a central articulation that has been always there but remained *insignificant* for the purposes of the model. The rhetoric of presentation makes visible this articulation and calls it to the foreground of signification.

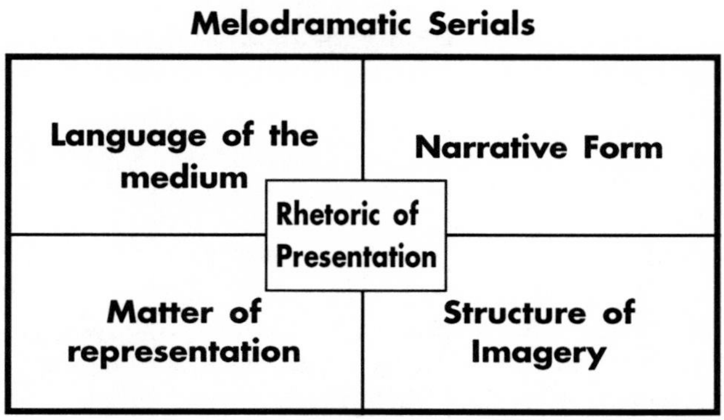

Melodramatic Serials

Figure 7.3. The *rhetoric of presentation* in televisual texts. This aspect of televisual semiosis cuts across the diverse planes of structural signification (my visualization).

What could that articulation be but the body? The body is the site in which structures break and emerge; in which codes are formed, informed, and conformed; in which merely referential structures become filled and charged with the ritualistic, the mythical, and the magical. The body is both the articulation and convergence of the four dimensions of signification, and the point from which the four divergent lines depart. The body is in itself articulation and materiality of a semiotic system inscribed in flesh, in the excess, voluptuousness and eloquence of gesture, posture, movement, gaze, embrace, grimace, face, and skin.

In fact, rhetorical, ideological, and epistemic systems cross the body and anchor it along lines of signification. Conversely, the body grounds them in processes of sense-making from which any signification or meaning is to be derived. Thus, fundamental ideological and discursive oppositions such as high/low, light/dark, and dexter/sinister are grounded on a basic sense of body posture, directionality, and orientation. In turn, these oppositions return to the body and inflect it with value, hierarchy, order, and ethics. Thus, the moral opposition good/bad becomes "physical" when it is reinvested on the high and the low, the right and the left, the upper and the lower, the forward and the backward. In turn, the body sense of light and dark, sound and silence, back and front becomes "moral" under the investment or contamination of the bodily with the valuative; the good and the bad, the ugly and the beautiful, the right and the wrong.

One knows the value of a text by knowing the body who reads it, who carries it, who *embodies* it. It was a popular understanding, when I was growing up, that telenovelas were made for maids, or that, in other words, *telenovelas* and maids *deserved* one another as an ideal text/reader couplet.[6] As much as *telenovelas* were considered trivial melodrama, so their readers embodied triviality and melodramatics. As in melodrama, the maid's life is organized in inverted priorities; the domestic over the public, the emotional over the analytical, the repetitious over the new, and the superstitious over the rational. As in melodrama's aesthetic and intellectual standards, the maid's standards are low. She is illiterate, peasant, and lower class; the embodiment of gender, class, and cultural "lowness." The latter can be "confirmed" by means of bodily resemblances, representation, and doubling. Thus, she speaks softly, with a "low voice"; she is short in height, shallow in character, down in walk and posture. She is, if one could say so, "dark-aged," as she carries the marks of that which has been already defeated by "progress" and modernization. As such, and in opposition to the *maiden*, the heroine of the melodramas, the maid is ugly, as the gods of a defeated culture appear to the victorious civilization.

Thus, value is invested in body, and body announces the principles of valuation. To understand the epistemic transformation of a time, the "setting on fire" of the archive, so to speak, is also to understand the shifts of bodily valuation and embodied evaluations (see Chapters 8–10). The body of the dancer in whose name the Greek tragedies are written (Dionysus and the Satyr) becomes, with the Middle Ages, the body of the devil, Satan, negation of the positive and the good. The body of the wisewoman, accompanied by the sacred cat and owl of ancient Egypt and Asia, becomes the body of the witch who performs sexual orgies with Satan, who is now incarnated in the cat and the owl, nocturnal animals, animals of the sinister (i.e., the left, the wrong, the evil). The sinister, conversely, reenters the body, so that it is wrong and suspect to prefer the left hand. The left hand leaves the body and enters politics, so that it is the "leftist" subversion and the corruption of the right.

The Rhemic Body[7]

Let us consider now the rhetorical constitution of the body in Latin American telenovelas. As is the case with other melodramatic forms, telenovelas are "minimalist" in technical resourses and baroque in terms of performance (Lozano, 1989). As was the case with classic melodrama, the silent film, or the sitcom, a minimalist setting implies the baroque nature of the performative body. This is especially evident in what I call "archaic" and "classic" telenovelas. In these telenovelas, face and body take to the extreme gesture and expression so that characters are not "realistic" representations but expressive masks. Emotions, attitudes, moral standings, and dramatic status are embodied and made flesh. Thus, a character's body is simultaneously a face (of an actor), a role (in a dramatic conflict), an index (of the telenovela's topic and pathos), a presentation (of a dramatic mood), and an icon (of a moral standing). The body is not only a dramatic vehicle but an extended face; a mask, a saturated text, and a node in a narrative discourse.

The body anchors and grounds the narrative form of telenovelas (and soap operas) and provides a flesh to the otherwise "empty" skeleton of the *Actantial Model* (see Chapter 10).[8] In fact, the otherwise structural semiotics cannot but become *material* in the face of the body and its narrative power. Indeed, a narrative is already and from the start a materiality, as it cannot be divorced from the instances, events, and faces that make the narrative possible. To call such a narrative "a structure" would be to abstract the narrative out of the multiple material from which it emerges. In an earlier study, I attempted to account for this situation by opening the *Actantial Model* to the tracing of the body (Lozano, 1990). In that study, I sought to convert this Greimassian narrative model into a *map* that could trace the narrative power of the otherwise "random" displacement of characters in the space of representation. Such an attempt showed how the narrative was as grounded on the content of events as it was on the bodily position and accommodation of the characters participating in those events.

However, one of the important conclusions that eluded me at the time was that the Actantial Model is less adequate to study narratives than to study the *narrative dimension* of non-narrative discourses. One of the model's limitations is, precisely, its requirement of abstracting the body and with it, bracketing the materiality of narration in "multilingual" or audiovisual forms such as theater, film, television, and video. In doing so, one is forced to treat these forms as written literature or oral storytelling (and not as performance). This should not be considered by any means an oversight of Greimas, as he explicitly grounded his Actantial Model on the study of literature and folk tales. The oversight could only be ours if we were to take Greimas' proposition as an axiomatic claim and "apply" it without examining its "interests" and commitments.

Narrative Materiality

The narrative materiality of the semiotic text has in the body its principle of patterning, articulation, and narrativization. That which in the Barbero/ Hjelmslev model (Figure 7.2) is called the "form of the narrative" spreads and overlaps into other semiotic aspects, as it is moved by the body-as-narrative. I would like to imagine it visually in the manner shown in Figure 7.4.

In turn, the narrative materiality points to and uncovers the textual materiality of television, the articulation and interconnection of televisual texts in the inscription of the bodily, the narrative, and the discursive levels mentioned earlier.[9] The textual materiality of television is a "flow," an extended

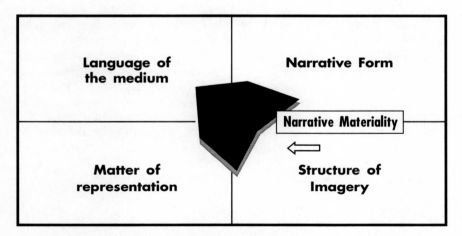

Figure 7.4. The *narrative materiality* of televisual texts. The figure shows the narrative dimension of the televisual text extending beyond the boundaries of the form of the expression and permeating both content and expression, form and substance.

and potentially infinite inscription that is anchored by the rhetorical resources of presentation, narrativization, and repetition. I have given the name of *textuality* to this inscription so as to emphasize the sense of weaving that the textual materiality of television carries. With textuality, a shift of focus takes place, from the text as foreground to the text as background in which crisscrossings and resonances extend in diverse directions, breaking the limits of texts. It is in terms of textuality that one could "read" the writing of a televisual system, for it allows the critic to see televisual texts as *intertexts*, that is, as intersections of discursive threads. As such, *textuality* would refer less to texts than to *discursive nodes*, densities that occur and recur across the televisual flow.

Archaic, Classic, and Modern Telenovelas

Rhetoric of Presentation

Telenovelas and soap operas are "melodramatic serials," a genre that combines the paradigmatic structure of melodrama and the syntagmatic structure of the serial (Martín-Barbero, 1986). That they belong to a common structural genre should not, however, undermine their differences. Whereas telenovelas, the most popular genre of Latin American television, are long tales of inter-twined stories that have a final resolution, soap operas are an epic edifice whose capacity for generating new stories is virtually unlimited. Telenovelas resemble the structure of the fairy tale; soap operas recall the family album that can be opened on any given page, without losing its dramatic force.

There are also differences among telenovelas, which I believe are located fundamentally at the level of the *rhetoric of presentation* and the *rhemic body*. Thus, while telenovelas have remained fundamentally unchanged structurally, their materiality of expression has changed based on what I call *archaic, classic,* and *modern* styles (Lozano, 1990, 1991, 1992).[10] In this case, the terms "archaic," "classic," and "modern" do not carry with them a value judgment or a strictly diachronic reference. They should be understood, instead, in a *genealogical* manner, as ways of denoting transformations of the semiotic rules by which the text is constituted.

The Matter of Representation

Archaic telenovelas are "rhetorized" as archetypal dramas whose setting is not a society or a community, but a place of drama. As such, they can be compared with the fairy tale and its central actors, the princess, the prince, the queen, and the villain. The setting of the drama in the fairly tale or the archaic telenovela is not Notre Dame, the Mississippi, or Macondo, but the castle and the woods, the mansion and the village. That is, an archetypal and *feudal* generality. The archaic telenovela does not tell the story of a woman (Madame Bovary or Candid Eréndira) but enacts the "human condition" or, better, the "woman condition." She is María, a poor young peasant to whom disgrace and dishonor have come. María is quite often a bastard child who has to leave her surrogate family and work as a servant of the region's wealthy family. She is deceived by a malicious man (who gives her a child) and an envious woman (who spreads the rumor). Her grace and purity win the heart of the good and wealthy heir, and while getting married, she might discover that she, herself, is the secret heiress of a family fortune.

In contrast with the archaic telenovela, the *classic* telenovela is "proto-typical," as it moves from the feudal place of drama to a provincial town or a small Latin American city. A "prototypical" community emerges in the classic telenovela, with its required priest, gamonal (i.e., the town's strong-man and virtual owner), brothel, witch, fool, doctor, hidden monster (a deformed child, quite often), and housewives. After being molested by the gamonal, blackmailed because of the monster, and injured with black magic, María emigrates to the big city, where her problems are just about to start. She becomes a maid, learns an art, overcomes her problems, and meets her would-be husband, usually a wealthy businessman.

A character who started appearing in the archaic telenovela will become more pervasive in the classic telenovela. This was *el extranjero* ("the foreigner"), usually an Italian, French, Spaniard, or Arab man who was often sinister and suspicious. He brought with him obscure practices from other lands and kept his true identity a secret. In the classic telenovela, the foreigner becomes more frequently the *gringo* (i.e., the Anglo American male). The gringo, a vital character as well in Latin American comedy, is often the entrepreneur (as he is in García Márquez's *One Hundred Years of Solitude*), the man who arrives with investment money and transforms the landscape.

Finally, the modern telenovela could be called "typical" because it empha-sizes both a generality and an increased sense of "realism" (in both storylines and codes of representation). The actions of the modern telenovela take place in either a specific Latin American location, *el Valle del Cauca, Rio, la Costa*, or a Latin American modern city, which can have a variety of names: *Buenos Aires, Mexico DF, Caracas*. María might not be a maid anymore but a poor girl from the city who struggles to study or get a job as a secretary or nurse, and, more recently, as a singer, model, dancer, or actress.

The Rhemic Body

Although the body is the stage of the drama in all of these telenovelas, archaic telenovelas emphasize the face, classic telenovelas focus on face and body, and the modern ones foreground both body and the space of action.

Thus, modern telenovelas deemphasize the closeup and provide weight to the contextual atmosphere.

Archaic and classic telenovelas emphasize the facial gesture and therefore maintain the body as an absence. But while the face of the heroine stands for her body, deeming the body irrelevant or merely indexical of her social status, the face of the bad woman is an extension of her body. In the case of the bad woman, the face announces the priority of the bodily, nonethical, and whimsical over the good-spirited, the spiritual. The goodness and badness of men is inserted in their skin, as possessors of base or honorable features (which do not require beauty but strong manhood). The goodness or badness of women is inserted in the difference between face and body as one carries the other, purifying the body (in the primacy of the face) or sexualizing the face (in the primacy of the body).

Thus, the repentant prostitute in *En carne propia* (produced in 1990), a classic telenovela, used exaggerated makeup and impossibly tight mini-skirts, which echoed the voluptuousness of her smile and body movement. Once she gives up her wrong ways, she stops wearing makeup, plain hair surrounds her face without adornment or fancy, and without her old mini-skirt she is revealed to be a young, inexperienced, and child-like woman rather than a seductress. The desirable woman has now turned into the good woman. It will take a while before she can become honorably beautiful, thus gaining a promised earthy redemption, beauty without poison, desirability without seduction.

Similarly, the protagonist of *Vivir un Poco* (produced in 1985) is not especially beautiful, while the evil women who fight her have outstanding beauty.[11] Nevertheless, a warm light illuminates her face and provides her with a literal aura of splendor. There is no doubt in looking at her that beauty comes from within. The true beauty is one who does not point to herself and who shines in spite of humility and simplicity. Beauty is a gift and a resemblance, not an instrument or an extension of success.

The narrative of the archaic and classic telenovela is structurally developed under the permeating discourse of aristocracy. In such a discourse, money is wrong and evil unless rightly inherited or morally deserved. Instead of money, in fact, one speaks of wealth, the already established condition of the lord and the king. Since wealth and money easily corrupt, the first requirement of the lord is to show equanimity and compassion. Such performance, the one that announces that one is of *buena cuna*, good birth, is the performance that makes someone beautiful. The face is its privileged site, as it irradiates compassion and makes present the good heart. Because eyes are mirrors of the soul, the mouth its trace, and wrinkles its map, the face reveals a true nature, even when it is "hidden" under rags or disguised by riches. Thus, while many characters are pretty or handsome, only the good one, especially the protagonist, is beautiful. Poor or rich, the beautiful woman shines. She is not the one with the "outstanding" physical attributes, but the one with the aura, the one who extends herself in what she touches; the one that invites life.

Within the context of U.S. Hispanic television, the above styles are not as clearly differentiated. There are virtually no telenovelas in the Hispanic programming that one could call "archaic," but many that combine in one degree or another elements grounded in the archaic, the classic, and the modern styles. A more powerful and fundamental criterion appears to make sense of these telenovelas, which has to do with the understanding of the *body* and, in consequence, with the rhetoric of presentation these telenovelas exhibit. The *selection* by Hispanic television of telenovelas makes apparent a transformation that is taking place in this Latin American genre. I call this a shift from *traditional* to *modern* telenovelas, a shift that is made particularly visible within the overall *modernization* that Hispanic television entails (if one compares it with the Latin American televisual systems). I will explore telenovelas in the Hispanic textuality in Chapter 10. Before that can be done, we must enter an emergent archive: Hispanic television.

Notes

1. See Foucault (1970, Chapter 4) on the relationship between modernity and the epistemics of representation.

2. Danish linguist Louis Hjelmslev (1899–1965) wrote *Prolegomena to a Theory of Language* (1943/1969) and developed "Glossematics," a theory of language. His work was the basis for the Copenhagen School of Linguistics, and his complex conceptualization of signification has been influential in Europe and Latin America. Some of the semioticians and philosophers who have used Hjelmslev's conceptualization of signification include French Deleuze and Guatari, Italian Eco, Lithuanian Greimas, and Colombian Martín-Barbero.

3. Martín-Barbero is one of the most influential scholars of Latin American cultural and media studies. A team of researchers under his direction undertook a multicountry Latin American study of telenovelas in 1986 and subsequent years. I participated in the earlier stages of this research and continued it in a different direction once in the United States. What is discussed in the next pages is the result of my research on the matter.

4. For example, *Mi Corazón Insiste . . . en Lola Volcán* is a modern telenovela whose *rhetoric of presentation* mixes traditional elements of melodramatic composition with action, outdoor sequences, and camera shots *anchored* in a Hollywood aesthetic (see Figure 10.1 and subsequent discussion in Chapter 10)

5. The work of the phenomenologist Alphonso Lingis (1984) could be understood as moving in the direction of such a semiotics of the body, the "inscription in flesh" of signifying systems.

6. I have referred to the "maid" in Lozano (1990, 1991).

7. I use the word "rhemic" to suggest the textual articulation of the body as rhetorical and semantic presence; as a combination of the rhetor and the *seme* (Lozano, 1990).

8. Clearly, the body is not a prerogative or privilege of melodramatic serials. However, I wish to focus specifically on telenovelas because this is one of the televisual forms in which the body-as-narrative is more predominant.

9. This can be related to the "great syntagmatic" of Christian Metz. For Metz (1982), film is not articulated as a language but as a rhetoric, along the lines of the metaphoric and the metonymic, the syntagmatic and the paradigmatic. Thus, for Metz, the minimum unit of signification in film is the "Great syntagmatic," the sequence or act in which an event, a conflict, or an action is articulated. In the case of television, the rhetorical syntagmatic establishes units and segments that can be read on their own but are also tightly connected—structurally and textually—with that which precedes and proceeds.

10. A distinction can be made as well between Colombian and Brazilian telenovelas, on the one hand, and Mexican and Venezuelan telenovelas, on the other. While contemporary Colombian and Brazilian telenovelas tend to be more anchored in national geographies and memories, Mexican and Venezuelan telenovelas tend to be more anchored in a Latin American generality. Incidentally, Mexican telenovelas are the most exported not only to the United States but also to the rest of Latin America.

11. *Vivir un poco* and *En carne propia* are both Mexican productions of *Televisa*. Several clips of both can be found on *YouTube*.

III

READING THE ARCHIVE

Hispanic Tele-Visions

8

Despierta América![1]

Rearranging the Field of the Real

Univision and Telemundo are TV networks that exist within the U.S. boundaries without being fully *American* and within the Latin American borders without being Latin American. They constitute a regional flow whose waves are both narrower and larger than those of national networks. The Univision and Telemundo networks are borderland television, transnational enterprises with a local color, and U.S. investments with an immigrant accent. The economic,

Figure 8.1. Washington, March 28, 2011. President Obama speaks with Univision co-host Ramos at an Education and Latinos town hall meeting. [Photo: Bloomberg]/[Bloomberg collection]/Getty images.

professional, cultural, and technological resources of Univision are as grounded in L.A. and Miami as they are in Mexico City and Caracas.[2] Telemundo also has strong ties to Mexico, via TV Azteca, as well as to Colombia and Brazil (it used to import Brazilian telenovelas). Telemundo prides itself on producing or co-producing its own melodramas (unlike Univision), a practice started in the early 2000s to cater directly to Latinos under the argument that most telenovelas fail to speak to Latinos' U.S. reality. Some of these telenovelas are co-produced with Colombia's RTI and are shot in the United States, Mexico, and/or Colombia, with Mexican and Colombian actors. Such is the case with the 2008 telenovela *Sin tetas no hay paraíso* ("Without Breasts There Is No Paradise"), which was shot in Girardot and Bogotá (Colombia) as well as Durango (Mexico).

As a transnational enterprise, U.S. Hispanic television is a Hollywood-like project, able to produce and reproduce relatively cheap and successful formulas for an enviably faithful and captive audience. But unlike its English-speaking counterparts in the United States, Hispanic television networks do not face the competition of a U.S. Hispanic film industry.[3] Neither Latino nor Latin American cinemas are in a position or disposition to compete with a homogenous industry, which relates to its audience as Spanish-speaking clients at the U.S. mall (more on this later). Thus, in many ways, Telemundo and Univision may perform like the 1960's U.S. broadcast networks, which held a great deal of control over viewers' time and attention.

At the same time that Univision and Telemundo are successful transnational businesses, they are also a "minority" media, with the multiplicity of meanings one may attach to such denomination. While Univision has at times surpassed NBC as the fourth largest network in the United States in terms of reach and revenue (James, 2011; Wentz, 2011), it remains safely out of reach of the U.S. mainstream in symbolic and material ways. Univision uses rhetorical themes that are alien (pun may be intended) to the mainstream, and it broadcasts in a language other than English, which it proclaims is at the core of its televisual identity. Maybe not surprisingly, the programming of Univision and Telemundo is ignored by the mainstream media and public, with the occasional exception of the coverage of events of great "cross-over" appeal, such as the Univision/CNN democratic presidential debates of 2007 and 2008, the Telemundo/NBC broadcast of Miss Universe in 2008, and international soccer tournaments.

Some satirical references to Hispanic television emerge from time to time, however, suggesting increasing familiarity with its iconic style and dramatic codes. In 2008, political comedian Stephen Colbert invited his "good friend" TV host Esteban Colberto to interview Lou Dobbs on immigration (The *Colbert Report*, January 2008). The audience is told that Esteban's show, "Colberto

Reporto Gigante," broadcasts on "Yonomundo," an allusion to Univision's iconic variety show *Sábado Gigante* and to its rival network Telemundo. A mustachioed man with slick shiny hair, Colberto is seen crossing the U.S.–Mexican border at night with his two scantily clad models in tow. Sporting *zoot suit*-type pants and a purple jacket with a rose on its lapel, Esteban strikes a few salsa moves with his back dancers before sitting with Dobbs for the interview (carried in Spanish with English subtitles). The dancers are then shoved off the balloon-filled studio.[4]

Univision and Telemundo are indeed prolific and reliable sources of cultural stereotypes, which are often grand enough to constitute their own best satire. The TV programming relies on formulas; on structural, narrative, and expressive repetition and redundancy. Its nonverbal dimensions require no knowledge of Spanish—or English, for that matter—and can be rather memorable (as the Colbert skit above described shows). These dimensions of televisual signification cross the linguistic borders without much obstacle, given their highly recognizable and generic nature. However, the verbal component, Spanish, performs as the main source of difference and therefore of identity, as a source of alien-ness and of in-group complicity, as marketing strategy and tactical subversion.

United by a Common Language

In a 2003 interview with E. Tiegel, Univision's famed journalist and writer Jorge Ramos cited a study by the Tomas Rivera Policy Institute in Claremont, California, according to which "nine out of 10 Latinos speak Spanish at home, eight out of 10 are bilingual and 57 percent of that group chooses to watch the news in Spanish. This is a major attitude change. Ten years ago, one in four bilinguals watched in Spanish" (Tiegel, 2003). In the interview, Ramos estimates that

> There are 8 million undocumented immigrants living in the country. These undocumented people have no voice in the English-language newscasts for obvious reasons. They speak Spanish and are afraid of being interviewed. For us they are part of our life. If they are interested in what's going on in Venezuela or Peru on a regular basis, they won't find anything on the three networks. (Tiegel, 2003)

A decade earlier, Ramos' assertions were mirrored by Univision's marketing vision. In celebration of its 30 years of broadcasting, Univision's corporate jingle proclaimed, "We are united by the same language; we are the vision of America."

> Juntos estamos de aniversario
> treinta años cumpliendo
> hemos crecido y estamos de fiesta
> treinta años sirviendo

> Univision es . . . Noticias . . . deportes . . . novelas . . . Variedad . . .
> tradición . . .Univision es tu gente

> Juntos unidos por un mismo idioma,
> Univision:
> La Visión de América[5]

This jingle worked as a nutshell of a discourse on Univision: "We have grown and we are celebrating thirty years with you. Univision is . . . news, sports, novelas, variety and tradition. Univision is your people. We stand together, united by a common language. Univision, The Vision of America" (my translation). The network proposed itself as a United Vision from the United States and to *Am(é)rica*. The network's slogan at the time, "La Visión de América," remains an eloquent "revelatory phrase," a statement on the rhetorical self-positioning of the network.[6]

"Vision of America" appears to be a fairly straightforward statement. It has recourse to a cliché—to have vision—and to a national referent—America. And yet, in their interplay, these dead metaphors, *vision* and *America*, recover their ambiguous flexibility. Univision's slogan worked across semiotic and rhetorical fields defined by cultural ambivalence, expressed in the conflicts of two languages and their social and historical memories.

"La Visión de América" does not fully translate as "The Vision of America," even if the words do correspond to one another one by one. The map of America (in English) is not necessarily that of *América* (in Spanish).[7] The former has the United States as its semantic center, the latter has Latin America. *The Vision of America* proposes to us a play of mirrors or a double reflection: the vision of America and America's vision. Univision is not only "our" vision but also a view on "us." It does not only allow us to see America; it allows us, "Americans," to contemplate our own image and see our *perspective*. Thus, we are both subjects and objects of Univision. We are the subject gazing and the object gazed at; both Univision's represented body and the grounds of its narrative discourse (see Chapter 7). Furthermore, that (uni)vision is verbalized "our" way, in "our" language—*en nuestra lengua*. As the jingle states, estamos juntos, unidos por un mismo idioma: "We are together, united by the same language."

La visión de América

Who are "we," the subject and object of this televisual textuality, the ones with the vision of *América*? "We" do not share a particular nationality, ethnicity, or class, but the complicity of a common language, and, more important, of a common *speech*. It is a speech that can be encountered "anywhere" in América; a speech that may carry the accents of Argentina and Cuba, Mexico and Venezuela, Colombia and Puerto Rico. Although the speaking could originate anywhere in *América*, the listening takes place in *America* (in both a metaphoric and literal sense). Univision positions the Spanish-speaking resident of the United States as its ideal listener and the totality of the American continent as the territory of reference. Thus, the "Vision of America" suggests the network as the eye of the continent staring at itself, in a vision given and received by Spanish-speaking people. Univision is the gaze of Latin Americans over the United States and the gaze of the United States over the rest of the continent. Univision would supply a people with a (national, even *nationalistic*) vision and give sonic *image* to a practice, the speaking of Spanish.

Telemundo's slogan "Hecho para tí," *made for you*, implies a similar understanding of Spanish as an embodiment of social practice and cultural difference and identity. Telemundo is "designed" by Hispanics and for Hispanics, and in its beginnings, it was Puerto Rico's "window to the world" (Información corporativa, Telemundo, 2010). As in the case of Univision's slogan, Telemundo's *hecho para tí* cannot be accurately translated into English because its meaning resides *precisely* in the fact that it is said in Spanish. "Made for you" is not *para tí* in this context because "you" refers to an anonymous everyone, and *tu* or *ti* connotes a member of a linguistic minority to whom I am referring affectionately (in Spanish one may use the colder, formal, and respectful "usted" or the warmer, closer, informal "tu"). Telemundo has made friends with us and has our audience interests at heart.

Speaking carries with it much more than the actualization of a language or the articulation of a linguistic grammar, syntax, or lexicon. Speaking embodies the density and complicities of the voices that speak; it carries with it a lived memory and a cultural depth. In the case of Univision and Telemundo, such memory is Latin American (with Mexico at its most influential axis) and gives shape to a U.S. Spanish customer who remembers Zapata, Bolívar, Ché, and Martí and consumes in English. This new reader and consumer presuppose a *deterritorialization* of traditional distinctions and geopolitical boundaries and the emergence of another continental topography. Such deterritorialization is present as well in literature, film, poetry, music, religion, and political movements. Hispanic television engages this new geopolitical topography as a market issue whose complex logics propose interesting discursive tensions and contradictions.

For example, the networks' stated intent to speak for and to a unified Latino community is not universally welcomed by an audience that originates in at least 20 different countries and that differs greatly in taste, politics, outlook, and social status. For example, Univision's reliance on Mexican Univisa makes for some disgruntled audience members who deplore the network's "Mexican-ness" and its perceived catering to a Latino lowest common denominator. This discomfort is occasionally expressed via cultural prejudice. Responding to a blog by *Advertising Age*'s Laura Martínez, commentator Jaime Borromeo describes the network as that "Mexican garbage" they show on "*Indiovision*" (Martinez, 2007, my translation). Elsewhere, commentator "Pitirre" describes *Indiovision* as "that station with the *mejicanadas* which has turned to be a . . . propaganda channel for those who cross the border illegally" (Cuba Forum, 2008, my translation). Most tellingly, a forum for "White pride world wide" considers that Spain's culture is being destroyed by Univision/Indiovision and their "darkie" Latin American invasion (Changing face of Spain, 2004).

Indiovision is a made-up word that expresses national, class, racial, and ethnic prejudice in the economy of one label. *Indio* or Indian denotes an indigenous person and, as such, a source of national pride in Peru, Colombia, Ecuador, Bolivia, Mexico, Guatemala, and other Latin American countries. But *Indio* can also be used in these countries to connote an inferior, uneducated, impressionable, simplistic, rural, unintelligent, and dishonest primitive. As in the case of N----r in English, *Indio* becomes an embodiment of despised otherness. Unlike N----r, the word still holds its original denotative significa-tion. Thus, *Indiovision* (a.k.a. Univision) is the vision of a *low culture*; the perspective of the poor, the dark, the illiterate, the (illegal) immigrant, the maid, the clueless housewife, the unwashed masses, the threatening mob.[8] Similarly unflattering word plays are used for Telemundo (e.g., *Teleinmundo*, "telefilthy," or "teletrash") in ways that suggest that, because of their affiliations, the two networks come to signify "Mexico" as an inferior yet overwhelming influential Other, which in turn appears to stand for a multiplicity of qualities the bloggers cited seemingly despise. In the view of these bloggers, Univision is "anti-American," "pro-Castro," "pro-*illegal*," non-White entertainment for uneducated immigrants.

These sentiments appear to be echoed by online channel *nomoreblather.com*, which found it necessary to unearth the seemingly hidden truth that Univision anchorman Jorge Ramos was a Mexican citizen. Ramos, who hosted a CNN presidential debate on February 21, 2008, was "not only" a Mexican citizen but did "not want to become a U.S. citizen." Additionally, the channel noted, Ramos believes that "the Melting Pot 'is a myth'" and has "promoted cultural separatism and . . . demographic '*reconquista*'" ("CNN forgot to tell you something," 2008). This fact, *nomoreblather* concludes, disqualifies Ramos from hosting a U.S. presidential debate.

If one is tempted to dismiss *nomoreblather*'s position as inane, one need only remember the "birther movement" that forced Obama to release his Hawaii birth certificate (the short form in 2008 and the long form in 2011). In both situations, a metonymic displacement has occurred, and physical resemblance has been taken into the role of legal identity. Obama may be a U.S. born citizen, but he does not look "Anglo" enough. Ramos may be Mexican, but he looks too Anglo; he can "pass." Both are suspect, and both need to be unmasked.

By the same token, Telemundo and Univision are not only U.S. corporations that sell Spanish speakers to advertisers. They also represent a dangerous "reconquista" from the south, a cultural invasion of noncitizens, a debasement of Latin American high culture, and a corruption of U.S. mainstream pop culture. These corporations embody a multiplicity of meanings, ideological positions, and contradictory values both within the United States and in relation to Latin America.[9]

The Spanish Difference

In most Latin American countries, Spanish is the common speaking ground, a tabula rasa that organizes the field of identities and differences. It is because Spanish is the common language that one can use it to tell apart the multiple peoples and regional accents that constitute Latin America.[10] However, in the case we are examining, Spanish becomes a marker of difference; not a ground but a positivity, not a given but a signature. One could not be "united by a language" unless such a language had become a distinction, a differentiating trait, or an identity within national Identity, as is Catalan in Spain, French in Canada, Quechua in Perú, gypsy *Roma* in Europe, or Jewish *Ladino* in Mexico or Argentina. In the presence of a host who does not understand it very well, a natural language becomes a secret code, a complicity, and (the possibility of) a counter-discourse.

Only when it is not a given that "we" speak a common language could we discriminate between those who speak and those who don't (i.e., erecting language as a marker of difference, and of cohesion). Colombian television, for example, could not characterize itself as Hispanic or Latin American because 20 other countries speak Spanish, and most of them call themselves Latin American. Only a transnational television aiming at a generality of countries sharing a common language or a local system speaking to a national "side stream" could emphasize Spanish as the site of communion. "We," the Spanish speakers who live in New York and Chicago, Buenos Aires and San Juan, could not be "united by a language" if that language were not a marker of difference.

Markers of Difference

By a marker of difference, I am referring to those discursive dimensions, nodes, or articulations that can be recognized as belonging to more than one semiotic system. These articulations mark simultaneously their inclusion and exclusion from the systems; their difference from and identity with those systems, and the porosity of the systems' boundaries. Markers of difference are not necessarily *signs of identity* (for they can only be understood in the thick overlapping of discursive practices). Awareness of that which differs does not necessarily imply the existence of a homogenous field of difference. In other words, the cultural differences that televisual and other discursive practices articulate are not necessarily a constant running across multiple planes of action. "Differences" are differently articulated at different times and in different spaces, and their presence grows or diminishes in intensity and extensionality. To speak of identity, in contrast, forces one to propose homo-geneity, to even out uneven fields, and to reduce an irregular topography to a paved road with conveniently located signposts. To seek out cultural identity (e.g., of the Hispanic) requires understanding ambiguity as an impediment, ambivalence as an indecision, and contradiction as a faulty logic that needs corrective analysis.

The *effect* of identity cannot be experientially denied (i.e., "I know I belong in here," "This is my group," "We are a family"). However, such an effect is always relational, multidimensional, and coextensive with an engagement and immersion in a field of action. The moment we "isolate it" for a better analysis, we lose it because there is nothing intrinsically sufficient, positive, or self-defining about identity. The latter implies *identifying*, and, as such, it is intentional, engaged, reflective, and retroactive. Certainly, we are continuously engaged in decisions concerning the definition and identification of ethnici-ties, groups, trends, or fashions. These decisions are a rhetorical act in the best sense of the word. They come out of a field of practice, acknowledge a commonality hitherto ignored, unidentified, or implied, and become true as they respond to an emergence in the cultural field.

In the particular case of the Latino/Hispanic, one cannot posit its identity without missing the complexity of its constitution, as it emerges within and without the Anglo and the Latin American fields, which are multiple and porous. The difficult task of the critic is that of dealing with the cultural field (television in this case) without imposing differences *not given* by it and without positing identity or difference as a given.

One can deconstruct the metaphysics of presence that underlies the con-cept of identity, but one cannot deconstruct the experience of belonging to a place or longing for it. There is no point in deconstructing the song that states, "si mi suerte cambiara a mi Portorrro yo me marchara" (*If I had a strike of good luck, I would go back to my Puerto Rico*) or "I will find Aztlán, that magic heart of our land," a mythical place no map can locate.[11] Instead of deconstruction, the aforementioned statements call us to interrogate the cultural and discursive fields in which this longing and belonging is articulated; the connections, extensions, and articulations in which the moment of *identity-in-difference* appear.

Instead of the task of identifying (so as to differentiate) or differentiating (so as to identify), the cultural field seems to demand the tracing of emerging and merging vectors, articulations, and nodes. As in the case of the quilt, neither the affirmation of identity nor that of its perfect twin, the affirmation of difference, can account for the shapes, textures, and thickness of the quilt's fabric.[12]

Reading the American Map

In the Spanish-speaking television of the United States, Spanish is not a neutral mediator but a language with a memory, a body, and a style.[13] Whether one assumes Univision and Telemundo to be Latin American broadcast systems operating in the United States or U.S. networks for Spanish speakers, the networks reveal the peculiarity of being situated in *Am(é)rica* (i.e., within and between the United States and Latin America). Such a positioning can be seen in the news and the talk shows, the commercials and the melodramatic serials—and these programs' intertextualities.

It is interesting to note in this regard that there are some surprising absences in Hispanic television, absences that one is not expecting, given its "Hispanic" nature. Thus, neither Colombian coffee nor Juan Valdés, perhaps the only recognizable Colombian figure in the U.S. mainstream marketplace, are much present in Hispanic television. This is the case as well with Taco Bell, Cancún, and the 365-days-a-year-fiesta Mexican towns, central images of the Mexican "flavor" in Anglo American television. In contrast, the American—or otherwise—airlines that "break the distance," flying to more (Mexican/South American/Caribbean) cities than any other airline; the ATT and Sprint special international services in Spanish; the psychic and astrological advice that guarantees you a better future; and the English learning programs that offer you the same acquire enormous centrality and relevance in Hispanic television.

More notorious than the absence of Juan Valdés is the absence of *Miami Vice, The Simpsons, CSI, Desperate Housewives,* or *Married: With Children,* programs that are "typical" of Latin American television—to reference Fiske's (1987) notion. Latin American TV programming includes local productions, imports from other Latin American countries, Anglo American TV shows, and occasionally British and Spanish series as well as Japanese *anime*. In contrast, absent from U.S. Hispanic television are any of the U.S. TV shows that are broadcast around the world and that have helped define "Western commercial television." Telemundo and Univision seldom run anything other than Latin American (e.g., telenovelas) and Latino programs (e.g., news, variety shows), with the exception of dubbed Hollywood feature films during weekends.[14] While during weekends the Hollywood content may constitute 30% of the U.S. Hispanic programming, during weekdays U.S. Anglo productions are virtually nonexistent. In contrast, 21% of Mexico's weekday programming is imported from the United States, and in Brazil that percentage is 31%. During weekends, that percentage increases to 38% in Mexico and decreases to 28% in Brazil (Martínez Garza, 2005). Interestingly, Mexico and Brazil, the largest exporters of television in the region, are also the largest importers of U.S. television. In an odd way, one could conclude that right now (in the first decades of the new millennium), Telemundo and Univision are more "Latin American" than their Brazilian and Mexican counterparts.[15] However, their advertising, the very material that weaves the televisual textuality, anchors the programming in a distinctively hegemonic U.S. Latino discourse, in which Anglo, middle-class values are seamlessly woven with Latin American mythologies and delivered in Spanish by *la abuelita* and *los vecinos del barrio*.

Univision and Telemundo are simultaneously external and internal to the United States, internal and external to Latin America. Its "twisted" relationship with *America* manages to uncover or register the contradictory and unresolved pluralities of the United States and of the Americas; the polysemic value of Am(é)rica. The inscription and writing of this continental field creates new and peculiar dynamics at the semiotic, rhetorical, and discursive levels.

Arranging the Field of the Real

One of these dynamics concerns the semiotic and discursive displacement of the United States and its relocalization within the geography—and topography—of the continent. The United States is discursively positioned as a component of América, so that its "Latinhood" becomes foregrounded (i.e., why not think of the United States in terms of its Hispanic heritage?). This situation is especially present in the narrative structure of the news broadcast.

Semiotically speaking, the news genre "maps out" the territory of the real and provides codes for the identification and selection of the newsworthy. Given its explicit duty to inform on the real and eventful, the news requires it to implicitly give answers to questions such as: What is newsworthy and what is its hierarchy of value? Who constitute credible authorities? Who can speak with the voice of the "average citizen"? Who can report and anchor news? What is familial/familiar and what is foreign or alien? Some excerpts from Univision news broadcasts suggest answers to these questions:

- "Recent polls show a national dissatisfaction with the state of the economy and the rate of unemployment," announces the anchorwoman. She cuts to the reporter, who then proceeds to interview Hispanics in the streets of Miami.

- "The riots of L.A. have caused distress in many residents." Several Chicanos and Central Americans voice their discontent.

- "Democrats unsatisfied with the Bush administration." A Hispanic congressman explains.

- "Miami residents protest the government's actions against the Haitian refugees." A Cuban civic leader and a Haitian are interviewed.

- "The Soviet Union has failed today. We will tell you what this means for Fidel Castro."

- "Don't miss the trial the whole world has been waiting for. We will keep you informed daily, live from San Antonio, on *The Trial of Yolanda Saldivar*." Two weeks after the Simpson trial had concluded—properly covered by Hispanic lawyers, reporters, journalists, and analysts—Hispanic television will have the chance to cover another trial the "whole world" will watch—the world for whom "is Saldivar Selena's murderer?" is as dramatic as "is Simpson Nicole's murderer?" Stay tuned.

- Argentine Esteban Creste, from Telemundo's Canal 47 (New York), conducts a special report on New York's 9/11/01 terrorist attacks (aired September 16, 2001). He recalls his life in the United States for the last 15 years, his fondness for New York, and the personal and collective shock of finding the Twin Towers converted to a ground zero war zone. "Duele mucho ver los escombros," he says, and his voice breaks. It hurts so much to see the destruction.

- In his first visit to the Guantánamo detention facility, Creste points out the concentration camp-like conditions of imprisonment. Interviews are conducted in English with high-ranking officers and in Spanish with Puerto Rican and Cuban personnel.

- Five years later and in remembrance of the attacks, Telemundo-New York interviews William Rodriguez, a "9/11 hero." Rodriguez

held the master key to the towers and became an advocate for
the Latinos affected by the attacks. "Six hundred *Hispanos* died
in the towers," we are reminded.

- Chávez was stunned "cold" by the July 2008 rescue of Colombian Ingrid Betancourt and 14 other FARC hostages, Univision
  Chicago tells us. The rescue forces him to make a 180-degree
  shift in rhetoric.

- Would a Hispanic take the place of Obama in the Illinois legis-
  lature? Vicente Serrano from Telemundo's "Contexto" discusses
  with Latino activists.

What appears to be framed as "newsworthy" here is a Spanish and English
nation, the United States. Its political and cultural borderlines, defining it apart
from South and Central America, are no longer thicker than those between
Colombia and Venezuela or more definite than the distance between Puerto
Rico and Cuba. The order, hierarchy, and organization of the news express,
among other things, what counts as newsworthy, nationally and internationally.

The speaker, actor, and average citizen of the United States is Hispanic.
She is María Montoya, street vendor; Felipe Alou, baseball coach; Sergio
Benixen, political analyst; Rosie Ornelus, L.A. county prosecutor; Jacinto Rojas,
drug smuggler; Lincoln Díaz-Bulart, state senator; Alfonso Lozano, convicted
rapist; Julio Meza, L.A. rioter; Pedro Otálora, odontologist; Paul Rodríguez,
comedian; Lola Benavides, Harlem resident; Henry Cisneros, politician; Tito
Nieves, musician; Anni Linares, Cuban refugee; Maria Luisa Branco, travel
agent; Salma Hayek, TV producer and film star; the López siblings, tae-kwon-
do Olympians; Janet Ramírez, pregnant Texan with a brainless child.

On Miami's *Noticias 23* (from Univision), Fidel Castro seems to "make"
more news than any other political leader in the world. Castro is in fact one
of the most important figures in the political panorama of Hispanic television, especially, and not surprisingly, in Florida. Castro occupies a place there
perhaps as central as that of the U.S. president, although for opposite reasons
(i.e., one is a Dictator, the other is the leader of the Free World). However,
the statements of the U.S. president, or of any other English-speaking figure
for that matter, are fully translated into Spanish and very often mediated by
Hispanic commentators and politicians. At this level, Clinton, Bush or Obama
are not different from Sarkozi, Putin, or Lula Da Silva. All are very important
to the "nation," and all are foreign leaders given the distance of language,
culture, and interests.

There is no difference between the Hispanic and the Anglo news programs in terms of the formal structures of news reporting. However, there
are important differences in these programs' ordering of the newsworthy and

their consequent arrangement of the field of the real. Hispanic television speaks of "our countries" to refer to Latin America and the Caribbean and of "our brothers and sisters" to refer to those who live on the other side of the frontier. Colombians, Peruvians, Nicaraguans, and Latin Americans in general would use the same terms to refer to Latin America and the Caribbean. The United States is, at this level, no more than the country in which "we" live; a country that is related by blood and tradition to the rest of the continent. It becomes closer to "other" Spanish-speaking countries by virtue of the lived territory, the common language, the continuous cultural breeding, and the family linkages.

The fate of *America*, in contrast, is quite different. While CNN reported on "America under attack" after 9/11, Univision was covering *The United States at war* ("Los Estados Unidos en guerra"). When I asked South American-born Alejandro why he prefers to say "the United States" instead of "America," he replied "todos somos Americanos."[16] *We are all Americans.* Whether South, Central, or North, we all are Americans.

Although the United States is the territory "we" live in, *America* is a distant land; the mythical space of Thanksgiving, in which a European pilgrim conquers the frontier and colonizes the natives with their help.[17] This *America* is as mythical as *Aztlán* or *El Dorado*, a land in which the One is not the European conqueror but the indigenous civilizations and their "bastard" offspring. We, the children of the raped Mother Land, now speak like our (Spanish) father, but we dance and dream like our (Indian) mother. The One and the Same is now a Criollo, a Mulatto, or a Mestizo, a mixed offspring of conquerors, slaves, and colonized peoples. *America* and the Americas are Other to one another, exclusionary myths united by a common magic, that of "opportunity," as the promise of technology, efficiency, and the possibility to *make*; to actually effect an alchemy that works.

Marked and Unmarked Spanish

Hispanic television speaks a flow of Spanish that is constituted by the rhythms, intonations, paces, and colorations of different Latin American and U.S. accents. The voices participating in this textuality—hosts/hostesses, anchormen/anchorwomen, members of the audience, actors and actresses, public figures and "average citizens"—speak as Mexicans, Chileans, Colombians, Dominicans, and/or U.S. residents. The latter is a Spanish lived within the rules of Anglo interaction, performance, and competence; a Spanish that cannot be thought of anymore without the co-presence of English. Seen in this way, the Spanish of Hispanic television is a heterogeneity that follows the "law of the more." That is, it is Latin American and more; it is North American and more; it is of the Americas and more; and it is the latter and *less*, for each one of these distinctions keeps its function within and without the others. Connecting and weaving this plurality of "marked" voices is the "nonmarked" Spanish. It is a Spanish spoken by the disembodied voices of the corporate announcement, the presentational advertisement, or the public service announcement. Instead of a face or a body, the neutral Spanish is a detached and impartial "talking head" that enunciates without mood, color, or land. The neutral Spanish could be integrated within the "official discourse" of any Spanish-speaking television (Latin American or otherwise). However, it is also the closest to Anglo American mainstream television as it emulates the principles, codes, and styles of the global language of television. In fact, the neutral Spanish is often in charge of introducing "English" within the flow.

English is carefully avoided by Univision and Telemundo, a situation that makes its eventual appearance more significant and noticeable. English appears in the grammar structure of the Spanish spoken by the *guests*, the "plain people" interviewed, reported on, or participating in talk shows, the news, or advertising. English is also the language of the sporadic technical reference (if it lacks a Spanish translation), of the urban geography (streets, shops, brand names), and of the conative expression (e.g., OK, come on, please, welcome, looks good). English is also the language of those leaders and public figures who do not speak Spanish. If their declarations are included, Hispanic television translates, so that there is no statement in this televisual flow that is not eventually Hispanic.

It Is a Good Idea to Learn English

As in *any other* Latin American country, it is important to learn English in the United States. Several commercials and service announcements boast how important English is and the difference that it makes to be able to speak it. It can help you get a new job, advance in your career, facilitate your business transactions, or even widen your circle of friends. As in any Latin American country, it is not obvious that the listener knows English or its rudiments. The BBC announced a program with cartoons that "help the adult listener memorize more easily the new information learned." Listeners would learn, with the help of the cartoon characters, to say, for example,

"How do you do?" dijo el rey (said the king).

"How do you do?" dijo la reina (said the queen).

As is the case in South or Central America, English is a nicety in the U.S. America of Hispanic television. It is something one wants to learn when one is upwardly motivated—something, however, one does not desperately require for survival. English is treated as an externality. It is clear that an Anglo American could not live in a Spanish-speaking Latin American country without knowing Spanish. It is not obvious that a Latino must learn English in the United States. The speaking of English is a secondary feature, an advantage, and a skill that does not come "with the territory." As with a college diploma, English might be very important to succeed, but it is not an essential condition for survival.

Commercials encourage readers to learn English as they will do in an environment in which Spanish is predominant. In fact, Spanish *is* the official language in the topographic territory that Hispanic television (re)constructs. It is not only the language in which all programs and advertisements are spoken, but it is also the one into which a multilingual world of news, events, gossip, music, trivia, business, and information is translated.

The world becomes present through Spanish, and Spanish sets up and transforms orders, privileges, and voices of authority. Thus, the United States becomes a nation spoken in Spanish, lived in Spanish, and often represented by Hispanics. The Hispanic ceases to be a minority and instead becomes us, *the people*, the standard against which the Anglo and other "foreigners" are measured. That learning to speak English is a good idea might be the loudest declaration of the hegemony of Spanish within the cultural territory that this flow (re)creates. If there is a potential political force in Hispanic television, it is not to be found in party manifestos, community activism, or nationalistic agendas. It is here, in the presence of a language that refuses to fade away or resign itself to the acculturation of the well-behaved American. Advertisers are learning to speak "Hispanic," we are told (see Chapter 1). "They" are too many to be ignored. They have been earning some money throughout the years. They even own houses and businesses. And they might not (want to) speak English or give up Spanish. In the process, they are transforming both English and Spanish and creating an in-between space that is only partially accessible to either Spanish-speaking Latin Americans or English-speaking Anglo Americans. Because it is a "minority" language, Spanish in the United States can be a potent form of resistance not unlike indigenous languages under the homogenizing power of imperialistic Spanish in Peru, Guatemala, Mexico, or Colombia. It can also be particularly creative and restless, as it is not subject to the systematic purifying and homogenizing oversight of a national linguistic body. The masterful work of writer Junot Díaz is an example of what it means to resist English within English with Spanish codes, to subvert Dominican Spanish with the new rules of the New Jersey barrio, and to critique the moral codes of both countries with a language that includes and excludes both, refusing to be contained by either.

It may or may not be used politically, but speaking Spanish in an Anglo setting carries in itself a dimension of resistance, complicity, and memory nourishment. This underground "Spanish power" and "tactical" colonization might be adequately synthesized by Paul Rodriguez when he asks his American audience in one of his standup acts, "Don't you hate it when you hear those people in the streets speaking in languages that you don't understand?"

> "I hate it, man. This is America. When somebody comes here, they should learn to speak like everybody else. I tell them, man: *Hey, mister, this is America: Speak Spanish!!!*"

Rodriguez could have been responding to this annoyed internet commenter who, ten years later, makes a similar point, with the "in your face" style proper of Internet anonymous exchanges. The Springfield, Ohio, resident responds with displeasure to the first democratic presidential debates aired in Spanish by Univision in 2007, to the catering to Spanish-speaking people that this implies, and to the use these people make of their perceived linguistic privilege.

He (or she) states:

> The REALITY is that MANY Spanish speaking immigrants (legal or not) USE their native language to assert a dominance over non-Spanish speaking people. It's a little game that they play and EVERYONE knows when they're doing it. It's a purposeful behavior MEANT TO disrespect. You know plenty of people who do it, if you don't do it YOURSELF. It's mean-spirited and hateful and it becomes something to RIDICULE natural-born Americans about. THAT is rude, obnoxious and low class behavior and it happens A LOT or no one would ever mention it. (September 7, 2007)

Hecho para ti [18]

That which may have appeared culturally or commercially compelling but politically innocuous in 2000 carries today striking political significance. Regardless of the conservative nature of its programming, both Telemundo and Univision can become positioned as virtual training grounds for ethnic subversion: uniting by means of a common language, a force stronger than flags, border disputes, class prejudice, or soccer rivalries. The significance of Spanish, or of any other cultural marker, as a unifying and differentiating source of identity can be made evident in how networks frame historical events. For example, in the coverage of the tragic events of 9/11, familiar slogans such as "one vision" or "united by a common language" would have appeared too emphatic of a difference that needed to de downplayed or else be read as nonpatriotic. Then it was important to shift full force to another "we," which otherwise remains in the discursive background: We, the people of the United States. We, the victims of *their* attacks. We, the heroes, the witnesses, the reporters, the writers, the musicians, the volunteers, and the victims. If, for the few starting minutes, the events reported by Univision and Telemundo were happening "there," in New York, Washington, or Philadelphia, they rapidly became events happening "here," in the United States. Univision, like every TV network, struggled for a few minutes with the right way to name and frame the horrifying events. Unlike other networks, Univision and Hispanic television needed to provide further assurance of their rightful belonging to the U.S. mainstream; to this "US," now attacked. Univision and Telemundo need to strike a difficult balance: to be mainstream and yet "ethnic" enough to fulfill the often conflicting expectations of advertisers, consumers, and investors.

Rearranging the Field of Fiction

Typical Latin American television includes both *Simplemente María* (or *María del Mar*, *Doña Barbara and Victoria*) and *Dallas* (or *Star Treck*, *The Simpsons*, and *ER*). Both are spoken in Spanish, with the difference that the former might include idiomatic "incorrections," whereas *Dallas* has the perfected and impeccable Spanish of professional dubbers. *Dallas* is Latin American in the same sense that the Amazonian rainforest has a place in the U.S. American imagination. If the Amazonian rainforest and the Andean mountains are the "exotic" places of Anglo American television, the vice of Miami, the wealth of Dallas, and the sins of Las Vegas are the exotic items of Latin American television. Both refer to spaces and places that are mythical, as they are accessed basically through storytelling and dramatization. Neither Miami nor Dallas need in principle to be "factual" cities in order for their televisual "versions" to make sense dramatically. Places such as San Francisco, L.A., New York, or Chicago become as mythical on television as the West, Disneyland, or the Starship Enterprise.

In the case of Hispanic television, an inversion takes place. Miami, New York, or L.A. are the places one hears from in the local news and the local commercials; the ones with the weather report, the toll-free numbers, the tax deadlines, and the immediate and factual referentiality. The mythical land is now somewhere else. It is the provincial Argentina town from which María comes, the beaches of Rio where Mariana falls in love, and the Venezuelan hacienda that Barbara struggles to keep. *Archaic and classic* telenovelas such as the aforementioned become invested with mythical dimensions, as they are increasingly opposed to the contemporary and modernized telenovelas, which bridge the "gap" between Latin American melodramatization and Hollywood realism.

Conversely, Hispanic television is marked by the absence of Anglo programming and the "omnipresence" of English, which is not spoken but pervades the televisual flow in ways that will be discussed later. In other words, Hispanic television lacks the Anglo American *documents* (i.e., the recognizable programs or advertisements), but it shares the principles of the Anglo *archive*. The markers of difference in Hispanic television emerge *within* televisual spaces, divisions, and codes already "naturalized" by the mainstream television of the United States.

Notes

1. "Wake up America" is the name of a Univision early morning news show.
2. Venezuela's Venevision and Mexico's Televisa share interests in Univision.
3. Some of the most interesting Latino and Latin American cinematic productions are independent projects at odds with the ideological and aesthetic preferences of Latin American/Latino broadcast television. For example, the cinematic movement known as "New Latin American Cinema" is as remarkable for its independence and budgetary modesty as it is for its willingness to take aesthetic and political risks. "New Latin American Cinema" films express resistance against the Hollywood aesthetic, economic, and political model so successfully emulated by television giants such as Televisa, Venevision, and Brazil's RedeGlobo.
4. Colberto turns out to be as conservative as his friend Colbert and to outdo Dobbs in his defense of the rights of the rich. A clever manipulation of footage has Dobbs expressing compassion for undocumented immigrants while the undocumented Colberto questions Dobb's kindness.
5. Univision's corporate jingle broadcast in 1991.
6. In the new millennium, the Univision corporate slogan is less imaginative but factually undeniable: *La empresa líder de medios de comunicación en español al servicio de la creciente población hispana en Estados Unidos.*
7. I am using two spellings, America and *América*, to mark materially the semantic, ideological, and cultural differences that this name envisions and embodies: the America that the Anglo world names and the América of which the Latin American world speaks. In Derridean terms, I am making visible the *erasure* that takes place under the homogenous "America."
8. It is interesting to note how these assumptions about the Indian are also made about a variety of Third World Others and their taste. The maid and her affinity for melodrama is a case in point.
9. In Figure 8.1, President Obama speaks with Ramos about Latino education. Ramos' power as an emblematic Latino figure became apparent when the Obama reelection campaign used Ramos' image in a polical advertisement. Ramos protested the inclusion publicly (Costantini, 2012)
10. Spanish is not, by any means, the only language spoken in Latin America. But it is, in most countries, the official one. Indigenous languages, such as Quechua or Guaraní, are spoken in different countries and constitute important sites of cultural and political resistance. Spanish is, after all, an "imperialistic" language in its own right.

11. The first quotation is from Ray Barretto's (1965) "Si mi suerte cambiara." Barretto was an acclaimed Puerto Rican salsa and jazz musician born in New York. The second quotation is from *Heart of Aztlán*, a novel by the Chicano writer Rudolfo Anaya (1976, pp. 122–123).

12. Thus, I have chosen to speak of "markers of difference" instead of "difference." The former is the moment of differentiation, whereas the latter is the *state* of difference and, as such, is as vertical and ontological as identity (e.g., essential, stable, and self-sufficient).

13. The political, social, and cultural implications of reading "us" in relation to "America" were forcefully expressed in *Nuestra América*, "Our America," the celebrated essay of Cuban poet José Martí (1977), originally published in Cuba in 1891. Said Spillers (1991), "Martí's 'our' and 'America' do not usually embrace the U.S.—except by the logic of a clearly defined dualism of antagonists who . . . must contend, in effect, for the right to name and claim 'America'" (p. 1).

14. According to Fox (1988), Hollywood constituted the *"lingua franca"* of Latin American television until the 1980s, when almost half of Latin American TV shows were U.S. imports. That percentage was reduced significantly in the next decade, and, by the turn of the century, only 18% of prime-time Latin American TV programming on average was imported from the United States (Martínez Garza, 2005). U.S. influence decreased, and Latin American TV giants (such as TV Globo, TV Azteca, Televisa, and Venevision) gained greater influence in the region due in part to the new market logics of globalization (Fox & Waisbord, 2002). While no Latin American country controls the regional market, globalization "contributed to the consolidation of a three tier structure formed by large producers and exporters of audio-visual content based in Brazil, Mexico and Venezuela; medium-sized producers and exporters in Argentina, Chile, Colombia and Peru; and modest producers with virtually no exports in Bolivia, Central America, Ecuador, Paraguay and Uruguay" (Fox & Waisbord, 2002, p. 18).

15. Other networks have been created to cater to Latinos who prefer Anglo or bilingual programming. Among them are "Telefutura" (owned by Univision) and cable Mun2 (owned by Telemundo).

16. Personal communication, June 2008. Alejandro, not his real name, has been working with U.S. Hispanic TV networks for more than two decades.

17. Martí (1977) expressed this unresolved continental tension in his reference to "Our America" and the "Other America" (Spillers, 1991, pp. 1–2). The former is "Mother America," constituted by "long suffering . . . republics raised up from among the silent Indian masses . . . to the sounds of battle between the book and the processional candle" (Martí, 1977, p. 86). The latter is the United States, "that avaricious neighbor who admittedly has designs on us" (Marti, 1977; cited in Spillers, 1991, p. 2). I mark this distinction by referring to América and America.

18. Slogan, Telemundo, "Noticias Chicago" (2008).

9

Televisual Archeology

Premodern and Postmodern Discourses

The study of Univision and Telemundo reveals a multiplicity of discourses that constantly cross the programming, often contradicting one another with equally valid premises. The discourse of instrumental beauty overlaps with that of magic-religious invocations, the discourse of tradition emerges alongside postmodern nomadism, the "born-again" Anglo optimism crosses indigenous Latin American nostalgia, and the discourse of gallantry faces that of sexual emancipation. Not unlike the overlapping of temporalities one faces in countries like Colombia or Peru (see Chapter 2), Hispanic television articulates, mixes, and transforms distinct cultural and ideological "times": Premodern legacies, modern aspirations, and postmodern technologies.[1] In this chapter, I take a tour through some of these overlapping temporalities.

An advertisement announces the powers of quartz to give happiness and love to its user. The next promises a spectacular diet that would allow you to lose up to 30 pounds in a week. While one advertisement promotes a BBC program for the learning of English and other languages, AT&T continues its campaign of a Spanish-speaking long-distance service to Latin America.

"We will be here tomorrow, God allowing," says Hector Lozano in closing today's sports section of Chicago's Canal 66. An anchorwoman in Miami's Canal 23 comments on *aplausos y trompetillas*, a news "cheers and jeers" section, by saying, "God forbid politicians would dictate our morals," referring to "Mr. Quayle" and his judgment on a TV character and her out-of-wedlock pregnancy. "Mr. Quayle has an evident lack of grey matter." Next, a reporter concludes enthusiastically his report about Annai Linares, a Cuban singer seeking asylum in Miami. "Now she will be able to sing in her own way . . . and in liberty." When the land of Dictatorship is confronted with the Land of Democracy, there is no need or use for the detached view or the political critical eye.

A Pepsi commercial puts "us" all together—brown, bronze, mestizo, mulatto, and criollo—in Spanish, Mexican, *campesino,* and Argentinean clothes, dancing to the rhythm of salsa. "A homage to the beauty of the Hispanic woman," announces the advertisement for the annual Hispanic pageant contest, sponsored by Oil of Olay, Colgate, and Max Factor. McDonald's is enjoyed to the rhythm of Miami Sound Machine, and *Telemúsica* brings us the music videos of Gerardo from L.A., Gimena from Mexico, The Gypsy Kings from Spain, and Michael Jackson from *America*. Next, a corporate advertisement announces a special one-month report on the social conditions of Hispanics.

In *Hola América*, a variety show, we hear, explained by an expert, about "women who steal husbands and what to do about it." Whereas last week we heard on *Cristina* a discussion on the sexual taboos of Hispanics, today we are confided the messages that extraterrestrial civilizations directly sent to a Puerto Rican, two Colombians, and a Mexican. Next week *Cristina* will be dealing with animal rights.

Discursive Nodes

The Moment of History

In one of his essays, Borges (1952/1981a) wonders whether history does not happen less in the battlefield or the heroic deed than in the humble occasion, the seemingly insignificant or forgotten moment in which something never spoken before was uttered for the first time. At that moment, something new entered the realm of cultural consciousness and transformed it in ways perhaps not readily apparent. These are moments in which a culture's change of awareness is made apparent, announcing the transformation of practices and discourses. Borges cited a Greek text, which states, "he brought in a second actor" (p. 246). "He" is Aeschylus, and this is the first occasion in which the ritualistic declamation of the Dionysian festivity turned into dialogue, in which the singing of a play became its performance. It was the humble birth of theater, the humble birth of a Western understanding of drama and representation.

Merleau-Ponty (1960/1964) referred to this phenomenon as the eruption, from the realm of silence, of something that was already present but not yet articulated or made visible. Foucault (1972) grounded his entire conception of the archaeology of knowledge in a similar understanding of the cultural field as a shifting, noncontinuous materiality that is articulated in the in-between spaces of discourses.

The moment in which something becomes verbalized, recognized, and legitimized is the moment we can call "historical." When Univision called itself "La visión de América" in the last decades of the 20th century, it gave materiality, by means of a statement, to the paradoxes, contradictions, and ambiguities of the Hispanic construct. As any moment in which history "emerges," such a statement forces us to reconsider the discourses by which we usually define exteriorities and interiorities. There are other "moments" in Hispanic television in which something is said whose implications are strong enough to unveil or reveal otherwise tacit or silent interconnections. I would like to call these *discursive nodes*, spaces or moments in which the crisscrossing of multiple discursive threads has formed an unusually thick and complex texture. Such a texture has required, in order to be shaped, the confluence of a variety of semantic fields and dimensions of cultural awareness. Let me now discuss some of these discursive nodes.

Mirando/Admirando; Tasting/Taking

"Si quiere hacerle una pregunta, no le de pena, por favor." Paul Rodríguez, the Mexican-American comedian and talk show host, invites one of his guests, a Mexican pianist, to ask questions of his other guest, Barbara Eden, star of *I Dream of Genie*.[2]

"No, gracias. Me contento con estar aqui, *admirando*." The pianist politely rejects the invitation, explaining that it is enough for him to be there "admiring"—her, that is.

"Mirando? Yo se muy bien lo que estás *mirando*." Rodríguez, smiling, replies that he knows well what the pianist is *looking at* (playing with the phonetic similarity between *admirando*, admiring, and *mirando*, looking at/staring). Laughter and applause ensue from the audience, the host, and the male guest. They are sharing in the complicity of "catching" the pianist staring at Barbara's body (it is insinuated that he is looking at her chest in particular). Barbara looks around puzzled and smiles politely, unsure of what has prompted the collective laughter. Because she barely understands Spanish, Rodriguez translates.[3]

> *"What did he say?"* asks Barbara.

> *"Admirando, admiring,"* says Rodríguez, taking good care to not mention the subtle shift of words (from admiring her to staring at her).

> *"Admirando? Oh, that might be good,"* says Barbara.

> *"Claro que es bueeeeno."* "Sure it is goood," says Rodríguez, with a tone of voice and emphasis that provokes an even stronger laughter from the audience.

By now the previous double entendre has been multiplied. It started with "It is good to admire her" (shared connotation with Barbara), and "It is good to stare at her" (shared complicity with the pianist). It continued with, "It is good to stare at her" because Barbara "está buena" (Barbara is delicious, her body is ripe, good enough to eat, "eye candy"). At this time, Barbara looks more confused, unable to participate in the unexplained laughter.

Barbara has been spoken to by three intertwined discourses present in Hispanic TV programming (among other cultural sites): courteous gallantry, profane picaresque, and Anglo American otherness. According to the discourse of *gallantry,* a well-groomed man is expected to be *caballeroso* (gentlemanly), praiseful, and protective. He has a duty to celebrate the beauty of woman. He must treat her with delicacy and care and be able to stand by her. Woman is, ideally, a radiant and delicate flower to be kept, trimmed, and admired. If she is a rose, he is the gardener, as an old Latin American song goes. Ideally, woman, like the rose, should be kept close enough to be admired but remote enough not to be touched, taken, or stained.[4] Naturally, when she is cut and *deflowered*, she loses her most cherished attributes, her very nature, and may die unless her one and only gardener is willing to keep her. At that point, she must reproduce to justify her new (uprooted) condition. She enjoys her own fragrance through him, and he is the measure of her beauty. She is bodily present but distant as she is external to any reflective action.

The Profane/Picaresque

In her exchange with Rodríguez and the pianist, Barbara is touched by a second discourse, in which the sublime rose gives place to the ripe fruit. Barbara is not there anymore to be admired but to be savored, as the discourse of gallantry has ceded place to that of the *picaresque.* A polite and idealizing talk has been transgressed by the profane twist, anchoring the otherwise "sublimating" discourse in the lower body. The fact that Rodriguez is a comedian facilitates this shift, for as a joker, he is expected to be mischievous. If gallantry requires speaking with elevating and distancing eyes (i.e., the aesthetic principle), the picaresque speaks with touching, intruding, and carnal eyes (i.e., the profane turn). It is not a coincidence that the discourse of the picaresque sexualizes food, bringing to the fore the eroticism of smelling, tasting, savoring, licking, biting, eating, and devouring.

Sensuality and violence are only one step away from one another in these discursive narratives, as *"el pícaro,"* the profane jokester, may stain the flower or eat the fruit that rightly belongs to the gentleman, *el galán,* whereas the latter may dispose of his garden as he pleases.[5] Because of their pervasive cultural nature, the discourses of the picaresque and gallantry can be traced across multiple cultural expressions. For example, Colombian salsa band *Grupo Niche* expresses the picaresque as sensuous playfulness when they sing "póngale la mano al pan pa que suba y suba."[6] In contrast, a poem by

Mexican-born, Chicana poet Lucha Corpi expresses the (patriarchal) violence of these discourses.

Grupo Niche's verse, "stick your hand in the bread so that it grows and grows," describes the baking of bread, but connotes sexual action. Put your hands in her "bread" (vagina) so that "it" would rise and rise. The poem from Corpi (1980), in contrast, counters that joyful "manipulation" with a very dark one:[7]

> Guadalupe was bathing in the river
> that Sunday, late,
> a promise of milk in her breasts,
> vanilla scent in her hair,
> cinnamon flavor in her eyes,
> cocoa-flower between her legs,
> and in her mouth a daze
> of sugarcane.
>
> He came upon her there
> surrounded by water
> in a flood of evening light.
> And on the instant cut the flower
> wrung blood from the milk
> dashed vanilla on the silence
> of the river bank
> drained the burning liquid
> of her lips
> And then he was gone,
> leaving behind him a trail of shadow
> drooping at the water's edge.

Although the poem is charged with the metaphors of food and nature, it depicts violence. Guadalupe is tropical nature, spice, and nourishment—vanilla, sugar cane, cinnamon, cacao flower, and milk. He is thirsty rage, uncontained devourer, dismembering force, and penetrating aggression. Her spontaneous sensuality is truncated, her cacao flower violently uprooted, and her joyous swimming transformed into bleeding silence. No eroticism guides his hands but the thrill of objectification—sterilizing, disintegrating violence.

El Gringo/ Anglo American Otherness

The third discourse by which Barbara was spoken is that of the *gringo*. The already "comic" value of the double entendre is magnified by the added interest of playing it at the expense of someone who "does not get it." This in turn creates an immediate complicity among those who "get it." Barbara is not only a woman worthy of gallantry and a body worthy of seduction, but also a *gringa* whose innocence is worth some laughter. She is the naive gringo/a who, according to the Latin American narrative, is always lost in the double entendres, connotations, and insinuations that populate Latin American speaking. That which is said in a conversation is very often not what is being said. This situation constantly fools gringos, so the saying goes, for they are ceaselessly seeking "just the facts" and taking information literally. The gringo is plain, clean, and unable to grasp subtleties and nuances.

This moment in a 1990's talk show is as trivial as it is significant; both revealing and predictable. The interaction between host and guests is a unique and unrepeatable moment in time, but it is also a consistent and repetitious discursive enactment. In fact, one could follow it discursively across other statements in the programming and ponder its cultural resonance and intertextuality.

Gallantry: El Amante y La Rosa

La Rosa/The Rose

La Marquesa de Santos, a Brazilian series, tells the historically based story of a courtesan who wins the love and favor of Don Pedro, Emperor of Brazil.[8] A woman with no morals or scruples, the marquise is astonishingly beautiful, a beauty that makes the fooled empress look especially fragile and insignificant. The marquise is a rose-like beauty of pink cheeks, green eyes, and silken skin. When the marquise is introduced to the empress as a new lady-in-waiting, the empress is gardening. She nervously plays with a rose in her hands while trying to be proper in front of the woman who is "stealing" her husband and ridiculing her in front of the European court and Brazilian society. When the marquise leaves, the empress's hands are bleeding, pinched with the rose's thorns.

As with a rose, beauty can be both good and evil, a spiritual achievement or an instinctual and carnal victory. In *One Hundred Years of Solitude* (García Márquez, 1970), Remedios the Beauty is the most beautiful woman the town of Macondo has ever seen. Men become sick at her sight; she can make someone insane or provoke his death. Her beauty is an incomprehensible omen as she leaves behind her an air of disgrace and an aura of desperation. Remedios does not have any awareness of her influence, nor does she understand social conventions or good behavior. She has lunch at midnight, walks naked around the house, eats with her hands, and sleeps most of the day. As the wildflower of mythical fame, she does not have any reflection of herself, no consciousness of body or self.

Woman is a rose, our grandmothers repeatedly told us. You should never hit your sister, not even with a rose's petals, my mother told my brother. Woman is naturally beautiful; earthy, aromatic, and ephemeral like the flower. However, if she has the natural beauty of the rose, she also has the thorns. Woman is the rose, both petals and thorns, a face of ultimate splendor, and a dangerous body, a potential inflictor of injuries and pain.

In telenovelas, the most important Latin American mass-mediated narrative, the plurality of the woman-rose is expressed in a splitting of body and face, the thorns and petals of the rose. A classic telenovela implies a battle over the upper and lower regions of the body. The good woman is a beauty of the upper region, whose spirituality is threatened by the manipulative urges of the body. However, her beauty can only be maintained if she is *intact*, distant, and disengaged. Once deflowered, her roots, the ones that provide beauty, are lacerated and damaged. She, as the rose, gets stained and dies sooner if taken or caressed. In the telenovela *Sin senos no hay paraíso*, Catalina, the protagonist, a young small-town Colombian beauty who obsesses over breast implants, is raped by *Caballo*, a drug dealer's bodyguard.[9] She had a fresh rose in her hair. While wrestling with her attacker, the rose falls to the ground. As Caballo pins her to a pool table, he smashes the rose under his shoes. Along with her virginity goes her whole fresh and pure self. Breast implants may become more necessary and unavoidable. Months later, Catalina has sex with her boyfriend for the first time. He thinks he is her "first." He calls her his pure "flower" and promises to always take care of her. He is very happy, Catalina explains, for he thinks he is her *dueño*, her "owner." In this cultural iconography, a desirable woman remains a flower, and a flower is required to be untouched, protected, and owned.

El Amante/The Lover

"It is well known that the Latino is a great lover . . . of coffee," states a commercial for a coffee-related product. While voicing the wonders of a coffee maker, the ad inscribes and enacts two well-maintained and intertwined Latino narratives.

The first narrative can be seen enacted by the Ecuadorian rapper Gerardo (1991) in one of his videos, "Latin till I die (Oye como va)." *Not even James Bond does it as suave as a Latino*, sings Gerardo, his body gestures performing for the camera the phallic goodness of the male Latin lover. Speaking of himself in the third person—his actions not merely his, but "generically" Latino, prototypically "suave"—Gerardo wonders who would be the lucky girl "Gerardo" might choose tonight. His song intertwines Spanish and English, as Gerardo sings for those who do not know Spanish and those who should be learning English. His presence, his rhetorical style, makes a similar point. He has the required bandanna (if you are a street-wise Hispanic), the required half-open jeans and hand gestures (if you are a rapper), and the required *sexed body* (if you are about to do the Hispanic-Anglo crossover).

Look at me, I am a Latino, says Gerardo with his body and gestures (i.e., I am not you; I am not the sum of the bodily gestures I am performing for you). "I do everything you do best" (i.e., I have women, a great look, and an athletic body), and still, "I'll be Latin till I die."

I will be translating for you (at least partially; I laugh at you from time to time) the Spanish lyrics you don't understand, and doing it softer, "mas rico y suave," than you possibly could.

The second narrative, the lover of coffee, is interestingly related to the first. Coffee is the social drink par excellence in many Latin American countries; the beverage of hospitality and friendly interactions. It is also a compelling pleasure: "What are the three best things in life?" asks one of my Colombian friends. "A coffee before and a cigarette after," comes his joyful reply. As in the Rodriguez case presented earlier, the picaresque in these two examples is the unspoken insinuation that breathes within the spoken (once it's uttered, the innuendo loses its power). The sexual dimension here is the burning omission that all recognize, for its absence is not a lack but an intensification, a presence that floats and pervades. The less "sex" is directly stated, the more present it can become, for it is ceaselessly invoked in callings that carefully avoid its name. Conversation surrounds the sexual, contemplates it from a prudent distance, and makes it the very "heat" of complicity, joke, and seduction. But when Latino narratives embrace the Anglo crossover, the sexed speech of the above utterances tends to become "speech about sex," and the sexed body becomes a body *with* sex appeal. This crossover space is where one can locate Gerardo's music, Gloria Estefan's style, and Shakira's astonishing new body at the turn of the new millennium.

Sexed Speech/Speaking About Sex

The Picaresque

Every Saturday Univision broadcasts *Sábado Gigante*, a popular four-hour variety show exported to 16 Latin American countries and watched by about 40 million people. Today we have learned about the magic powers of stones, stars, and pyramids, the audience's skill imitating *ranchera* singers, the ability of Hispanic couples to keep their marriage together for 20 or more years, and the reduced sexual potency of the host.

A policewoman ("La Cuatro," a female comedian) approaches Don Francisco, the host of the program. She explains to him how she does her professional work:

> "Look, these are my professional devices. I have here all I need to do my job. For example, this one . . . oh, why would I waste it with you!! This is to know if you still."

> (Laughter of the audience at the insinuation of the sexual impotency of Don Francisco.)

La Cuatro reaches for another "professional" device. This time the device sets off an alarm:

> "See? I was sure that I was still OK," says Don Francisco.

> "Oh, no. This one only runs when there are parabolic heads around!" answers La Cuatro.

> (Laughter of the audience at another insinuation of sexual inadequacy, "parabolic head." In Latin American speech, being "big-balled" implies being a fool. If your balls are bigger than your head, so to speak, you are inadequate socially and sexually.)

Sábado Gigante has not only referred to or hinted today at Don Francisco's sexual performance or lack thereof. Today's show has insinuated for us the sexual standing of the models, the guest comedians, and some of the members of the audience. Colgate gives an award to the member of the audience who has "the most beautiful smile." Today the winner is Martha Escobar, a Colombian. The camera follows her (or, at least, her upper body) as she descends the stairs and comes to the center stage. As she descends, Don Francisco comments, to the delight of the public, "What a biiig . . . happiness!!" and then proceeds to congratulate Martha for her award. The reader might suspect by now that Don Francisco (and the laughing audience) has something other than money in mind. Neither the camera nor the gaze of Don Francisco allows for much doubt, as both are focusing on the woman's generous chest.

> "What was it that you liked most about your wife?" asks Don Francisco in another program, while interviewing a couple who married a week after meeting for the first time.

> "Well," the proud husband answers, slightly blushing, "her personality. . . ."

"No," interrupts Don Francisco. "I mean, physically. You just met her. What was it? Her legs, her chest, her face?"

"Oh, no. All of her body," he answers, blushing more.

"Señorita Greta," asks Don Francisco to an audience member in another segment of the program. "Do you believe in extra-terrestrials?"

"Oh yes, I do."

"How do you imagine them?"

"Well, muy *raros* (weird, strange)."

"*Raros*?" Don Francisco repeats. "You mean. . . ."

(and now Don Francisco makes the bodily mannerisms that signify effeminate, for *raro* also means *voltiado*, twisted, inverted; which means *dañado*, bad seed, perverted; which means *del otro equipo*, playing for the other team; which means gay).

Much hilarity ensues.

In "*De humor con Don Francisco*," a comedy sketch segment within the program, we see the two owners of a restaurant struggling over their huge restaurant's bills. A man overhears them. He approaches them with the cartoonish walk, hand gestures, and dandy look that are meant to signify "gay."

"Do you need money? I can lend you some," he tells the associates.

"But I don't have any way to pay you," answers José, one of the owners.

"Don't worry, we can negotiate how you pay me."

(Laughter of the audience)

José is now furious. He grabs a kitchen knife.

"Get out of here right now!" he yells.

"Put that thing away," says the gay man in a seductive tone. "Sharp objects used to penetrate make me nervous."

(The audience laughs appreciatively.)

The gay man is fair game in Hispanic television, as is the impotent, the prostitute, the dwarf, the lascivious old woman, the ugly wife, and other forms of sexual or anatomic "deviation."

Two anchormen are discussing the sports on *Noticias 23*, with the "usual" informality that is typical of the coverage of sports on television, Anglo or otherwise:

"So how did you like the game last night?"

"Oh, it was great. I stayed up until 2 a.m."

"2 a.m.?" (inquisitive) "What were you doing up at that time? The game finished at 12!"

"Shut up!!" (smiling) "Don't say that aloud: My wife will kill me!"

The picaresque insinuation and the play on male and female sexuality are aired on Hispanic television at moments in which it would seem unexpected and, indeed, inappropriate—if one read it against the expectations of "typical" Anglo television. In Hispanic television, there is less talk about sex than a *sexed speech* that floats across programs, and that emerges less in specific genres (e.g., the comedy, the late night series) than in *live dialogue*, in the news, the talk shows, or the variety shows. As such, the sexed speech is not a specialized discourse (as the talk about sex is) but a level of discourse, a dimension that might enter interaction at any moment, provided that the conditions of complicity and intersubjectivity are in place. It, in fact, provides a continuous motive for the social wink, a common ground to which the speaker can always resort in order to gain the favor of the audience and the complicity of the "insider."

Talking About Sex

The show *Cristina* might stand, at one level, as the stylistic opposite of *Sábado Gigante*. This "modern" Anglo-like talk show and hostess contrasts highly with the 1950s-like, archaic-looking, jingle-singing game show of Don Francisco. *Cristina* is, according to its own description, a daring, unique, controversial daytime talk show in which "hot" topics are discussed openly and without censure. "Sex manuals," the topic being discussed on this occasion, makes the point clearly. In fact, it is unusual to find "sex manuals" as the object of discussion of a Hispanic or Latin American TV program. "Are they any good?" is the question that the guests, a Spaniard sex therapist, three Puerto Rican women, and a Mexican couple from Texas, are discussing.

The guests are discussing, with "typical" American sophistication, the effectiveness of sex manuals. The couple from Texas joins the discussion via satellite. Their image has been silhouetted and their voices disguised. The couple speaks about their "excessive" sex practices. It is the audience's turn to ask questions. A young woman, perhaps age 16 or 17, speaks:

> "I want to ask you, what could a woman do if she does not want to have sex with her boyfriend? Mine is always asking me to have sex with him. I tell him no, but I feel guilty."

> "Don't feel guilty," interjects Cristina.

> "You have to think what is that you want to do with your life and whether you are going to marry this man. Above all, remember the good morals that your parents have taught you. Besides, you have to remember that what you are learning here today can only be practiced after you get married."

> (The public erupts in applauses of approval.)

An interpellation has broken the established rules of "realism" of this talk show and of a sex discussion that has been held under the premise "everything goes provided that it feels good." The young woman's question has broken the smoothness of the discussion and revealed a set of implicit rules under which the discussion was sustained.

The young woman has failed to recognize that her question cannot be treated as those of other audience members. Her question has positioned her as an outsider and an intruder revealing, simultaneously, the implied rules of today's program. That is, "everything goes . . . provided that you are an adult, legally married, morally correct and mindful of your limits" (a great amount of "things" do not go).

Cristina's gesture reestablishes the confidence of the audience and evens out a suddenly uneasy space, a space of unexpected *intrusion*. In the middle of a discussion in which sophistication, modernization, and open debate defined the scene, a surprising interpellation has broken the smoothness of the "modern discourse" and called for a radical shift. Provoked by her irruption, the "speaking subject" of this show (i.e., those who participate in its enactment: the hostess, the guests, the live audience, the viewer) has now entered another discourse, another logic.[10] Such a discourse was not absent from the show, but it was backgrounded and tacit. The young woman's question reveals its presence and its force, provoking in fact an illumination of that which was staged prior to her question.

The young woman's intervention has *revealed* an aspect of the field so far invisible and prompted a revelatory phrase, Cristina's answer. Such an answer is able to express and summarize, in the uniqueness of a moment, the complexity of the discourses that are being played against one another. Cristina has shifted her voice. The sophisticated hostess of the "most controversial program" in Hispanic television has turned into a mother; a *madrina*, a godmother adviser of youth. For it is now a matter of children and sex, and the discourse of sophistication cannot but stop right there.

Cristina could not possibly support sex out of wedlock, let alone discuss it "casually," that is, within a setting that was not ready for its address. Teenage sex would have to be the *explicit topic* of another program, say, one on troubled youth and what to do about their behavior. Her demands as "modern" hostess are countered by her demands as "local" role model, which require her to speak with great caution about a topic such as teenage sex. Cristina's action is not "hers," but "ours," as it is demanded by a field of discursive and cultural complicity. The conflicting demands of the modern and the traditional, the mainstream and the "sidestream," appear here proposed and resolved, as global sophistication requires obeying the call of cultural tradition (incidentally, upholding a time-honored practice of double morality).

If Cristina's show were part of another textuality (e.g., Anglo American), neither question nor answer may have been considered nonproblematic or worth applauding. First, the question can be read as misplaced or irrelevant to the topic, as it invokes the atmosphere of counseling more than that of opinion or information. In fact, the young woman's question is not dealing with the content of the discussion (sex manuals), but with the field of discourse and practice that it opens up (i.e., it is good to actively seek pleasure, to practice sex, and to become well versed on its technology). However, Cristina's answer seems to go beyond that which the question "demands" and deviates from the requirements of her role as mediator of "controversy." Instead of considering the question, the answer is an emphatic "go upstairs young lady; don't sneak into adult conversations." Thus, Cristina is answering explicitly to the discursive field that has been opened and taken good care in setting up its limits and rules. The answer has stated clearly and for the benefit of anyone who doubted: "We all know sex is only a feasible practice for married adults." The audience claps in relief and support, as a possibly damaging moment has been avoided by the (apparently intrusive) appearance of the right discourse.

The discursive splittings and juxtapositions that make possible this interaction in *Cristina* could not be understood in the absence of the televisual textuality at large. As many U.S. mainstream TV shows, *Cristina* has positioned sex as a public object of discourse. Unlike many of those shows, *Cristina* carries out this novel task with difficulty and some disturbances. In this way, the show expresses the tensions between Anglo and Latin American legitimate approaches to "sex" as an object of discourse and illuminates them. Such tension could be articulated in the following manner: In Anglo American television, sex is addressed as a lay space, or even more, a homogenous, external, and functional space. One refers to *it*. It has an existence of its own, a territory of its own, and its own recourses of legitimation. There is nothing wrong or strange about talking about sex—provided that it is done at the appropriate time and with the appropriate purpose. "Sex" is a word that does not have anything sexy about it, as it has been polished, cleaned, and distanced from the burning territory that it indicates. This has become more and more the case in Latin American television, aided by accelerated processes of globalization and neoliberalism (we will see an example of this in the next chapter). Generally speaking, however, in Latin American television, "sex" tends not to be publicly discussed, as it is too immediately connected with its referentiality, too contiguously inflected by what it denotes. However, if one does not speak *about* it, one constantly *speaks it* and performs it. In fact, it is hard to find a conversation in which the erotic is not playing a role at one level or another. Its frequent irruption is, in fact, one of the most powerful forces of Latino humor, satire, and discursive profanation. To catch the serious authority in sexual talk is a major entertainment, as it is to tease friends and enemies with the constant slipping of their words in the territory of the sexual and erotic. Interstitial spaces and silences are filled more often than not with the embracing presence of the erotic, the picaresque, and the indirect fire of sexuality.

Reaccommodating the Latino Archive

This earlier reflection traced some of the discursive threads of Hispanic television and focused on the emergent differences between Hispanic and Anglo American television, or what I have chosen to call *markers of difference*. In the next chapter, I turn to explore a "complementary" field of difference—that between Latin America and the U.S. Hispanic, as articulated on Hispanic television. In order to do so, I focus on telenovelas and reflect on the *shift* that the female body as a site of signification is undertaking within the genre. Such a shift, as we will see, also extends across other aspects of the televisual textuality under a general discourse of modernization. Once these markers of difference are traced, we will be able to hint at the textual fabric of Hispanic television: its architecture (i.e., the social edifice) and its topography (i.e., its cultural territory).

Notes

1. The televisual statements cited in this and other chapters were compiled from taped national and local broadcasts of Univision and Telemundo in Miami and

Chicago, between the years of 1989 and 2009. An emphasis was made on the years 1989–1992, 1999–2001, and 2008–2009.

2. Univision's *The Show of Paul Rodríguez* (1990–1994) was hosted and produced by the stand-up comedian Rodríguez, who has appeared in several U.S. TV shows and films (including *Born in East L.A.*).

3. Latino and Anglo guests were equally present in the *Show de Paul Rodriguez*. When the guests did not know Spanish, Rodriguez interviewed them in English and translated in Spanish for the audience. On some occasions, like today, the guest knows some Spanish, which makes Barbara an especially susceptible object for the play of double-entendres.

4. See Dealy (1992) for a brilliant analysis of the singular place that the public/ private, feminine/masculine spaces have in Latin America. Man has a public duty to assert his manliness, expressed, also in other ways, in his charismatic and seductive powers. Woman, in contrast, strives between two María's, so to speak, the Virgin and the prostitute. One is "home" and the other is "public" and has succumbed to man's seductions.

5. Note as well that joker and gentleman may be two expressions of the same masculine figure.

6. From the song "Doña Pastora" by Grupo Niche (1990 track 4).

7. Excerpt from the poem "Romance Negro," *Dark Romance* (Corpi, 1980, pp. 126–129).

8. *La Marquesa de Santos*, produced by Rede Manchete in 1984 (Brazil).

9. *Sin senos no hay paraíso*, "Without breasts there is no paradise." Co-produced by RTI-Colombia and Telemundo in 2008. This telenovela was a remake of Colombian telenovela *Sin tetas no hay paraíso* (2006).

10. I am referring to the Foucaultian sense of "subject," that is, the subject that is required and demanded by a given discourse. The subject who speaks varies constantly in the fluidity of a text or a document, as it requires following one or another discursive logic. Thus, the speaking of a single individual can be populated by a multiplicity of subjects.

10

The Melodramatic Body

From "Just María" to Catalina's Breasts

In the last two chapters, I have explored some of the central discourses that permeate Hispanic television and stand in contrast and tension with those proper to Anglo American television. The latter assumes the United States as the universe of reference (instead of the Americas), the American as the given standard (instead of the Latino), the Latino as one among many Others

Figure 10.1. From the Colombian countryside to L.A: Image from video taken on the set of *Mi corazón insiste. . . . en Lola Volcán*, in August 2011. This telenovela from Telemundo is a remake of *Yo amo a Paquita Gallego* (Colombia, RTI productions, 1998).[1]

(instead of the Gringo as its necessary cultural other), English as the given language (instead of English as *the other language*), "gender equality" as the official norm (instead of gallantry and seduction), and Protestantism as the underlying ethical logic (instead of Catholicism).

It is important as well to examine those discursive aspects of Hispanic television that converge with or approximate the discourses of Anglo American television, and that as such are marking a divergence, or even a shift, from traditional Latin American discourses. One of the most intriguing aspects of this convergence is the transformation of the valuation of the body, as seen in *telenovelas*.

A Melodramatic Shift

One of the teasers for *Vivir un Poco*, a Mexican telenovela of the mid-1980s[2] opens with the close-up of a middle-aged woman crying[3] The close-up opens to reveal eight faces surrounding the woman's: four men and four women. All of them, except the crying woman, have something dark about them, something somber and disturbing. The woman is the victim/heroine; the others are her opponents, the multiple faces of deception, cowardice, greed, envy, immorality, ambition, and crime. Someone in this collection of portraits has committed a crime of which the heroine was accused and for which she went to prison. Everyone has good motives to have committed the crime. Everyone behaves—and looks—like a (potential) criminal, although each one has his or her own territory of wrongdoing. Thus, the group includes the manipulating mother, the coward husband, the ambitious sister-in-law, the envious cousin, the immoral sister, and the unlawful business partner. The telenovela will be resolved when the heroine uncovers the criminal, recovers her children, and discovers her fortune. The story ends with a return to the way things should be (the heroine is rewarded and the wrongdoers punished according to their faults).

The Mirror-Face

As in almost all televisual programs, openings in telenovelas are extremely revelatory, for they constitute the rhetorical self-presentation of the program: Nothing in their construction has been left to chance. To study them, then, is to study what the telenovela wants to say about itself. As it is the case with other telenovelas, the opening of *Vivir un Poco* works as a leitmotif of the story and an allegory of its fundamental drama. The opening synthesizes, in an image, the narrative logic of *Vivir un Poco*, its melodramatic conflicts, and its *point of articulation*—the heroine in despair.

Opponent1	Opponent2	Opponent3
Opponent4	**HEROINE**	Opponent5
Opponent6	Opponent7	Opponent8

Figure 10.2. *Vivir un Poco*'s melodramatic square. The heroine, *Woman* writ large, constitutes the node and intersection that articulates the semiotic planes in this traditional telenovela. The good woman is the focus and the explicit common ground of conflict. Her goodness is impressed in her face—as are the evil ways of her multiple and ethically ambiguous opponents. My visualization.

Vertical and horizontal planes position the heroine and her antagonists (or their faces) in a narrative grid. She is, quite literally, at the articulating center of a semiotic square; or better, at the center of a narrative structure, occupying the "subject" position; the force that animates the conflict and moves the story (see Figure 10.2).

In *Vivir un Poco*, the face is a central articulation of drama, and it is so in several ways. First, the face is the site of emotion, conflict, and expression. Each one of the faces in this "melodramatic square" presents more than physical features: It *features* character. The face not only presents a character as a synecdoche, but it also re-presents that character's ethical standing. A moral and perverse ambiguity is present in the eight faces that surround the heroine; twisted grins, evasive eyes, cruel mouths, and imperious looks.

Second, whereas the face of the heroine, tearful but illuminated, gives presence to and embodies the "higher" attributes—spirituality, virtue, and sensibility—the faces of her opponents, calm but somber, embody the "lower" ones—materiality, vice, and conniving. Thus, the face becomes a mediation or a transitional space between spirit and body. It foregrounds "spirit" (which is made visible; inscribed, expressed, and revealed in the face) and glosses over "body" (which is made invisible or insignificant in this portrayal arrangement). Flesh and heart, mind and spirit find in the face their acting stage. In *Vivir un Poco*, there is little dramatic attention given to the body (that below-the-neck physical presence) for here the body is no more than the extension of that expressed in the facial close-ups that carry the drama.

And yet, as the telenovela unfolds, we find out that the body carries a moral standing. The good and the bad woman have different "centers of gravity." One is spiritual and oriented upward. The other is material and oriented downward. The former has no body or a nondramatic body. It is proper, it is acceptable, it is plain, it is silent. Her body is a background. The good woman's wicked rival, in contrast, is a body. She is voluptuous, curvaceous, and earthy. She is snake-like. She has a dramatic body.

The good woman thinks, feels, and acts with her heart, whereas the bad woman *calculates* with a rational mind and acts with her belly. The upper and the lower body indicate the profound and the superficial, the righteous and the wicked, the authentic and the fake, morality and temptation. "Lower instincts," which command the bad woman's actions, are also instincts of the surface, passions of the flesh that reverberate in the skin, superficially. They are opposed to the "higher values," which are intuitions of the heart, the immaterial core of righteous action. In the traditional telenovela (of which *Vivir un poco* is an example), the mind is part of the lower body, and indeed it can be located somewhere around the hips. The heart and the spirit, in contrast, occupy the highest place in the human anatomy, and thus they reorganize the topography of the body. From this perspective, the face is a center, a synecdoche from which it is possible to reconstruct the coordinates of the person, both the material and the immaterial features. Above the face there is the spirit and the heart. Below the face there is the flesh, the rational, and the instinctual.

The Extended Body

Let us now shift attention to another opening. Four adolescent women wearing swimsuits are lying on a floor forming a circle. Their heads touch one another, their backs are against the floor, and together their bodies compose a sort of iridescent flower, a star of four points. The camera sees the women from above, capturing the synchronicity of their movements and the symmetry of their bodies and shapes. The flower, the four bodies united by their heads, changes composition when the bodies raise one or another leg. There is no woman at the center of this drama. Instead of a narrative grid whose central articulation is the heroine, we have now an articulation of four axes. Although at the center of such articulation there is nothing but a positive absence, its periphery is woman reproduced four times; four replicas of noncapitalized woman who carry perfectly symmetrical bodies and faces (see Figure 10.3).

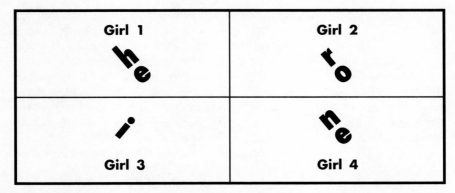

Figure 10.3. The (fractal) heroine in *Muchachitas (Little young women)*.[4] The woman writ large proper of traditional telenovelas is replaced in *Muchachitas* by the dispersion of the female body across the semiotic space. In this contemporary telenovela, there is no single heroine standing as central articulation of the narrative. The center is both emptied and multiplied.

Instead of a narrative structure, the opening of *Muchachitas* proposes to us, if one may, a *semiotic square*; a melodramatic semantic field in which an empty sign, "woman," is displayed in multiple semiotic valences with an added common qualification: extreme youth (the protagonists are all teenagers). Girl1 (the rich), girl2 (the poor), girl3 (the dreamer), and girl4 (the rebel) make up the four faces of one empty, absent, totalizing figure: the heroine (see Figure 10.4).

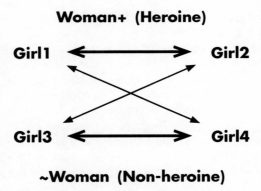

Figure 10.4. *Muchachitas* and the Semiotic Square. Using the Greimassian semiotic square, we can visualize *Muchachitas'* play of positive differences: the four embodiments of a de-centered heroine.

If at first woman was the articulating point of the drama (and her face her spiritual mirror), now she is dispersed across the space of signification (and her body takes center stage). Instead of *woman* as heroine, we now have *women*, whose *duplicated* bodies, homogenized as one, cross the text evenly. This *modern telenovela* has "disseminated" the good woman and homogenized the body, so that now a "good body" is a capitalistic asset and a "good woman" a fractured presence. The modern telenovela distinguishes less between the good and the bad woman (who are now more ambiguously depicted) than between the significant and the insignificant body.

Accordingly, the semiotic valuation of beauty undergoes an important transformation. In the first case (i.e., traditional telenovelas), beauty radiates from the face and comes from within and above, with the power of virtue and honesty. This is the case of *Vivir un Poco* (Univision, 1988) but also of *Victoria* 20 years later (Telemundo, 2008).[5] In the second case (modern telenovelas), beauty is as deep as the skin and spreads horizontally. In other words, the moral division between upper and lower body is replaced in modern telenovelas by a division between the right and the left; *the right* body and the *left* bodies, so to speak; between the "dexterous" and the sinister use of the same homogenous instrumental body. It is not anymore the evil woman who generously displays her skin and flesh. Both the good and the evil women have killer abs, fantastic long legs, flawless skin, and a generous bosom. Both wear impossibly tight outfits. But, while the evil one often breaks the rules, the good one follows them.

In the modern telenovela, of which *Muchachitas* is a good example, a good woman is a good body, which is an anatomically correct body, which is, by definition, a *sexed body* (i.e., sex brought to the fore of body shape, to the surface of the skin and across all available flesh). The "modeled" body becomes a condition for virtue and not its impediment. A body without a perfect shape cannot but aspire to be bad, inferior, or harmless. Thus, it should not be surprising that the heroine of the traditional telenovela (e.g., *Vivir un Poco*) might now be the comic relief of the modern telenovela (which is in fact the case in *Muchachitas* or in *Alcanzar una Estrella*, another mid-1990s Televisa production). She might still be a maid (this time not by accident) whose good heart, naive intellect, and nonathletic body stop her from being heroic material. What were the conditions for heroism are now the conditions for domesticity—and secondary roles—and what were traces of nonspiritual impulses are now heroic traits. The heroine might now be driven by ambition to succeed, by a will to become something she never was, or by a decision to transform herself. In the traditional telenovela, such a transformation would have been proof of inauthenticity, hypocrisy, or sin. The ones who transform themselves are the sinister stranger (who hides his identity and on occasion undergoes plastic surgery), the ambitious woman (who becomes arrogant once she gets money), the cunning former lover, or the false priest. At the end of a traditional telenovela, the heroine becomes her(truest)self—she regains her identity and recovers what belonged to her all along. In the contemporary telenovela, she achieves that which she was not. One goes back to the origin—*viaja a la semilla*—the other progresses.

Beauty is no longer a quality that comes from within but a productivity. It has been removed from the status of natural expression and reorganized as a territory of hard work. The protagonist now has to work for her beauty, as she goes to the salon, does aerobics, and keeps a healthy diet. Beauty is no longer a manifestation of virtue or vice, but the presence of discipline, success, and cleanliness. Thus, it becomes technological, accessible, and reproducible. The virginal heroine, the sovereign Rose of traditional telenovelas, is now a mass-produced floral arrangement. One may suggest that a Protestant, puritan, and postmodern capitalistic ethics has started to replace a Catholic pathos (see Figures 10.3 and 10.4).

Contemporary Telenovelas: Between Tradition and Modernization

Contemporary telenovelas (those produced and broadcast in the new millennium) reveal traces of an unsolved discursive tension, between a tradition and its modernization. This is expressed in an oscillation between a "local," premodern melodramatic imagination and its "cosmopolitan," neocapitalistic, postmodern, urban expressions. The former is a discourse of honor, fate, and faith. It is a narrative of archetypal confrontations between the Bad and the Good, of innocent victims and virtuous heroines who fight against awe-inspiring odds and injustices. In the cosmopolitan discourse, in contrast, the outstanding and the incomparable have turned democratic, individualized, and practical. Feudal melodrama is now instrumental melodrama, the melodrama of training, competition, and success. Out of this tension between tradition and modernization emerges the contemporary telenovela.

I would summarize this shift from the traditional themes to the contemporary tensions appealing to the rhetorical and ideological displacement that is suggested by the names of two melodramatic serials ten years apart: *Simplemente María* (the famous 1969 Peruvian telenovela) and *Dancin' Days* (a 1978 Brazilian Rede Globo production). Between these two melodramatic serials, there is a shift from "Woman" to "women," from resemblance to reproduction, from face to body, and from the (mythic) memory of the "simple" María—rural, feudal, local—to the (mass mediated) memory of the "worldly" dancin'—cosmopolitan, Anglo-capitalistic, nomadic, urban. The *body* is one of the central sites in which this modern discourse and its traditional traces are inscribed.

The name and theme of a third telenovela, three decades later, makes this shift from virginal beauty to manufactured body explicit to the point of irony: *Sin senos no hay paraíso* ("Without Breasts There Is No Paradise,"

2008). This U.S.-Colombian production is based on *Sin tetas no hay paraíso*, a successful 2007 Colombian telenovela, which is in turn based on a book by Colombian journalist Gustavo Bolívar (2006).[6] Telemundo/RTI *Sin senos* follows the struggles of a gorgeous teenager, Catalina, to get the breast implants she considers essential for her dream career. In the process to become beautiful and valuable in her own eyes, Catalina is raped three times, becomes a prostitute, and unwittingly smuggles heroin to Mexico. According to Catalina, her high school girlfriends, and the copious drug leaders they encounter along the way, there is no joy, no stability, and no money without a good pair of full breasts. Paradise is an achievable state of economic success that can be obtained by body manipulation. If one is a young woman, that body manipulation entails surgery, fashion, cosmetics, and seduction. If one is a man, that manipulation entails the control of others' bodies by means of money, guns, and seduction. The opening sequence of *Sin senos* eloquently stands in rhetorical continuity and opposition to those of *Vivir un poco* and *Muchachitas*. If in *Vivir un poco* there is a dramatic emphasis on faces and in *Muchachitas* the focus extends to the protagonists' bodies, in *Sin senos* there is no face anymore, but a naked and anonymous female body that has been marked for cosmetic surgery. The drama is, literally, *written in her body*, which becomes, therefore, the full text of the enacted narrative. The young female body has become in this case an embodiment of narrative: Her body is hero and villain, opponent and helper, subject and object of desire.

Face, Body, and Conflict

The transformation of face and body also marks a shift in the materiality of conflict and a redesign of the melodramatic discourse. One of the young women in *Muchachitas* tells her mother:

> El problema contigo es que eres una conformista. Estás acostumbrada a la pobreza, y no aspiras a nada más. Yo no. Yo quiero ser famosa; no quiero ser pobre.[7]

In a traditional telenovela, this statement would be framed as negative (most probably as an indication that this is a false heroine or a good seed gone bad). The traditional heroine gets what she deserves not thanks to ambition but to devotion, to persistence more than investment, and to faith more than rebellion. The final reward is more a result of good behavior—a morally deserved award—than the result of a will to succeed—an entrepreneur award.

In the traditional telenovela virtue is beauty, whereas in the modern telenovela beauty is a material condition for virtue. In fact, the spirit is revealed in the material gain, so that success is already the guarantee of spirit and virtue. This shift could be visualized with the help of the Greimassian Actantial Model (Chapter 6). Applying the model, traditional and modern telenovelas could be visualized as shown in Figures 10.5 and 10.6

Feminine beauty was previously coded as exceptional, superlative, or refined; as an expression of moral and communal extremes—the cultured or the peasant, the sacred or the prohibited, the divine or the evil, the pure or the malicious. In the modern telenovela, beauty is the discourse of the ideal average, the democratic, the accessible. Beauty has changed from that which is made present to that which gives presence—material support—to something else: the desirable, the good, the dangerous, the deceiving. Thus, beauty does not guarantee virtue anymore, but signification.

Shifting Inscriptions

Many contemporary telenovelas on Univision and Telemundo express a shift toward a plot, "Americanization," and an undermining of the "ideal reader" of traditional telenovelas. Another reader is now suggested. Telemundo co-productions such as *Sin senos* and melodramatic series such as *Decisiones* (Telemundo) and *Así es la vida* (Telefutura/Univision) speak to a young, contemporary reader who appreciates the "nontraditional," Latin American North (i.e., the United States). This contemporary "young" telenovela speaks less from the South than *with* the South. In the contemporary telenovela, the North is

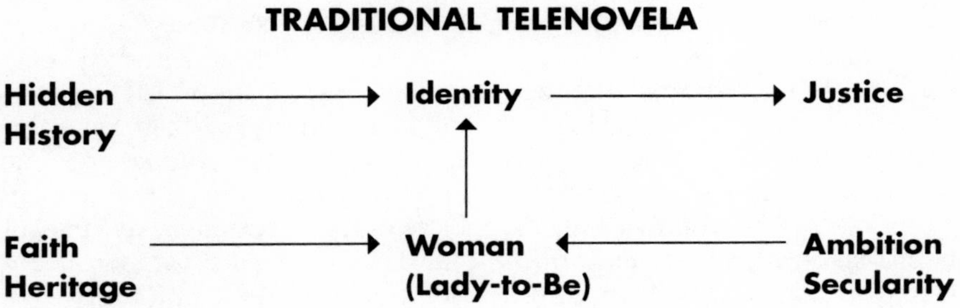

TRADITIONAL TELENOVELA

Figure 10.5. The Actants in traditional telenovelas. In terms of the Actantial Model, traditional telenovelas entail a subject (woman) who seeks an object (her lost identity) with the purpose of achieving justice and motivated by the weight of an undeciphered past. Woman is helped in her efforts by her faith and her community's tradition and attacked by the forms of personal and social ambition and disrespect for tradition.

MODERN TELENOVELA

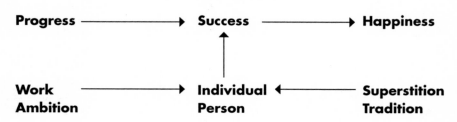

Figure 10.6. Actants in modern telenovelas. In terms of the Actantial Model, modern telenovelas entail a subject (the individual) who seeks an object (success) with the purpose of achieving happiness and motivated by an ideal of progress and realization of potentials. The individual is helped in her or his quest by hard work and ambition and slowed down by communal superstition and restrictive traditions.

no longer an exteriority but a complementarity.[8] If in traditional telenovelas the gringo was a foreigner, indeed an alien, in the contemporary telenovela the gringo is a neighbor. The visitor, in turn, may no longer be the gringo, but rather María who has gone North. She may even be Norteña. In *Al Filo de la Muerte* (produced by Univision in 1990), Mariela is a Chicana who has been forced to go to Mexico. She has to face now the envy of women who cannot believe that "she has earned her prestige and money working" and who call her, with disdain, *chicanita* (i.e., a sell-out, an "Americanized," fake Mexican). One of the envious women downplays Mariela's success as a nurse by explaining that, "In the United States women have much better chances" (i.e., she, as a secretary in a Mexican hospital, finds success much harder to achieve). Mariela's boss explains back that good workers have better chances anywhere (i.e., this implies, first, that there is gender equality in Mexico, and, second, that Mariela's success is attributed to her own merit).

Similarly, the wealthy family may not be defined anymore by its land but by its business connections with the United States. A good vacation might take place now in San Francisco, New York, or L.A. These cities may even be home: Andrés and Lola, protagonists of *Mi corazón insiste*, live in L.A. (Figure 10.1).

Instead of spending her honeymoon in a Latin American coastal resort, Mariela went to New York. Twenty years later, Andrés and Lola elope to Las Vegas where an Elvis impersonator marries them.[9] The United States, as embodiment of urban modernity, fights center stage with the Capital City or the Hacienda of traditional telenovelas as the site of danger, sophistication, novelty, or success. By adapting the codes of modern realism and leaving behind those of allegoric melodrama (Lozano, 1990, 1991), telenovelas are appealing to a Hispanic who has met the Protestant ethic; a "realistic," "modern," urban viewer who consumes an assorted diet of international and local media. This realism implies an adaptation of the recognized codes of Hollywood and its "modern" codes of drama.

A Rhetorical Intertextuality

The previous discussion suggests the ways in which modern telenovelas express a transformation on the valuation of the body and a shift in the cultural place granted to technology and the (capitalistic) magic of individual transformation.[10] This shift is expressed rather clearly by Sam Quinones (1997) when he states that Mexican telenovelas, due to new competition, "have changed from *teary household tales* to dealing with such issues as homosexuality, corruption, and now drug trafficking. Characters now drink, they work, they speak a more slangy and sometimes dirty Spanish. Heroines are frequently strong, well-educated, middle class, unwilling to suffer unremittingly for their men" (p. 2, italics added). Later he adds, as a sort of final explanation, "[Mexico] was a society unaccustomed to competing, in politics, television, in anything. Now it's beginning to get used to it."

Quinones was announcing "progress" in the melodramatic text. Now the text is not so teary or domestic (i.e., no longer for housewives); it has the middle class as a new protagonist and celebrates a will to compete (intra- and extra-textually). This new melodrama rejects household affairs and goes for the worldly, "serious and important" issues: drug trafficking, homosexuality—which we are told, therefore, are never "teary," household affairs. Clearly, for Quinones the capitalistic drive, the will to compete, is not only a guarantor of democracy, but also of realism and aesthetic value.

But this aforementioned melodramatic shift is not only or necessarily a narrative matter, but also a matter of textuality and intertextuality; that is, of the place that telenovelas have within a televisual flow and of the rhetorical weaving of that flow. When these telenovelas are read within the context of Hispanic television, it becomes apparent that this discursive shift permeates the rest of the Hispanic programming, from advertising to talk shows and from the news to music television. There is, in other words, a semantic and semiotic transformation of melodrama in Hispanic television:

1. The contents of the melodramatic serial have become "international," Catholic-Protestant, neocolonialist, and post(non) modern.

2. The melodramatic imagination spreads beyond the melodramatic serial to become a trademark, a rhetorical naming for the Hispanic programming and the Hispanic reader. We are Latino: We have a (Uni)Vision and a (Tele)mundo; that is, one televised world. That vision is melodramatic and cosmopolitan, and it is how we know who we are. There are few places (if any) out of the mass-mediated texts where we could find "us"; the U.S. Hispanic. We know what we are when we are on television: talking, singing, narrating, and expressing ourselves, melodramatically.

Notes

1. This photo accompanied a report by Paula Bustamante (2011) which discussed the success that Telemundo has had developing its own telenovela "formula" by using actors from many Latin American countries and creating stories with a "twist." Telenovelas are no longer "love stories," a Telemundo producer is quoted saying. "There is a lot of action in every episode. Characters are very strong . . . and the stars are not victims; they are fighters" (Bustamante, 2011).

2. *Vivir un Poco* was produced by Univisa in 1985 and voted by fans best Mexican telenovela of that year. It aired on Univision in 1988.

3. See the trailer at http://www.filmaffinity.com/es/film134876.html

4. *Muchachitas*, a popular telenovela, was produced by Televisa in 1991, broadcast on Univision in 1992, and rerun by cable channel Galavision in 1997. It was remade in 2007.

5. As I stated earlier, I do not use "traditional" and "modern" to identify chronological periods (e.g., 1970s vs. 1990s), but stylistic, rhetorical, and discursive transformations. Thus, whereas there is a general shift occurring from traditional to modern imaginaries, it is also possible to find "modern" and "traditional" telenovelas produced in the same year, one grounded on the old María and her identity quest and another on the new Marías and their quest for success. For example, *Viviana*, a traditional production, and *Sin senos no hay paraíso*, a modern one, are both Telemundo co-productions from 2008, and both were produced with Colombian TV networks.

6. A poster for this telenovela can be found here: http://2.bp.blogspot.com/_6RJQ3tvJtr4/St-W9leaJKI/AAAAAAAACC4/LJaI36EayzM/s1600-h/Slide02.jpg

7. "Your problem is that you are a conformist. You are used to poverty and don't aspire to more. Not me. I want to be famous; not poor" (my translation).

8. In the traditional telenovela, the feminine/masculine discourse followed the logic of dichotomies such as tradition/progress, nature/culture, and spirituality/materiality. Such a situation was expressed in extreme opposites (poverty/wealth, good/evil, innocence/perversion, desire/duty). The modern telenovela transforms some of these traditional tensions into oppositions that are more agreeable to cosmopolitan, modern, and technologically correct sensibilities. Such oppositions include law/crime, dependence/autonomy, success/failure, and progress/superstition.

9. *Mi corazón insiste . . . en Lola Volcán* (Fig. 10.1) was produced by Telemundo and aired in 2011. This telenovela was shot primarily in L.A. and Miami.

10. Earlier on, I discussed the differences between Venezuelan and Mexican telenovelas, on the one hand, and Brazilian and Colombian telenovelas, on the other. Although such a distinction was valid for telenovela productions in the 1980s and 1990s, they do not seem to be appropriate in the 2000s, as Brazilian telenovelas have all but disappeared from the U.S. Latino screens, Colombian production has adopted the melodramatic values of Mexican fare, and Mexican telenovelas have gone Hollywood. The majority of the telenovelas broadcast in the United States remain Mexican, followed by Colombian and Venezuelan productions. Although Brazilian telenovelas are widely exported throughout the world, they have become rare in the U.S. Hispanic networks.

11

Weaving a Hispanic Textuality

The Market Place, the Hyphen, and the Third Text

The Space of Television, the Place of the Market

Television is not only a collection of texts or a discursive site—an archive—
but also a social and cultural practice. The televisual experience supersedes,
from the start, the empirical boundaries of *the television*, for it is also the
space in which viewing takes place; the domestic scenario that transforms
and is transformed by television. With television, the living room extends into
airports and bars, malls and hotel lounges, gyms and beauty salons (Figure
11.1). From this perspective, television is not but a moment in a social *web
of intertextuality*, in constant dialogue with (Internet) sites, mall settings,
virtual realities, avatars, billboards, and urban dwellings.

Television erupts into the daily, into the space of home, redefining the
coordinates of domesticity and the look of "everyday life." It becomes not
only a vital part of the domestic setting, but also a central element in the
topography of the city; in the contemporary experience of the street, the barrio, the town, and the waiting room. Television transforms the street space
into a domestic place and brings the topography of the street into the house.
This mixing and blurring of public/domestic boundaries can be clearly seen
in the "family resemblance" between television and malls.

Television is the virtual mall; the mall, a three-dimensional video-scope
(Morse, 1990).[1] One is a public realm gone private, the other is a private
realm gone public. Whereas the mall compartmentalizes space, television
compartmentalizes time—and transforms time into virtual space. There is
prime time and daytime, night time and late night shows; shows fragmented
by the unavoidable presence of other shows in simultaneous times and parallel
frequencies. There are times for children, youth, women, men, and families;
there are times for drama, comedy, health, and "reality." These are "remote-
controlled" times, further compartmentalized and fragmented by the playfulness

Figure 11.1. Television in the public living room: Waiting for a haircut at Rosita's. In Fremont, CA, customers wait as a Spanish-language show plays on the television.[2]

of the interlocutor in this *heterologue*. As the mall, television invites window shopping and does not separate consuming from hanging out, socializing or drifting aimlessly. As the mall, television is not only open to polymorphous consumption but also to distracted wandering or engaged interaction. Like the mall, television is not only a supermarket but also a fair: a place in which trade is also entertainment, seduction, and spectacle.

Fair and Mall

The traditional fair of the Middle Ages and the Renaissance was a noisy space in which melodrama and parody, theater and popular medicine, debate and intrigue took place alongside trading (Bakhtin, 1965/1984, Chapter 2). At the fair, talks, genres, and rhythms of diverse status took place simultaneously and expressed polyphony in a temporary and "hetero-logic" setting. The setting of the fair was a situated arrangement of things and bodies, constituted by the temporal and circumstantial settlement of sellers, buyers, casual visitors, and curious passers-by.

The mall has compartmentalized these activities, homogenizing them and "cleaning" them up. While the mall's setting is a stable, fixed, and functional architecture, its customers are the temporal and circumstantial element of an edifice designed for efficiency. The fair extended the domestic space outdoors and made the public space intimate; the mall extends the public space indoors and privatizes the public. Whereas the premodern fair was communal and interpellated unknown persons, the mall is social and deals with anonymous individuals. The former could be seen as a metaphor of premodern city dwelling, the latter as a metaphor of the postmodern city, a place of highways and speedy circulation in which *no-lugares*, "nowhere places," proliferate (Augé, 1995; Martín-Barbero, 1996).

Whereas at the mall transactions can be accomplished by barely speaking, at the fair trading is built in talk and negotiation. The principles of the fair, still present in farmers' markets, small town festivals, and carnivals, suppose plural engagements, as buyers and sellers continually interpellate one another. It relies, one can say, on the principle of "sympathy"—contiguity, concatenation, and overlapping.[3] At the fair, the one who sells products also pauses to confide an anecdote, rearrange the goods, flirt with the passers-by, or tell jokes to the potential clients. Selling is contiguous and sympathetic to body, mood, situation, and accident.

The ordering principle of the mall, in contrast, requires transforming the sympathetic body into a "body of organs," which is a carrier of functions rather than a source of action and expressivity. In such a way, the polymorphous body is segmented into functional organs that rule out ambiguity and ambivalence.

At the mall, transaction requires the meeting of complementary and dualistic functions. Thus, the clerk charges a bill and the client runs a credit card; the customer tries on some dresses while the clerk waits. Anonymity is the rule by which transaction is achieved efficiently and appropriately. The mall is built in such a way that customers or visitors can go about "their business" without being bothered by the context. Things and bodies are clearly identified, designs are simple and functional, and directions are available in carefully coded maps. At the fair, anyone could be interpellated at any time because transactions required a public performance.

Television, Mall, and Fair

Television recuperates both the heterogeneous offerings of the fair and the homogenous display of the mall. Like the fair, television weaves together, in the same (temporal) setting, a "loud" variety of market displays and styles of address. The mall has carefully segmented its market offerings and created a stable edifice that keeps on displaying. Television also inverts the logic of "stasis" and "flux" proper to the traditional market. Whereas television is a stable apparatus, its viewers are a temporal and circumstantial element. This does not imply that television—or malls—can survive without customers, but that television follows a logic of exchange instead of bargaining. That which remained "constant" in the traditional fair fluctuates in the postmodern mall, so that the supremacy of space has given way to the supremacy of time.[4]

But within the solid blocks of time programming and its market compartmentalization, television explodes in a multitude of reiterative tones, moods, and colors that supersede programming, overlook compartments, and provide the virtual archive with a sense of "carnival" (Fiske, 1987). A carnival-in-a-loop, one might say, TV is endlessly repetitious and endlessly new. If television resembles the mall as an apparatus, it is a *fair-like* textuality.

Weaving Temporalities in Hispanic Television

Fair-like juxtapositions and mall-like segmentations are particularly visible in Hispanic television. Produced by transnational corporations, Hispanic television stands at a crossroad, speaking a Spanish "born" in various Latin American locations but "raised" in the United States. Hispanic television waves two flags and pledges allegiance to two forms of nationalism. A Latin American flag (by way of Mexico, Brazil, and Venezuela) and an Anglo American flag (by way of L.A., Miami, and New York) articulate both a U.S.-specific patriotism and a "transpatriotic" allegiance. Such allegiance is ambiguously defined as that which is "ours," *lo nuestro*. What is *"ours"* may range from our Mexican *dia de los muertos* to our Argentinean *yerba mate*, from our Inca *Machu Picchu* to our Brazilian *Ronaldinho*, from our talented Shakira to our talented Sonia Braga. In this context, "my" country is subsumed under "ours," without necessarily disappearing in the mix but making cultural, national, and political boundaries problematic.

This linguistic and cultural bilingualism enacts, additionally, a confluence of Catholic discourse and Protestant practice so that I may appeal to collectivist principles while pledging allegiance to individualist success and competition. Thus, while Hispanic television may look back to Virgin of Guadalupe with reverence, it also makes it imperative to "conquer all adversity" by sheer individual hard work—and the speedy consumption of the appropriate products.

Hispanic television, therefore, reveals discursively a willingness to reconcile a "motherland" and a "fatherland," a Latin American background with a U.S. Bill of Rights, a Spanish *apellido* and an Anglo first name. This reconciliation includes the weaving of *criollo* and immigrant storytelling, of home-town nostalgia and "American dream" optimism, of Amerindian and Indiana Jones mythologies. This also implies the redrawing of the symbolic map of América, with "Hispanic America" as its integrating core and cultural undercurrent.

Latin America is indeed a nation, and *a nationalism*, in Hispanic television (see Chapter 8). It is a nation spread throughout different countries, regional identities, and cultural alliances, from Juárez to Buenos Aires and from Puerto Rico to Chile. However, it is a group of peoples whose local histories and lives find mass-mediated unity in common icons, common myths, and common Others. Hispanic television re-creates and helps create these icons, these puns, and this *imagined community*. It offers archetypes, prototypes, and stereotypes through which the Hispanic is given a face and endowed with a Pan-American voice. Hispanic television provides a "memory of memories": A Latin American, cross-national, highly distilled memory of home, place, and identity. In the house of mirrors of mass-mediated narratives, the Hispanic finds her most certain face in Hispanic television and its mediated intertextuality. Everywhere else she turns, she might find that image gets blurred and confounded in the multiple demands, pushes, and pulls of everyday life.

Tradition and Modernization

In the discourse of Hispanic television, *América Latina* stands for idealized tradition and *America* for an idealized horizon (see Chapter 3). The United States is the battleground in which the two meet, confront each other, and negotiate a new market, a new language, and a new consciousness. This negotiation implies a sort of pull toward "modernization" and a renunciation of tradition in the name of universalization (a horizontal synchrony). In the case of Latin America and in relation to the United States, this pull between tradition and modernization may be seen, among other examples, in the following realms: (a) a tension between *orality* and *videocy*,[5] (b) the social status of self and body, and (c) the character of public discourse.

Many Latin American cultures carry strong oral traditions in which pedagogy and mythical storytelling go hand in hand. Orality presupposes the primacy of the sonorous, the attuned, and the ambivalent over the semiotic, the digital, and the functional (Mickunas, 1983). The modernizing process requires, however, instrumental rationality and the instrumentalization of the body. It requires homogenizing functions, forces, codes, and practices. The visual becomes more central than the oral, and it surpasses even logos with the visual assertion of the signal. In a similar way, a rational magic replaces mythical logic so that television talks of and praises homogenous and ceaselessly duplicated bodies; the bodies created or perfected by technology. Television also speaks of endless consumption, endless change, and endless improvement.

The Public Body

The tension between tradition and modernizing instrumentalization can also be seen in *the status of self and body*. As opposed to its Anglo-Saxon Protestant counterpart, the Latin American body is not a private property but a public domain (Lozano, 1994). There is no distance between "I" and my body, so that I cannot possibly have a relationship of ownership with "it." That I own my body becomes reduced, given the aforementioned, to the tautological "I own I." This tautology carries the interesting consequence that I become a property of myself, and with it, this "I" ceases to belong to the community (as it would be in a collectivist setting) and starts viewing itself as an individual commodity. That I cannot possibly "own" myself can be seen reflected in the sinister connotations that the willing manipulation of the body (e.g., through plastic surgery) carries in traditional telenovelas, as well as the importance of *authenticity* within this discourse. However, if I am my property, I can do whatever I wish with myself, including transforming my body.[6] To transform my body is a willingness to hide my soul (for one will not mirror the other anymore), and therefore implies a confession of hypocrisy and maliciousness. In doing so, I break the natural relationship of belonging that exists among me, the community, and the world. The argument according to which a woman "owns her body and therefore has a right to control it" makes little sense within a cultural mindset that has not separated community and body via State and Law.

Modernized Tradition

The fair-like dimension of Hispanic television appears more noticeable when the programming requires a degree of impromptu dialogue and interaction; its mall-like dimension is more strongly revealed, however, at the moment in which the televisual textuality emphasizes the video performance and patterning proper to music videos and MTV-inspired aesthetics.[7] *Contemporary telenovelas* are an interesting case, in that they seem to be a meeting ground for orality and videocy, where the body at the fair meets the body at the mall, so to speak. This seems to be the case for two reasons. First, contemporary telenovelas emerge within an otherwise traditional Latin American narrative, thus highlighting the contrast between two understandings of the body (i.e., the traditional Catholic and the modernized Protestant). Second, if contemporary telenovelas aspire to be considered "realistic" in the Hispanic context, they need to enact rules of representation that would gain the complicity of a reader who is not only Latin American but also U.S. American. Thus, they have "modernized" their rules of realistic representation (i.e., made them more Hollywood-compatible), which includes a certain valuation and positioning of the body.

In fact, a strong rapport and intertextuality exists between *contemporary telenovelas* and U.S. commercials, as they praise the same homogenous body (e.g., *la mujer de hoy*, "today's woman"). It is understood that *la mujer de hoy*—the ideally constructed female consumer—goes more often to the mall than to the fair, and that her bodily needs and rhetoric have been transformed accordingly. A modern understanding of beauty, body, and virtue resonates from telenovelas to commercials and through each other.

The increased pervasiveness of the sexed body in telenovelas and advertising speaks of a new form of melodrama that is more in accordance with U.S. soap operas and their own modernized subgenres (the melodramatic procedural, the YA soap opera, the "reality" melodrama). Telenovelas might be becoming more "secular" as sex leaves its traditional place as a sacred or profane topic and enters the democracy of "social issue," the detached status of *an object* of speech (see Chapters 9 and 10).

But Is It Transmodern?

The aforementioned televisual characteristics suggest the intertwining of three epistemic modalities in Hispanic television. These are premodern, modern, and postmodern modalities, evidenced in the treatment of the body; the status of orality, literacy, and videocy; the rhetorical construction of Self and Other; the overlapping of various temporalities; and the mixing of different forms of address, from carnivalesque parody to fragmented information. Equally important in this context is the fact that Latin America's modernity is not akin to Europe's. "Modernity" does not in fact correspond to an inescapable and linear development; there are many modernities and forms of being modern, and, therefore, postmodernity may have arrived to some places in Latin America before or at the same time as modernity. Colombia, for example, fully experienced globalization—a postmodern condition—before fully experiencing national identity—a modern project (Lozano, 2011).

Interestingly, following a different path of analysis, John Hartley (1999) has argued that television *itself* must be understood as containing characteristics of these three categories—premodern, postmodern, and modern—and that it is, therefore, necessary to think of television as *transmodern*, accepting that television simultaneously enacts ideals of modernity, reaches beyond those to medieval practices, and embodies fundamental principles of postmodern communication. This, according to Hartley, makes television a form of "transmodern teaching" (1999, Chapter 4). Most interestingly, we both arrived at a similar conclusion through rather different approaches. I would not claim that the characteristics of Hispanic television are common to all television. But I would argue that it is of utmost interest to inquire as to how contemporary, transnational, yet local media such as Univision and Telemundo deal with the rhetorical demands of different temporalities and cultural imaginaries.

The Third Text: Reorganizing the Archive

Hispanic television provides a different topography for the American territory and another way of mapping the Americas in which borders are reconsidered.

Some of the main features that reorganize this map are (a) the "marked" and "unmarked" Spanish across the programming, (b) the marked absence of English, and (c) the marked externality of the Anglo as reader, consumer, and object of discourse.

In Hispanic television, cultural foreground and background constantly shift position. In the same manner that what is "marked" announces that which is "unmarked," in Hispanic television, the traditional points to the modern, the presence of the mall announces the fair, and both rhythms resonate through one another. Now the defining field becomes the defined figure, and now the framed figure reveals the extended field, and its clear-cut limits dissolve. The writing of Hispanic television opens a space in-between traditional memories and postmodern logics. In semiotic terms, the articulation of the "vertical" tradition and the "horizontal" modernization produces a diagonal textuality that provides the horizontal and the vertical with a curvature, a dimension that cannot be accounted for in linear terms; a syncretic text. This dimension reveals the conditions that make the Hispanic text readable and profitable.

I would like to say that this cultural syncretism announces "the right to existence," of a Third Text in which Anglo and Latino popular narratives are interwoven. Such a text supposes the emergence and legitimation of an Anglo-Latino fabric, a cultural and textual logic in which traditions intersect, revealing and transforming their cultural backgrounds. Hispanic television, with its documents, its inscribed body, and its pervasive textuality, constitutes an instance of this emergent fabric: one that resonates with the accent of the mythical land of origin—Latin America—and performs with the attitude of the pragmatic land of action—the United States. In this ideological and discursive syncretism, a new reader has been positioned and constructed. This reader's existence is "real" within the text and ambiguous or ephemeral without.[8]

This syncretic construction of a new "us" is somewhat analogous to the one that characterizes *mestizaje*, although it can be argued that syncretism is a far more conservative, less dynamic process; more guided by the short temporality of markets—or crises—than by the long and slow processes of cultural cross-pollination (Levine, 2001). In Latin America, *mestizaje* is both a cultural process and a mythical narrative (see Chanady, 1994; Pick, 1993). We, Latin Americans, are West and not West, says Fuentes (1988). We are Black, Indian, and Mediterranean. We are the intersection of three worlds.

In countries such as Peru, Colombia, Mexico, or Ecuador, our sanctioned and mainstreamed myth of origin provides us all with a common mother, an Indian, and a common father, a Mediterranean European. Under the guise of this common trait, the mestizo is celebrated as the new race that erases racial difference. But underneath this mestizo harmony, the "maternal" indigenous line is both glorified and silenced, and the African ancestry is dismissed. The paternal Spaniard line is questioned and criticized, but it is also embodied and practiced; it is the one expected at the Polis. We visit "mother" in the museum, and we see "father" everywhere else.

In a similar fashion, Hispanic television calls proudly to Latin America, the motherland, *la madre patria*, invoking images of origin, authenticity, and difference.[9] However, it is the fatherland, the much questioned, feared, and praised Uncle Sam, that defines social rules and the legitimate practices of everyday life. While the motherland is visited in postcards of nostalgia, the he-State, *el pais*, is the place of dwelling.

Hispanic television expresses its motherland allegiance in body comportment and orality; in a memory of landscapes, folklore, and popular music; of *criollo* foods and festivities; and of nationalistic celebrations. The Colombian, the Mexican, the Chilean, and the Ecuadorian "Independence Day" are officially announced, covered in the news, and celebrated. The adopted fatherland, in contrast, is carried on the televisual formats and organizing logics of "blocks" and "breaks," of genres and advertising—of realism and pragmatism.

Archival Transformations

Archives and libraries suffer transformations, crises, and ruptures. On occasion a new document added to the archive forces a transformation of orders and divisions; entire sections are judged apocryphal, or hitherto "irrelevant" material is judged worthy of conservation. Sometimes the library is besieged by the enemy, set on fire, and reduced to dust, supposing not only the disappearance of an edifice but also the rearrangement of the surrounding topography. Sometimes the library's ruins become in themselves documents or a neighboring edifice takes over the functions of the burned archive.

The moment when the constitutive principles of the cultural archive are transformed to give room to a new set of principles, a new epistemic understanding has emerged. Let us call these dramatic transformations or ruptures "cultural epistemes" or discursive formations, the exploration of which was Foucault's undertaking.

On occasion a document emerges whose writing requires the merging of cultural logics that were hitherto separate. Paraphrasing Borges (1952/1981a), one could say that this is the moment of history, in which distinct semiotic systems intersect one another and produce a new construction, a *third text*, both different from the originating matrices and recognizable along their lines.[10] This "third text" can be related to Kristeva's (1969) *intertextuality* (see also Ducrot & Todorov, 1979).[11] Kristeva sees intertextuality as an inescapable condition of the text, for any text is already a "permutation of texts" (Moi, 1987). If this is the case, the third text could be understood as a *radical intertextuality*, for that which emerges is not only a text but also a *new kind of textuality*. The third text, to paraphrase Foucault (1970) and Kristeva (1984), cannot be deduced or inferred from its precedent systems, but needs the precedent as founding or grounding strata.

The emergence of a third text might imply a moment of breakage away from historical hermeneutics as understood by Gadamer, as a given cultural context will be besieged by the presence of an externality that cannot be resolved or denied.[12] To break the smoothness of the given context is to hint, at least momentarily, at the presence of alien logics that may soon become another smooth space, both as continuation and breakage from the tradition.

Following Foucault's (1970) archaeological reading of history, one might suggest that a *third text* might have appeared three or four times in the last five centuries. It appeared as material form in *The Quixote* (a "negative of the Renaissance world"), *Las Meninas* ("the representation, as it were, of Classical representation"), and *Ecce Homo* (Foucault, 1970, pp. 16, 47). The latter, expressing Mallarme's and Nietzsche's question *Who is speaking?* would be a sign "of the very first glow, low in the sky, of a day scarcely even heralded as yet, but in which we can already divine that thought . . . is about to re-apprehend itself in its entirety" (Foucault, 1970, p. 306). If *Las Meninas* were a "spiral shell" in which "representation is represented at every point" (p. 307), the question "who is speaking?" signifies the rejection of representation as a self-contained endeavor, announces a break from classical thought, and foresees the crisis of modernity.[13]

Postmodern platano or syncretic rubbish?

Besides the aforementioned radical transformations, however, the life of cultures is one of ongoing intersections, borrowings, and juxtapositions (Stewart, 1999). In this sense, cultures are engaged in an ongoing process of hybridation (García-Canclini, 1997) made the more visible now by increased global diasporas (Brah, 2003), nationalistic impulses, and multiple technologies of communication.[14]

In a much more local sense, therefore, one could say that the third text unfolds the logic of that which is "neither nor, but both and more." A logic that is, which announces the co-presence of different semiotic systems or cultural matrices (Martín-Barbero, 1982) without being reduced to any of them or to their combination.[15]

In this sense, the third text's logic is that of hyphens, the logic that manifests ruptures as it announces encounters, the one proper to material and symbolic borderlands, the logic that underlies cultural mestizaje. One can see the third text in new forms or practices for which there is more than one identifiable cultural, social, or semiotic system of reference. It is present in *conjunto music*, a Texan music that is played halfway between

Mexican *corridos* and U.S. country rhythms. It is also present in Spanglish and code switching, the transformation of both Spanish and English in the speaking of Chicanos, Nuyoricans, and other Spanish-speaking peoples of the United States. Luz María Umpierre (1980), a Nuyorican poet, inscribed it in the following manner:

Vivo en el pais de los amaestrados
    I beg your pardon, excuse me, I'm sorry
Fila india para coger la guagua   pisotón
    I beg your pardon
Ir por la calle siempre a la derecha   encontronazo
    Excuse me
Hablar siempre en voz baja   CARAJO!
    I'm sorry
No dejar que un papelito se te caiga en la
acera   FLOP
    Excuse me
Coger un número y esperar   Colao!
    I beg your pardon
Estacionar a quince pies, ni uno menos,
del fire-hydrant   Déjalo ahí al
                    frente!
Twelve inches from the curve   Párate en la
                curvita!
    Excuse me
Caminar siempre de prisa   Acangana!
    I'm sorry
            I b-e-g yul paldon, escuismi
            am sorri pero yo soy latina
            y no soporto su RUBBISH.

                        (p. 108)

This poem expresses with singular force a bilingual and bicultural awareness and the unstable site from which such duality can be observed and experienced. The poem describes the social environment where "she," the Latina, lives. "I live in the country of the tamed," starts the poem. While the English lines speak the forms and ways of that domestication (politeness, correctness, rule-following), the Spanish lines answer back with disorder, rebellion, or impoliteness. One is understood as the Latina's legitimate speech in the U.S. public space, and the other is her exasperated but constrained response to that public space. Throughout the poem, English and Spanish follow this play of dual voices, the legitimate and the irreverent, the social and the personal.

In the last part, nevertheless, Spanish takes over (visually and linguistically, as it now occupies one centered line).

First, "she" starts by using a bad English, an English that is marked by Spanish and heavily mispronounced by the Spanish intonation:

> ""I b-e-g yul paldon, escuismi am sorri. . . ."
> I beg your pardon, excuse me, I am sorry. . . .

Second, the mispronounced English opens room for the assertive Spanish, now voicing, simultaneously, the linguistic and the cultural tension:

> "pero yo soy latina y no soporto su RUBBISH."
> but I am Latina and I cannot stand your RUBBISH.

Umpierre's poem also expresses the experiential situation of one who speaks in two languages but might not be understood in either one (García, 1983; Lavandera, 1981; Trueba, 1988). In fact, some (e.g., Aparicio, 1988; R. Durán, 1981) speak of "Spanglish" and other variations of the Hispanic's mixed use of English and Spanish as a dialect or language in its own right (as the last sentences in the poem suggest). Such a dialect implies, nevertheless, that both Anglo Americans and Latin Americans look down on the Hispanic as an outsider or a misfit. The Hispanic is either a "sell out" or an "ignorant." That is, either she *favors* an "American" accent and a repertoire of English words over the "purity" of her first language or she is unable to speak correct English and behave as a full member of the "American society" (R. Durán, 1981; Peñalosa, 1981).

Writer Junot Díaz unfolds brilliantly the expressive beauty and exuberance of this "dirty" and organic language mix, revealing a moment in which the *site of the hyphen*, that unstable and porous "in-between," becomes poetry itself. In his novel *The Brief Wondrous Life of Oscar Wao*, the narrator describes what happens to anybody who conspires against the life of Dominican dictator Trujillo:

> Every single Dominican, from the richest jabao in Mao to the poorest güey in El Buey, from the oldest anciano sanmacorisano to the littlest carajito in San Francisco, knew: that whoever killed Trujillo, their family would suffer a fukú so dreadful it would make the one which attached to the admiral jojote in comparison. (Díaz, 2007, p. 3)

This is genuinely a New Jersey-Dominican voice, a "postmodern plátano" (p. 145) writing that refuses to reduce Spanish to mere adornment or occasional "local color," and in which the supremacy of English is fought from within, with the subversion of time and memory. Spanish is, in this text, intrinsic to the texture of the writing and intrinsic to the lived experience of a Dominican boy in the New Jersey "ghetto" (Díaz, 2007, p. 22).

Univision and Telemundo so far have taken a different approach to the organic, joyful, and angry "third text" manifested by Umpierre, Díaz, and other Latino/a writers. Instead of a constant and unpredictable mixing of language and experience, Hispanic television proposes a clean juxtaposition of language and experience, so that Spanish is kept in relative purity as speech, and English is kept absent as language *but brought back as discourse*. The result approaches more of a "syncretic" than a hybrid text as seen by Levine (2001) and Naficy (1993). Levine states that

> syncreticism is the impregnation of one culture with the contents of another (or others) to create a third. It is a more stable, longer lasting and less ambivalent condition than that of hybridity into which two (or more) cultures blend and shift into an indeterminate array of positions, sometimes displaying the features of one culture more prominently. For Naficy [1993], hybridity constantly tries to resolve itself into syncreticism for syncreticism offers a means of symbolically expressing the boundaries of a community in a way that the ever-shifting nature of hybridity does not. (p. 34)

Univision and Telemundo are a "third text": Both Latin American and Anglo American; neither one nor the other, but both and more. By weaving Anglo and Latin American discourses, Hispanic television breaks and reorganizes the limits of those discourses, keeping them unstable and unresolved. The intrinsic difficulties and unresolved political tensions of a "syncretic" text may become particularly apparent in situations of crisis. Such was the case during, and immediately after, the terrorist attacks of 9/11.

Allow me for a moment to break the "fourth wall" of academic writing. When the news of the attacks reached me just minutes after the event, I, like thousands of others, ran to the nearest television to see what was happening. In front of me a "moment of history" was unfolding; a moment unique and unrepeatable not only because of the nature of the attacks on U.S. soil, but also because of the crisis of discourse, representation, and, indeed, of the "real" that the attacks generated. I went back and forth between the major U.S. English and Spanish language networks, taping this curious channel flipping. What unfolded on TV screens was an authentic, rhetorically naked moment, in which uncertainty took over the clean predictability of televisual time. Commercials stopped. Fiction was replaced by news. The explicit market interrupted operations. "Reality" took over in a frantic way, and the networks struggled to contain that rawness with an appropriate rhetoric of address: the right descriptors, the right slogans, the right tone of address. We were witnessing a discursive and an ideological laboratory. In the case of Telemundo and Univision, the discursive struggle included how to properly refer to New York and Washington, and indeed to the United States, while doing so *in Spanish*. As discussed elsewhere (Chapter 8), Spanish is a marker of difference in the televisual programming and, as such, a practice that distinguishes the Hispanic viewer from the Anglo mainstream. On this particular day, Spanish felt acutely foreign, alien, and, by extension, unpatriotic.

At that time, the ambiguity of *nosotros*, the Spanish-speaking audience and supranational community, was temporarily resolved. That collective identity moved away from the "nosotros-in-the-U.S." stance to the "us-of-the-United-States" vs. them, the outside threat. This became the legitimate national discourse regarding the attacks. For a few weeks, the Hispanic ambiguity of identity was resolved, and in the discourse of Univision and Telemundo, *we* were insiders; citizens united in sorrow before attacks against our "way of life." Bush ceased to be the U.S. president and became our president.

Levine (2001) states that "it is by becoming consumate consumers that exiles or immigrants become an identifiable, syncretic ethnic group that can be given a place within the larger culture" (p. 35). The paradoxical result in Univision and Telemundo is that Hispanic television maintains itself "at the border," as a sort of first-generation immigrant television, constantly addressing the Spanish speaker as newcomer but constantly reiterating the United States as fatherland. It is, therefore, simultaneously a stable and conservative text and a potentially subversive textuality, in which contradictory discourses are juxtaposed and intermixed, and nationalities are celebrated and broken.

Epilogue

In this work, I have studied the textual construction of a cultural reader, the *Hispanic*, as it is chronicled and recorded, envisioned and embodied by one of the powerful apparatuses of cultural and social legitimation: television. I have examined the "disturbances" that such an invention carries, the rhetorical deconstructions that it performs, and the cultural paradoxes that it uncovers. By studying an aspect of the discursive life of the contemporary Americas, I attempted to advance an understanding of the rhetorical constitution of culture, ethnicity, and identity as situated, intentional, and ambivalent. The discursive emergence and constitution of ethnicity already implies and requires a de facto, lived deconstruction of naturalized cultural boundaries, identities, and differences. "New" ethnicities and identities unfold among and across diverse discourses, thus announcing the viscosity and irregularity of common sense and empirical certainties. In this moment of revelation, we witness, even if only for a moment, a discursive slippage, the moment in which names and orientations we have maintained as natural and necessary become contrary to or at odds with our practices or our bodies.

To study an ethnicity or an identity as being constituted or even "invented" is to interrogate or question its authenticity; its characterization as origin, seed, root, essence, or exclusionary orientation. At a time when the boundaries of the contemporary society are no longer those of the nation-state (Featherstone, 1990), there is a contemporary "proliferation" of cultures that cannot be contained anymore, either within the geopolitical boundaries of the world or within the limits of the logical Word. Both in the plane of action and in the plane of discourse, cultures explode and supersede formal boundaries.

Cultural traditions are coming to the fore of national disputes, articulating difference, foregrounding distinction, and proclaiming authenticity. Paradoxically, the very centrality of the "authentic" in this dispute points to the fact that culture has no virginal cleanliness, as its authentic features are defined in the battlefield; broken, dispersed, and reconfigured in large and short temporalities. While identities, boundaries, and nationalisms are fiercely defended today, they are, because of the same reasons, challenged, denied, realigned, and *revisioned* in exhausting attempts to capture the essence of tradition, the essence of memory, and the essence of the Other. Paradoxically, the more radically "identity" is sought out, the weaker its constitution becomes, as it constantly demands an extra reduction, another step toward purification, a new cleansing technique. At the end of this quest, identity or ethnicity might have proven that, like the onion, it has no center, no core beneath its transparent layers, no essence different from its integral and multilayered presence.

But as in the case of the onion, this study also interrogates the equally common option taken to the claim of the authentic: If it is not authentic, then it is a fabrication, an imposture, a falsehood. If it is not natural, then it is merely "semantic": a creation of labeling, an operation born in language and restricted to the affairs of language, with no other intentionality than that of a closed and reflective system. As we may have seen in these pages, ethnicity is neither an act of sincere self-discovery nor an arbitrary convention in a linguistic system. Ethnicity manifests an uneasy, nonharmonic juxtaposition of lived and discursive spaces, sometimes at odds, sometimes complementary, and often over-flowing with signification.

Notes

1. Morse (1990) discusses television, malls, and freeways as cultural forms that "observe similar principles of construction and operation" including being loci of "distraction" and "derealized space" (pp. 193, 195).

2. The title of this photo reads "Immigrants stay in touch with their home culture through TV programming" (The Christian Science Monitor via Getty Images, April 27, 2011).

3. Foucault (1970) used the concepts of "sympathy" (attraction and rejection among things) and "resemblance" to describe the principles around which the epistemic order of the premodern was organized.

4. The status of time and space in modernity and its relationship to capitalism is studied by, among others, French sociologist and philosopher Henri Lefebvre in his books, *Critique of Everyday Life* Volumes 1 and 2 (1991a and 2002) and *The Production of Space* (1991b).

5. *Videocy* is the term that Ulmer (1989) used to speak of an epistemic videologic, of a cognitive competence similar to that of *literacy* and *orality*.

6. The sinister connotations of manipulating the body—and thus the self—may be found not only in Latin American traditions. They could also be traced in cultures or societies whose designs are not classically "modern." The body as private property seems to be a development of Western, modern rationality, whereas its transformation into segmented organs open to manipulation and improvement seems to be a development of postmodern, postindustrial logics.

7. This patterning is one of the traits that Ulmer (1989) describes as proper to videocy, to the logic of television in a postmodern age.

8. This is not only a characteristic of Hispanic television, but of mass-mediated audiences in general, as Hartley (1992) pointed out.

9. It is worth investigating the masculinization of the United States and the feminization of Latin America in national and international discourses. Two compelling collections addressing the relationship between nationalisms and sexuality are Parker, Russo, Sommer, and Yaeger (1992) and Lewis and Mills (2003). Burton's (1992) article is also illuminating.

10. I am indebted to philosopher Algis Mickunas for suggesting to me the term "third text," to which he referred in our many conversations. I use the term here to refer to the new textual pattern that emerges from the crossing and juxtaposing of previously independent textual patterns.

11. Kristeva (1969) coined the often used—and misused—term "intertextuality" in her *Recherches pour une semanalyse*.

12. Gadamer (1975) argues that one reads any alien text within the scope of one's cultural context. Thus, the hermeneutic circle is inescapable as it is not possible to leave one's own culture and read it "from outside." Habermas and Foucault disagree with Gadamer, although their disagreement stems from different conceptualizations of history, knowledge, and interpretation (see e.g., Foucault, 1972; Habermas, 1987; Mickunas, 1996).

13. According to Foucault (1970), Nietzsche's question points to the emergence in the 19th century of an "epistemic consciousness of man" (p. 309). One should remember that Nietzsche is for many the first postmodern thinker, the inspiration for Heidegger, Bataille, Foucault, Derrida, Deleuze, and Guattari.

14. Argentina-born, Mexican sociologist Nestor García-Canclini (1997) has greatly influenced our collective understanding of hybridization as a "social concept." Of particular interest is his work *Hybrid Cultures: Strategies for Entering and Leaving Modernity* (1995). From García-Canclini's perspective, hybridization includes several types of cultural mixture that may range from mestizaje and syncretism, to resis-

tance hybrids and contemporary "multicultural fusions" in which all these types may "intermingle and draw strength from one another" (1997, Hybridity as an Explanatory Resource section, para. 4).

15. In his groundbreaking investigation of mass culture and of the modern concept of the "people," Martín-Barbero (1982, 1993) speaks of "cultural matrices" to refer to the grounds from which "mass culture" emerges at the turn of the 19th century. Martín-Barbero asserts that mass culture is constituted in the encounter of two *cultural matrices* that were previously separate and distinct: the high and the low; the "cultivated" and the "popular" culture. Mass culture is neither the popular nor the cultivated, but its mix and its transformation.

References

Aguirre, Jr., A., & Bustamante, D. A. (1993, January). Critical notes regarding the dislocation of Chicanos by the Spanish-language television industry in the United States. *Ethnic & Racial Studies, 16*(1), 121.

Alazraki, J. (1988). *Borges and the Kabbalah*. Cambridge, England: Cambridge University Press.

Allen, R. (1985). *Speaking of soap operas*. Chapel Hill, NC: University of North Carolina Press.

Allen, R. L., & Clarke, D. E. (1980). Ethnicity and mass media behavior: A study of Blacks and Latinos. *Journal of Broadcasting, 24*(1), 23–34.

Anaya, R. (1976). *Heart of Aztlán*. Berkeley, CA: Editorial Justa.

Ang, I. (1985). *Watching Dallas*. London: Methuen.

Anzaldúa, G. (1987). *Borderlands/La frontera: The new mestiza*. San Francisco: Spinsters/Aunt Lute.

Aparicio, F. R. (1988). La vida es un Spanglish disparatero: Bilingualism in Nuyorican poetry. In G. Fabre (Ed.), *European perspectives on Hispanic literature of the United States* (pp. 147–160). Houston: Arte Público Press.

Armstrong, J. (1999, June). *Santa Barbara around the world*. Retrieved June 15, 1999, from http://www.cybercom.net./-jima/sbhome.html.

Augé, M. (1995). *Los "no-lugares," espacios del anonimato. Una antropología de la sobremodernidad* (2nd ed.). Barcelona: Gedisa.

Avery, R. K., & Eason, D. (Eds.). (1991). *Critical perspectives on media and society*. New York: Guilford Press.

Bakhtin, M. (1984). *Rabelais and his world* (Heléne Iswolsky, Trans.). Bloomington: Indiana University Press. (Original work published 1965)

Barretto, R. (1965). Si mi suerte cambiara. *Viva Watusi!* United Artists.

Barthes, R. (1968). *Elements of semiology* (A. Lavers & C. Smith, Trans.). New York: Hill and Wang. (Original work published 1964)

Barthes, R. (1977). *Image, music, text* (S. Heath, Ed. & Trans.). London: Fontana.

Baudrillard, J., with M. Poster (Ed.). (1988). *Selected writings*. Stanford, CA: Stanford University Press.

Bea, K. (2005, May). *Political status of Puerto Rico: Background, options, and issues in the 109th Congress*. Congressional Research Services (CRS) report for Congress. Retrieved July 17, 2009, from http://www.census.gov/prod/2003pubs/p20-545.pdf

Bean, F., & Tienda, M. (1987). *The Hispanic population of the United States*. New York: Russell Sage Foundation.

Blosser, B. J. (1983, May). *Television for cultural affirmation: An approach to formative research*. Paper presented at the annual meeting of the International Communication Association, Dallas, TX.

Blosser, B. J. (1986). Modeling bilingualism on television: Shaping the linguistic environment. *The Journal for the National Association for Bilingual Education, 10*(2), 83–111.

Blosser, B. J. (1988). Reading and oral language development: The case of the Hispanic child. *The Journal for the National Association for Bilingual Education, 13*(1), 21–42.

Bolívar, G. (2006). *Sin tetas no hay paraíso*. Bogotá, Colombia: Oveja Negra.

Borges, J. L. (1981a). The modesty of history. In E. Rodríguez Monegal & A. Reid (Eds. & Trans.), *Borges, a reader* (pp. 246–248). New York: Dutton. (Original work published 1952)

Borges, J. L. (1981b). Pierre Menard, author of the Quixote. In E. Rodríguez Monegal & A. Reid (Eds. & Trans.), *Borges, a reader* (pp. 96–103). New York: Dutton. (Original work published 1941)

Borges, J. L. (1992, October). Some versions of Homer (Suzanne Jill Levine, Trans.). *PMLA, 107*(5), 1134–1138. Available at http://www.jstor.org/stable/462868. (Original work published 1932)

Borges, J. L. (1996). Las versiones homéricas. In *Obras completas* (p. 239). Buenos Aires: Emecé editores. (Original work published 1932)

Brah, A. (2003). Diaspora, border and transnational identities. In R. Lewis & S. Mills (Eds.), *Feminist postcolonial identities* (pp. 613–634). New York: Routledge.

Brunsdon, C. (1990). Television: Aesthetics and audiences. In P. Mellencamp (Ed.), *Logics of television: Essays in culture criticism* (pp. 59–72). Bloomington: Indiana University Press.

Burton, J. (1992). Don (Juanito) Duck and the imperial-patriarchal unconscious: Disney studios, the good neighbor policy, and the packaging of Latin America. In A. Parker, M. Russo, D.Sommer, & P. Yaeger (Eds.), *Nationalisms and sexualities* (pp. 21–41). New York: Routledge.

Bustamante, P. (2011, August 31). Telenovelas woo Hispanics with new twists. *AFP*. Available at http://www.google.com/hostednews/afp/article/ALeqM5hqVGgDbgIG8AUeoUclEVtsVKxlVQ?docId=CNG.6168b7edab1b101e6b881602004f54f4.221

Butler, P., & Logan, M. (1988, April). Soaps go international. *Soap Opera Digest*, pp. 98–102.

Buy me some arepa y buena noche. (1993, May). *Forbes*, p. 184.

Calderón, H., & Saldívar, J. D. (Eds.). (1991). *Criticism in the borderlands. Studies in Chicano literature, culture, and ideology*. Durham, NC: Duke University Press.

Caldwell, J. (2004). Convergence television: Aggregating form and repurposing content in the culture of conglomeration. In L. Spigel & J. Olsson (Eds.), *Television after TV: Essays on a medium in transition* (pp. 41–74). Durham, NC: Duke University Press.

Caughie, J. (1990). Playing at being American: Games and tactics. In P. Mellencamp (Ed.), *Logics of television essays in culture criticism* (pp. 44–58). Bloomington: Indiana University Press.

Chanady, A. (Ed.). (1994). *Latin American identity and constructions of difference*. Minneapolis: University of Minnesota Press.

Changing face of Spain. (2004, March 28). *Stormfront*. Available at http://www. stormfront.org/forum/t123395-5/

Civica Americana. (2008). *Mission*. The Hispanic-American Civics Foundation. Retrieved June 12, 2008, from http://civicamericana.org/Mission.html

CNN forgot to tell you something. (2008, February 21). *NoMoreBlatherDotCom*. Available at http://www.youtube.com/watch?v=cjOJPvDdB1c

CNN world report webpage. (2009). Available at http://www.cnn.com/CNNI/Programs/world.report/

Colbert Report. (2008, January 17). "Lou Dobbs." Episode 04008. Available at http://www.colbertnation.com/the-colbert-report-videos/147922/january-17-2008/lou-dobbs

Condit, C. M. (1991). The rhetorical limits of polysemy. In R. K. Avery & D. Eason (Eds.), *Critical perspectives on media and society* (pp. 365–386). New York: Guilford Press.

Corpi, L. (1980). *Palabras de Mediodía/Noon words* (Catherine Rodríguez Nieto, Trans.). Berkeley: Fuego de Aztlán.

Corporate Information (2013). Telemundo. Available at http://msnlatino.telemundo.com/legal_corporate_english

Costantini, C. (2012, June 11). Jorge Ramos, Univision anchor, criticizes Obama campaign for using his image in advertisement. *The Huffington Post*. Available at http://www.huffingtonpost.com/2012/06/11/jorge-ramos-univision-anc_n_1586487.html

Cota-Cárdenas, M. (1977). *Noches despertando inconsciencias*. Tucson: Scorpion Press.

Cuba Forum. (2008, March 5). *Topix*. Available at http://www.topix.com/forum/world/cuba/p56

D'Acci, J. (2004). Cultural studies, television studies and the crisis in the humanities. In L. Spigel & J. Olsson (Eds.), *Television after TV: Essays on a medium in transition* (pp. 418–445). Durham, NC: Duke University Press.

Dajani, N. (2005). Television in the Arab East. In J. Wasko (Ed.), *A companion to television* (pp. 580–601). Oxford: Blackwell.

Dávila, A. (2000, Fall). Talking back: Hispanic media and U.S. Latinidad. *Centro Journal, 12*(1), 36–47.

Dávila, A. (2001). *Latinos Inc.: The marketing and making of a people*. Berkeley: University of California Press.

Dealy, G. C. (1992). *The Latin Americans: Spirit and ethos*. Boulder, CO: Westview.

de Certeau, M. (1984). *The practice of everyday life* (S. Rendall, Trans.). Berkeley: University of California Press. (Original work published 1980)

Deleuze, G. (1988). *Foucault* (S. Hand, Trans.). Minneapolis: University of Minnesota Press. (Original work published 1986)

Deleuze, G., & Guattari, F. (1987). *A thousand plateaus: Capitalism and schizophrenia* (B. Massumi, Trans.). Minneapolis: University of Minnesota Press. (Original work published 1980)

Dempsey, J., & Schneider, M. (2007, June 27). Big finale for novella "Bella." *Daily Variety, 295*(61), 6–11.

174 / References

Derrida, J. (1976). *Of grammatology* (G. C. Spivack, Trans.). Baltimore: Johns Hopkins University Press. (Original work published 1967)

Derrida, J. (1978). *Writing and difference* (A. Bass, Trans.). Chicago: The University of Chicago Press. (Original work published 1967)

Díaz, J. (2007). *The brief wondrous life of Oscar Wao.* New York: Riverhead Books.

Ducrot, O., & Todorov, T. (Eds.). (1979). *Encyclopedic dictionary of the sciences of language* (C. Porter, Trans.). Baltimore, MD: Johns Hopkins University Press. (Original work published 1972)

Durán, L. I., & Bernard, H. R. (Eds.). (1982). *Introduction to Chicano studies* (2nd ed.). New York: Macmillan.

Durán, R. (Ed). (1981). *Latino language and communicative behavior.* Norwood, NJ: Ablex.

Eastman, H., & Liss, M. B. (1980). Ethnicity and children's TV preferences. *Journalism Quarterly, 57*(2), 277–280.

Eco, U. (1979). *A theory of semiotics.* Bloomington: Indiana University Press.

Eco, U. (1984). *The role of the reader: Explorations in the semiotics of texts.* Bloomington: Indiana University Press. (Original work published 1967)

Eco, U. (1986). *Travels in hyper reality* (W. Veaver, Trans.). San Diego: Harcourt Brace Jovanovich. (Original work published 1983)

Faber, R., O'Guinn, T. C., & Meyer, T. P (1986). Diversity in the ethnic media audience: A study of Spanish language broadcast preference in the U.S. *International Journal of Intercultural Relations, 10*(3), 347–359.

Fabre, G. (Ed.). (1988). *European perspectives on Hispanic literature of the United States.* Houston: Arte Público Press.

Featherstone, M. (Ed.). (1990). *Global culture: Nationalism, globalization and modernity.* London: Sage.

Fisher, C. (1994, January). Hispanic media see siesta ending. *Advertising Age,* pp. S1, S6.

Fiske, J. (1987). *Television culture.* London: Methuen.

Fiske, J. (1991). Television: Polysemy and popularity. In R. K. Avery & D. Eason (Eds.), *Critical perspectives on media and society* (pp. 346–364). New York: Guilford Press.

Fiske, J., & Hartley, J. (1978). *Reading television.* London: Methuen.

Flitterman-Lewis, S. (1987). Psychoanalysis, film and television. In R. Allen (Ed.), *Channels of discourse: Television and contemporary criticism* (pp. 172–210). Chapel Hill: University of North Carolina Press.

Foucault, M. (1970). *The order of things: An archaeology of the human sciences* (A. M. Sheridan Smith, Trans.). New York: Vintage. (Original work published 1966)

Foucault, M. (1972). *The archaeology of knowledge & the discourse on language* (A. M. Sheridan Smith, Trans.). New York: Pantheon. (Original work published 1969 and 1971)

Foucault, M. (1977). *Discipline and punish* (A. M. Sheridan, Trans.). New York: Vintage. (Original work published 1975)

Fox, E. (Ed.). (1988). *Media and politics in Latin America: The struggle for democracy.* London: Sage.

Fox, E., & Waisbord, S. (Eds.). (2002). *Latin politics, global media*. Austin: University of Texas Press.

Fregoso, R. L., & Chabrám, A. (1990). Chicana/o cultural representations: Reframing alternative critical discourses. *Cultural Studies, 4*(3), 203–216.

Frye, N. H. (1957). *Anatomy of criticism*. Princeton, NJ: Princeton University Press.

Fuentes, C. (1988). *Myself with others*. New York: Farrar, Straus & Giroux.

Fullerton, J., & Kendrick, A. (2000, Spring). Portrayal of men and women in U.S. Spanish-language television commercials. *Journalism & Mass Communication Quarterly, 77*(1), 128–142.

Gadamer, H. (1975). *Truth and method*. New York: Crossroads Publishing. (Original work published 1960)

García, H. (1983). Bilingualism, biculturalism, and the educational system. *Journal of Non-white Concerns on Personnel and Guidance, 11*, 67–74.

García-Canclini, N. (1995). *Hybrid cultures: Strategies for entering and leaving modernity* (C. Chiapari & S. L. López, Trans.). Minneapolis: University of Minnesota Press. (Original work published 1990)

García-Canclini, N. (1997). Hybrid cultures and communication strategies. *Media Development* (1). Special issue on "Cultural boundaries and identity in Latin America." Available at http://www.waccglobal.org/en/19971-cultural-boundaries-identity-and-communication-in-latin-america/940-Hybrid-Cultures-and-Communicative-Strategies.html

García Márquez, G. (1970). *One hundred years of solitude* (G. Rabassa, Trans.). New York: Harper & Row. (Original work published 1967)

Gerardo. (1991). Latin till I die (Oye como va). In *Mo' Ritmo* (Music Record). New York: Interscope.

Gibson, C., & Jung, K. (2005, February). *Historical census statistics on population totals by race, 1790 to 1990, and by Hispanic origin, 1970 to 1990, for large cities and other urban places in the United States*. U.S. Census Bureau, 20233. Retrieved October 1, 2009, from http://www.census.gov/population/www/documentation/twps0076/twps0076.html

Gimenez, M. (1989). Latino/"hispanic"—who needs a name? The case against a standardized terminology. *The International Journal of Health Services, 19*(3), 557–571. Retrieved June 12, 2008, from http://www.colorado.edu/Sociology/gimenez/work/latino.html

Gitlin, T. (Ed.). (1986). *Watching television*. New York: Pantheon.

Glascock, J., & Ruggiero, T. (2004, Fall). Representations of class and gender on primetime Spanish-language television in the United States. *Communication Quarterly, 52*(4), 390–402.

Goldsen, R. K., & Bibliowicz, A. (1976). Plaza Sésamo: "Neutral" language or "cultural assault"? *Journal of Communication, 24*(2), 124–125.

Greimas, A.-J. (1983). *Structural semantics*. Lincoln: University of Nebraska. (Original work published 1966)

Greimas, A.-J. (1987). *On meaning: Selected writings in semiotic theory* (P. J. Perron & F. Collins, Trans.). Minneapolis: University of Minnesota. (Original work published 1970)

Greimas, A.-J., & Courtés, J. (1982). *Semiotics and language: An analytical dictionary* (L. Crist & D. Patte, Trans.). Bloomington: Indiana University Press. (Original work published 1979)

Griego, E. M., & Cassidy, R. C. (2001, March). *Overview of race and Hispanic origin 2000. Census 2000 brief.* Retrieved July 17, 2009, from http://www.census.gov/prod/2001pubs/c2kbr01-1.pdf

Grossberg, L. (1988). Wandering audiences, nomadic critics. *Cultural Studies, 2*(3), 377–391.

Grupo Niche (1990). Doña Pastora. On *Cielo de tambores* [CD]. Miami: Sony Discos.

Guthrie, M. (2012, October 18). At 50 years old, how Univision owns the Hispanic audience. *The Hollywood Reporter.* Available at http://corporate.univision.com/2012/press/univision-in-the-news/the-hollywood-reporter-profiles-univision%e2%80%99s-successes-over-its-50-year-history/#ixzz2c4HWgRYg

Habermas, J. (1987). *The philosophical discourse of modernity* (F. Lawrence, Trans.). Cambridge, MA: MIT Press. (Original work published 1985)

Hale, M., Olsen, T., & Fowler, E. F. (2009). A matter of language or culture: Coverage of the 2004 U.S. elections on Spanish- and English-language television. *Mass Communication & Society, 12*(1), 26–51.

Hall, C. (1992). Missionary stories: Gender and ethnicity in England in the 1830s and 1840s. In L. Grossberg, C. Nelson, & P. Treichler (Eds.), *Cultural studies* (pp. 240–269). New York: Routledge.

Hall, S. (1980). Encoding and decoding. In S. Hall, D. Hobson, A. Lowe, & P. Willis (Eds.), *Culture, media, language* (pp. 128–139). London: Hutchinson.

Hartley, J. (1992). *The politics of pictures.* London: Routledge.

Hartley, J. (1999). *Uses of television.* London: Routledge.

Harvey, P. M. (1991). Drunken speech and the construction of meaning: Bilingual competence in the southern Peruvian Andes. *Language and Society, 20,* 1–36.

Havens, T. (2002, December). "It's still a white world out there": The interplay of culture and economy in international television trade. *Critical Studies in Media Communication, 19*(4), 377–397.

Hawkes, T. (1977). *Structuralism and semiotics.* Berkeley: University of California Press.

Hispanic fact pack: Annual guide to Hispanic marketing and media. (2007, July). *Advertising Age* [Special supplement], pp. 1–60.

Hispanic broadcasting and cable. (1995, January). *Broadcasting and Cable* [Special report], pp. 40–52.

Hispanic heritage month. (2007). The U.S. Census Bureau. Retrieved May 13, 2008, from http://www.census.gov/eeo/hispanic_heritage.html

The Hispanic market. (1988, July). [Special report]. *Television/Radio Age,* pp. A1–A45.

Hispanics in the U.S. are likely to be uninsured. (2009, October 9). *National Public Radio.* Retrieved October 9, 2009, from http://www.npr.org/templates/story/story.php?storyId=113107192

Hjelmslev, L. (1969). *Prolegomena to a theory of language* (F. J. Whitfield, Trans.). Madison: University of Wisconsin Press. (Original work published 1943)

History (2013). Spanish International Network. Available at http://www.sintv.org/sintv/history.html

Jakobson, R. (1960). Linguistics and Poetics. In T. Sebeok (Ed.), *Style in Language* (pp. 350-377). Cambridge, MA: M.I.T. Press.

James, M. (2011, April 5). Univision gains on NBC, signaling shifts in population trends. *Los Angeles Times.* Available at http://latimesblogs.latimes.com/entertainmentnewsbuzz/2011/04/univision-gains-on-nbc-to-vie-for-title-of-nations-fourth-largest-television-network-.html

Jameson, F. (1972). *The prison-house of language: A critical account of structuralism and Russian formalism.* Princeton, NJ: Princeton University Press.

Jameson, F. (1987). Foreword. In A. J. Greimas (Ed.), *On meaning: Selected writings in semiotic theory* (P. J. Perron & F. Collins, Trans.). Minneapolis: University of Minnesota. (Original work published 1970)

Kristeva, J. (1969). *Recherches pour une semanalye.* Paris: Seuil.

Kristeva, J. (1984). *Revolution in poetic language* (M. Waller, Trans.). New York: Columbia University Press. (Original work published 1974)

Kristeva, J. (1987). The system and the speaking subject. In T. Moi (Ed.), *The Kristeva reader* (pp. 24–33). London: Blackwell.

Kuznesof, E. A. (1989). The history of the family in Latin America: A critique of recent work. *Latin American Research Review, 24*(2), 168–186.

de Lailhacar, C. (1990). The mirror and the encyclopedia: Borgesian codes in Eco's *The name of the rose.* In E. Aizemberg (Ed.), *Borges and his successors: The Borgesian impact on literature and the arts* (pp. 155–179). Columbia, MO: University of Missouri Press.

Lara, M., Gamboa, C., Kahramanian, M. I., Morales, L., & Hayes Bautista, D. E. (2005). Acculturation and Latino health in the United States: A review of the literature and its socio-political context. *Annual Review of Public Health, 26,* 367–397. Retrieved October 2, 2009, from http://www.rand.org/pubs/reprints/2005/RAND_RP1177.pdf

Lavandera, B. (1981). Lo quebramos, but only in performance. In R. Durán (Ed.), *Latino language and communicative behavior* (pp. 49–67). Norwood, NJ: Ablex.

Laviera, T. (1985). *AmeRícan.* Houston: Arte Público.

Lefebvre, H. (1991a). *The critique of everyday life* (Vol. 1) (J. Moore, Trans.). London: Verso. (Original work published 1947)

Lefebvre, H. (1991b). *The production of space* (D. Nicholson-Smith, Trans.). Oxford: Basil Blackwell. (Original work published 1974)

Lefebvre, H. (2002). *The critique of everyday life* (Vol. 2) (J. Moore, Trans.). London: Verso. (Original work published 1961)

Levine. E. (2001). Constructing a market, constructing an ethnicity: U.S. Spanish-language media and the formation of a syncretic Latino/a identity. *Studies in Latin American Popular Culture, 20,* 33–50.

Lévi-Strauss, C. (1968). *The savage mind.* Chicago: University of Chicago Press.

Lewis, R., & Mills, S. (Eds.). (2003). *Feminist postcolonial identities.* New York: Routledge.

Lingis, A. (1984). *Excesses: Eros and culture.* Albany, NY: SUNY Press.

Lozano, E. (1989, May). *Soap operas and telenovelas: An intercultural critique of soap operas as feminine discourse.* Paper presented at the annual meeting of the International Communication Association, San Francisco, CA.

Lozano, E. (1990). *The televisual melodrama: An intertextual analysis of soap operas as rhetorical discourse.* Unpublished master's thesis, Ohio University, Athens, OH.

Lozano, E. (1991). Rhetorical constructions of the feminine: Feminine taste, melodramatic hours. *Media Development, 38*(2), 10–12.

Lozano, E. (1992). The force of myth in popular narratives: The case of melodramatic serials. *Communication Theory, 2*(3), 207–220.

Lozano, E. (1994). The cultural experience of space and body: A reading of Latin American and Anglo American comportment in public. In A. Gonzales, M. Houston, & V. Chen (Eds.), *Our voices: Essays in culture, ethnicity, and communication.* Los Angeles: Roxbury Press.

Lozano, E. (2008). Convertirse en una y en otra mas: Identidad y porosidad de la identidad étnica en los Estados Unidos. *Revista Oficios Terrestres, 23*, 194–207. Available at http://www.perio.unlp.edu.ar/oficios/documentos/pdfs/ofi_23/informe_especial-ensayos-lecturas.pdf

Lozano, E. (2011). I am the leader, you are the leader: Nonviolent resistance in the peace community of San José de Apartadó, Colombia. In M. Pilisuk & M. N. Nagler (Eds.), *Peace movements worldwide: Peace efforts that work and why* (Vol. 3). Santa Barbara, CA: Praeger.

Lozano E., & Mickunas, A. (1992). Gebser and pedagogy: The integral difference. In E. Kramer (Ed.), *Consciousness and culture: An introduction to the thought of Jean Gebser* (pp. 179–200). Westport, CT: Greenwood Press.

Lugones, M. (1990). Hablando cara a cara/Speaking face to face: An exploration of ethnocentric racism. In G. Anzaldúa (Ed.), *Making face, making soul/Haciendo caras: Creative and critical writing by feminists of color* (pp. 46–54). San Francisco: Aunt Lute.

Marin, C. (Director). (1987). *Born in East L.A.* [Film].

Marketing to Hispanics (1987, September). [Special report]. *Advertising Age*, pp. S1–S24.

Marketing to Hispanics (1994, January). [Special report]. *Advertising Age*, pp. S1–S10.

Martí, J. (1977). Our America. In P. S. Foner (Ed.), *"Our America": Writings on Latin America and the struggle for Cuban independence* (E. Randall, J. de Onís, & R.H. Foner, Trans.). New York: Monthly Reviews Press.

Martín-Barbero, J. (1982, June). Apuntes para una historia de las matrices culturales de la mass-mediación. In *Primer Foro Internacional de la Comunicación.* First International Symposium of Latin American Faculties of Communication, Universidad de Lima, Peru.

Martín-Barbero, J. (1986). *A semiotic model for the textual analysis of telenovelas.* Unpublished raw data.

Martín-Barbero, J. (1989). Repossessing culture: The quest of popular movements in Latin America. *Media Development, 2*, 21–24.

Martín-Barbero, J. (1993). *Communication, culture, and hegemony: From the media to mediations* (E. Fox & R. A. White, Trans.). London: Sage. (Original work published 1987)

Martín-Barbero, J. (1999). Recepción de medios y consumo cultural: Travesías. In G. Sunkel (Ed.), *El consumo cultural en América Latina.* Bogotá, Colombia: Convenio Andrés Bello.

Martinez, L. (2007, October 10). Why can't Hispanic TV be as good as Hispanic advertising? As agencies push boundaries, programmers push garbage. *Advertising Age*. Retrieved July 10, 2008, from http://adage.com/bigtent/post?article_id=121032

Martínez Garza, J. (2005). La oferta de televisión en América Latina. *Zer*, *19*, 145–172.

Mastro, D., & Ortiz, M. (2008). A content analysis of social groups in prime-time Spanish-language television. *Journal of Broadcasting and Electronic Media*, *52*(1), 101–118.

Meehan, E. (1990). Why we don't count: The commodity audience. In P. Mellencamp (Ed.), *Logics of television: Essays in cultural criticism* (pp. 117–137).

Mellencamp, P. (Ed.). (1990). *Logics of television: Essays in culture criticism*. Bloomington: Indiana University Press.

Merleau-Ponty, M. (1962). *The phenomenology of perception* (C. Smith, Trans.). London: Routledge. (Original work published 1945)

Merleau-Ponty, M. (1964). *Signs* (R. McCleary, Trans.). Evanston, IL: Northwestern University Press. (Original work published 1960)

Metz, C. (1982). *The imaginary signifier: Psychoanalysis and cinema*. Bloomington: Indiana University Press.

Mickunas, A. (1983). Civilizations as structures of consciousness. *Main Currents of Modern Thought*, *29*(5), 179–185.

Mickunas, A. (1996). Mas allá del racionalismo y del historicismo. *Cuadernos de Filosofía*, *8*(9), 115–134).

Mitchel, R. (1995, May 21). Selena. *The Houston Chronicle*. Retrieved July 4, 2008, from http://web.archive.org/web/20070709024550/http://www.chron.com/content/chronicle/metropolitan/selena/95/05/21/legend.html

Modleski, T. (1982). *Loving with a vengeance: Mass produced fantasies for women*. London: Methuen.

Mohr, N. (1990). The journey toward a common ground: Struggle and identity of Hispanics in the U.S.A. *The Americas Review*, *18*(2), 81–85.

Moi, T. (Ed.). (1987). *The Kristeva reader*. London: Blackwell.

Montanaro, F. (2007, September 10). Last night's Univision debate. *MSNBC*. Retrieved June 3, 2008, from http://firstread.msnbc.msn.com/archive/2007/09/10/353237.aspx

Moraga, C. (1986). From a long line of vendidas: Chicanas and feminism. In T. de Lauretis (Ed.), *Feminist studies/critical studies* (pp. 173–190). Bloomington: Indiana University Press.

Morley, D. (1980). *The nationwide audience: Structure and decoding*. London: British Film Institute.

Morris, M. (1990). Banality in cultural studies. In P. Mellencamp (Ed.), *Logics of television: Essays in culture criticism*. Bloomington: Indiana University Press.

Morse, M. (1990). An ontology of everyday distraction: The freeway, the mall, and television. In P. Mellencamp (Ed.), *Logics of television: Essays in culture criticism* (pp. 193–221). Bloomington: Indiana University Press.

Murray, K. (1994, April 10). Banging the drums as Spanish TV comes of age. *The New York Times*, p. 10.

Naficy, H. (1993). *The making of exile cultures: Iranian television in Los Angeles.* Minneapolis: University of Minnesota.

Newcomb, H. (2005). The development of television studies. In J. Wasko (Ed.), *A companion to television* (pp. 15–28). Oxford: Blackwell.

Nicolini, P. (1986). Philadelphia Puerto Rican community leaders' perceptions of Spanish-language media. *Mass Communication Review, 13*(1, 2, 3), 11–17.

Nietzsche, F. (1978). *Thus spoke Zarathustra: A book for none and all* (W. Kaufmann, Trans.). New York: Penguin. (Original work published 1883)

Olsson, J. (2004). One commercial week: Television in Sweden prior to public service. In L. Spigel & J. Olsson (Eds.), *Television after TV: Essays on a medium in transition* (pp. 249-269). Durham, NC: Duke University Press.

Parker, A., Russo, M., Sommer, D., & Yaeger, P. (Eds.). (1992). *Nationalisms and sexualities.* New York: Routledge.

Peñalosa, F. (1981). Some issues in Chicano sociolinguistics. In R. Durán (Ed.), *Latino language and communicative behavior* (pp. 3–18). Norwood, NJ: Ablex.

Pick, Z. (1993). *The New Latin American cinema: A continental project.* Austin: University of Texas Press.

Quinientos años de herencia hispana. (1992, January). [Special issue]. *Mas.*

Quinones, S. (1997, October 6–19). "Too much heart"—Mexican soap opera presents the flip side of Miami Vice [12 paragraphs]. *JINN Magazine* [Online serial], *3*(21). Available at pacificnews.org/jinn/stories/3.21/971013-vice.html

Radway, J. (1984). *Reading the romance: Feminism and the representation of women in popular culture.* Chapel Hill, NC: University of North Carolina Press.

Ramirez, R. R., & de la Cruz, P. G. (2002). *The Hispanic population in the United States 2002.* Current population reports, 20-545. Washington, DC: U.S. Census Bureau. Retrieved July 17, 2009, from http://www.census.gov/prod/2003pubs/p20-545.pdf

Ramirez Berg, C. (2002). *Latino images in film: Stereotypes, subversion, and resistance.* Austin: University of Texas Press.

Rebolledo, T. D. (1980). The bittersweet nostalgia of childhood in the poetry of Margarita Cota-Cárdenas. *Frontiers: A Journal of Women Studies, 5*(2), 31–35. Available at http://www.jstor.org/stable/3346032

Ricoeur, P. (1985). *Time and narrative* (Vol. 2) (K. McLaughlin & D. Pellauer, Trans.). Chicago: University of Chicago Press. (Original work published 1984)

Ricoeur, P. (1991). *From text to action: Essays in hermeneutics* (K. Blamey & J. B. Thompson, Trans.). Evanston, IL: Northwestern University Press. (Original work published 1986)

Ricoeur, P. (1992). *Oneself as another* (K. Blamey, Trans.). Chicago: The University of Chicago Press. (Original work published 1990)

Rodriguez, A. (1999a, Fall). Making Latino news: Race, language and class. *Aztlan, 24*(2), 15–47.

Rodriguez, A. (1999b). *Making Latino news: Race, language and class.* Thousand Oaks, CA: Sage.

Rodriguez, R. (1989). An American writer. In W. Sollors (Ed.), *The invention of ethnicity* (pp. 3–13). New York: Oxford University Press.

Rodríguez Monegal, E., & Reid, A. (Eds. & Trans.). (1981). *Borges, a reader.* New York: E.P. Dutton.

Rojas, V. (2004). The gender of *Latinidad*: Latinas speak about Hispanic television. *Communication Review*, 7(2), 125–153.

Rojek, C. (2003). *Stuart Hall: Key contemporary thinkers*. Cambridge, England: Polity Press.

Rosales, A. F. (1990). Chicano art: A historical reflection of the community. *The Americas Review*, 18(2), 58–79.

Rubin, M.G. (1986, February). FCC flags foreign ownership. *Advertising Age*, p. 42.

de Saussure, F. (1959). *Course in general linguistics* (W. Baskins, Trans.). New York: McGraw Hill. (Original work published 1916)

Schleifer, R. (1987). *A. J. Greimas and the nature of meaning: Linguistics, semiotics, and discourse theory*. Lincoln: University of Nebraska Press.

Sconce, J. (2004). What if?: Charting television's new textual boundaries. In L. Spigel & J. Olsson (Eds.), *Television after television: Essays on a medium in transition* (pp. 93–112). Durham, NC: Duke University Press.

Sebeok, T. (Ed.). (1986). *Encyclopedic dictionary of semiotics*. Berlin: Mouton de Gruyter.

Shorris, E. (1992). *Latinos: A biography of the people*. New York: Norton.

Sloterdijk, P. (1986). *Critique of cynical reason* (M. Eldred, Trans.). Minneapolis: University of Minnesota Press. (Original work published 1983)

Sobel, B. (1990, October). Hispanic stations. *TV World*, pp. 37–40.

Spigel, L. (2004). Introduction. In L. Spigel & J. Olsson (Eds.), *Television after TV: Essays on a medium in transition* (pp. 1–34). Durham, NC: Duke University Press.

Spigel, L., & Olsson, J. (Eds.). (2004). *Television after TV: Essays on a medium in transition*. Durham, NC: Duke University Press.

Spillers, H. J. (1991). Introduction: Who cuts the border? Some readings on "America." In H. J. Spillers (Ed.), *Comparative American identities: Race, sex, and nationality in the modern text* (pp. 1–25). New York: Routledge.

Steiner, L. (1991). Oppositional decoding as an act of resistance. In R. K. Avery & D. Eason (Eds.), *Critical perspectives on media and society* (pp. 329–345). New York: Guilford Press.

Stewart, C. (1999, Autumn). Syncretism and its synonymous: Reflections on cultural mixture. *Diacritics*, 2(3), 40–62.

Stroeker, E. (1987). *Investigations in philosophy of space* (A. Mickunas, Trans.). Athens: Ohio University Press. (Original work published 1965)

Svetkey, B. (2008, June 6). Presidential primaries: The surprise hit of the TV season. *Entertainment Weekly*. Available at http://www.ew.com/ew/article/0,,20204485,00.html

Teer-Tomaselli, R. (2005). Change and transformation in South African television. In J. Wasko (Ed.), *A companion to television* (pp. 558-579). Malden, MA: Blackwell Publications.

Tiegel, E. (2003, June). Hispanic leader Univision not resting on laurels. *TelevisionWeek*. Retrieved June 9, 2008, from http://www.jorgeramos.com/loquedicen32.htm

Trueba, H. T. (1988). English literacy acquisition: From cultural trauma to learning disabilities in minority students. *Linguistics and Education*, 1, 125–152.

Ulmer, G. (1989). *Teletheory*. New York: Routledge.

Umpierre, L. M. (1980). Rubbish. In E. Barradas & R. Rodríguez (Eds.), *Herejes y mitificadores* (p. 108). Rio Piedras, Puerto Rico: Ediciones Huracán.

Univision Story (2013). Corporate Univision. Available at http://corporate.univision.com/corporate/#axzz2btapifgU

Uriccio, W. (2004). Television's next generation: Technology/Interface culture/flow. In L. Spigel & J. Olsson (Eds.), *Television after TV: Essays on a medium in transition* (pp. 163–182). Durham, NC: Duke University Press.

U.S. Census Bureau. (2007, July). *Annual estimates of the population by sex, race, and Hispanic or Latino origin for the United States: April 2000–July 2006.*

Weldon, D. (Director). (1991). *Mi Macondo/My Macondo.* [Film].

Wentz, L. (2011, May 19). Grupo Televisa, the star at Univision's upfront presentation. *Advertising Age.* Available at http://adage.com/article/special-report-tv-upfront/grupo-televisa-star-univision-s-upfront-presentation/227677/

Williams, K. (2003). *Why I (still) want my MTV.* Cresskill, NJ: Hampton Press.

Zhao, Y., & Guo, Z. (2005). Television in China: History, political economy and ideology. In J. Wasko (Ed.), *A companion to television* (pp. 521-539). Malden, MA: Blackwell.

Žižek, S. (2008). *For they know not what they do: Enjoyment as a political factor.* London: Verso. (Original work published 1991)

Author Index

Subject Index

CPSIA information can be obtained
at www.ICGtesting.com
Printed in the USA
FFOW03n0414111213
2608FF

9 781612 891293